Beethoven, Performers, and Critics

Beethoven, Performers, and Critics

The International Beethoven Congress
Detroit, 1977

Sponsored by the Detroit Symphony Orchestra
and Wayne State University

Edited by
Robert Winter, University of California, Los Angeles
Bruce Carr, Detroit Symphony Orchestra

Wayne State University Press   Detroit, 1980

Library of Congress Cataloging in Publication Data

International Beethoven Congress, Detroit, 1977.
  Beethoven, performers, and critics.

  Includes index.
  1. Beethoven, Ludwig van, 1770–1827—Congresses.
I. Winter, Robert, 1945– II. Carr, Bruce, 1938–
III. Detroit Symphony Orchestra. IV. Wayne State
University, Detroit. V. Title.
ML410.B4I67 1977   780'.92'4   80-16881
ISBN 0-8143-1658-1

Publication of this volume has been made possible by a grant from
the Michigan Council for the Arts.

Contents

Foreword

Our age is one of specialization and specialists. This fact, while it produces an extraordinary development of various skills and crafts, is also a source of alienation. Only too frequently we do not manage to fathom the whole while we are submerged in one or another part of it; looking at the trees, we do not see the forest. This is true, one can regretfully say, for every facet of our lives.

Thus also in the art of music. Its creative, performing, and theoretical aspects have moved in divergent directions, insofar as its active participants are concerned, while the public—once also an active participant—has become increasingly passive and perhaps increasingly bewildered.

As one who is saddened by this development, one who is both a creative and a performing musician, and who has profited much from musicology and is actively and passionately engaged in direct service to the public, I am endeavoring to bring together, at least temporarily, all components of musical art "under one roof," so to say. It was from this desire that the idea for the music festivals I have instigated began, and it is that goal that they essay to approach.

With great pleasure I welcome here—as we are preparing our third annual music festival in Detroit—the records of the congress that was held during the first, in 1977. In each festival a special light is thrown upon a creative musical aspect by a specially chosen, congenial group of performing artists, and each includes a musicological congress discussing related matters. Musicians and musicologists meet, talk to each other, and also talk to and with the public during these brief, extraordinary festival periods. Not only do these proceedings bear witness to the lively, open, scholarly, and practical spirit of the discussions, but they also throw light upon the interrelations of all musical aspects, and of music to sociology, history, aesthetics, and more.

My profound thanks go to Professor Robert Winter, the organizer of our International Beethoven Congress of 1977, to the scholars whose writings appear in this volume, and to all others who were with us at that time.

Antal Dorati
Detroit, October, 1979

Participants in the International Beethoven Congress

Ilse von Alpenheim, Saint Adrien, Switzerland
Eva Badura-Skoda, Vienna
Otto Biba, Gesellschaft der Musikfreunde, Vienna
Malcolm Bilson, Cornell University
Sieghard Brandenburg, Beethoven-Archiv, Bonn
Bruce Carr, Detroit Symphony Orchestra
Robert Commanday, *San Francisco Chronicle*
D. Kern Holoman, University of California at Davis
John Hsu, Cornell University
Owen Jander, Wellesley College
Douglas Johnson, University of Virginia
Joseph Kerman, University of California at Berkeley
Karl-Heinz Köhler, Deutsche Staatsbibliothek, Berlin
Irving Lowens, *Washington Star*
Robert Marshall, University of Chicago
Sonya Monosoff, Cornell University
Frank L. Peters, *St. Louis Post-Dispatch*
John Rockwell, *New York Times*
Howard Serwer, University of Maryland
Maynard Solomon, New York City
Susan T. Sommer, New York Public Library
Peter Stadlen, *London Daily Telegraph*
Michael Steinberg, Boston Symphony Orchestra
Daniel Stepner, New England Conservatory of Music
Alan Tyson, All Souls College, Oxford;
1977–78 Ernest Bloch Professor, University of California at Berkeley
James Webster, Cornell University
Robert Winter, University of California at Los Angeles

Abbreviations

Anderson Emily Anderson, ed., *The Letters of Beethoven,* 3 vols. (London, 1961).

BH Beethovenhaus, Bonn.

DStB Deutsche Staatsbibliothek, Berlin.

GdM Gesellschaft der Musikfreunde, Vienna.

Hess Willy Hess, *Verzeichnis der nicht in der Gesamtausgabe veröffentlichten Werke Ludwig van Beethovens* (Wiesbaden, 1957).

JAMS *Journal of the American Musicological Society.*

Kinsky-Halm Georg Kinsky, *Das Werk Beethovens. Thematisch-bibliographisches Verzeichnis seiner sämtlichen vollendeten Kompositionen,* completed and ed. Hans Halm (Munich-Duisberg, 1955).

MQ *The Musical Quarterly.*

N I Gustav Nottebohm, *Beethoveniana* (Leipzig-Winterthur, 1872; rprt. New York and London, 1970).

N II Gustav Nottebohm, *Zweite Beethoveniana: nachgelassene Aufsätze* (Leipzig, 1887; rprt. New York and London, 1970).

ÖNB Österreichische Nationalbibliothek, Vienna.

SBH Hans Schmidt, "Die Beethoven Handschriften des Beethovenhauses in Bonn," *Beethoven-Jahrbuch* 7 (1971): vi–xxiv, 1–443.

StPK Stiftung Preussischer Kulturbesitz, Berlin.

SV Hans Schmidt, "Verzeichnis der Skizzen Beethovens," *Beethoven-Jahrbuch* 6 (1969):7–128.

Thayer-Deiters– A. W. Thayer, *Ludwig van Beethovens Leben,* con-
Riemann I–V tinued Hermann Deiters, completed Hugo Riemann,
  5 vols. (Berlin-Leipzig, 1901–11). (Vol. I again revised 1917, remaining vols. reissued 1922–23).

Thayer-Forbes *Thayer's Life of Beethoven,* rev. and ed. Elliot Forbes,
  2 vols. (Princeton, 1964).

Wegeler-Ries Franz Wegeler and Ferdinand Ries, *Biographische
  Notizen über Ludwig van Beethoven* (Coblenz, 1838).

WoO Werk(e) ohne Opuszahl [work(s) without an opus
  number], in the listing of Kinsky-Halm.

Introduction

Robert Winter

In November of 1977, the city of Detroit played host to a Beethoven festival of grand proportions. Under the direction and inspiration of the Detroit Symphony Orchestra's new music director, Antal Dorati, all nine symphonies, two string quartets, the Op. 16 Piano Quintet, and the *Waldstein* and *Kreutzer* sonatas were offered in an auditory feast intended to satisfy the appetites of the most enthusiastic of the composer's partisans. The symphonic performances were also videotaped and later telecast over the national public television network as "A Beethoven Festival." As a longtime friend of musical scholarship in the service of performance, Maestro Dorati also proposed that a scholarly congress of international scope be included as an integral feature of the festival. The participants in the International Beethoven Congress, sponsored jointly by the Detroit Symphony Orchestra and Wayne State University and held on November 4–6, 1977, at the McGregor Conference Center on the Wayne State campus, were treated to concerts by the orchestra and by the Amadé Trio, as well as to extensive discussions of musical performance during the congress itself.

It was more than a spirit of active music making that informed the Detroit congress. Between the bicentennial celebrations in 1970 of Beethoven's birth and the sesquicentennial of his death in 1978, there had been a sizable series of scholarly colloquia around the world, from New York to Berlin to Bonn to Vienna to Paris and back to Chapel Hill, North Carolina. To Detroit was afforded the luxury of sharing in the fruits of these earlier meetings and at the same time evaluating their accumulated impact; a welcome breadth of consideration established itself as a natural part of the deliberations. A grant from the Michigan Council for the Arts now makes possible publication of the proceedings of the Detroit congress.

Seven years ago, Alan Tyson stated that the impression that the main lines of Beethoven scholarship are fixed and settled is wholly misleading. Since then, the situation has not substantially changed, and the eight individual essays gathered here explore largely uncharted regions of Beethoveniana. Michael Steinberg opens the discussion by assuming the difficult guise of a critic contemporary with Beethoven (a critic who bears a more than passing resemblance to E. T. A. Hoffmann) reviewing a performance of a still fresh Fifth Symphony. "Writing about Beethoven," Steinberg points up anew, involves more than "recognition and acknowledgment of recognition"; it requires a recapturing of the freshness—even the shock value—that accompanied Beethoven premieres.

Douglas Johnson chronicles Beethoven's most extensive musical tour, one that took him to Prague and Berlin in 1796. Besides providing a greater understanding of why the composer undertook no further journeys, Johnson is able—with the help of recently developed techniques for studying Beethoven's music papers—to fill out our picture of the composer's musical output during this period, one that includes extensive sketches made in Berlin for a symphony in C.

It is not with composition but performance that Eva Badura-Skoda is concerned. Although a growing number of musicians are aware of the important role played by tradition in Beethoven's Vienna, few grasp the extent of its influence. Badura-Skoda shows that virtually every dimension of performance was affected, from details of pedaling to the role of improvisation. Otto Biba's survey of concert life in Vienna provides an appropriate sequel, for he broadens performance considerations to include their sociology: the kinds of halls available (most of them attached to restaurants), the economics of presenting concerts (many of which produced substantial profits for the artists), and the genres cultivated. He closes by revealing some new figures about contemporaneous performance forces in Beethoven's time that ought to send shock waves through today's traditional orchestral ensembles as well as through the growing numbers of groups committed to "historical" instruments.

James Webster's more traditional approach—that of style analysis—to traditional elements in Beethoven's middle quartets produces some novel findings. Among other things, Webster offers abundant evidence from the Op. 59 quartets that Beethoven's reliance upon Mozartean models and Haydn's dynamic sense of process did not end in 1800, but continued well into the so-called Heroic Decade.

The final trio of essays focuses on the Beethoven of the last decade. Karl-Heinz Köhler looks at the deaf composer who reveals himself in the conversation books: at his pugnaciously independent political views, his wide-ranging literary tastes, and the general taboo that surrounded discussion of musical projects. One of the most ambitious of these was the mammoth Ninth Symphony, and Maynard Solomon ponders Beethoven's spiritual relationship to Friedrich Schiller, the author of the "Ode to Joy." Solomon suggests that Beethoven's choice of the ode symbolized his fundamental allegiance to the ideals of an earlier, enlightened age, one which Schiller at least partly renounced, but to which Beethoven returned after his personal dreams of "brotherhood and reconciliation" and "a world of innocent joy" had ended in disillusionment. Building upon Solomon's insights, Robert Winter's essay explores the complex musical evolution of the finale. Drawing upon a large body of unpublished sketches, this paper demonstrates that Beethoven's renewed commitment to fundamental ideals exercised a profound influence upon the composition of the finale. Indeed, it led the composer to develop his own "devotional language," one born of "profound allegiance to archaic and associative styles probably not wholly understood by Beethoven, but simply raised by him to immortality."

The retrospective and reflective aims of this volume are served by condensations of two lively panel discussions held during the congress. If the debate on "Historical Problems in Beethoven Performance" points up more questions than it answers, this is in large part because the panel included distinguished representatives of every aspect of performance, with many different experiences to report. Finally, it is rare that a group of such collective achievements has been empaneled to consider the many issues raised by Beethoven's sketches, especially aided as it was by the added insights of specialists on Haydn, J. S. Bach, Handel, and Berlioz.

Writing about Beethoven

Michael Steinberg

Few of us, I dare say, spent March 26, 1977, in mourning, or indeed in any other manner of observing the 150th anniversary of Beethoven's death. I am also aware that I am here as the representative of an orchestra that is doing something unique, so far as I know, in the history of major American orchestras: going through an entire season without a drop of Beethoven. Some of you have attended Beethoven congresses in this country or in Europe, but by and large, outside the world of musicology, this Beethoven year has been ignored. And for good reason: the world of music is a perpetual Beethoven festival anyhow. True, in 1970 we celebrated Beethoven's 200th birthday with limitless application and vigor, and it nearly drove us all mad. That deluge of recordings, books, articles, and complete cycles in concert of sonatas, symphonies, and quartets showed how hard it can be to make a fresh response to something as familiar as most of Beethoven's music.

Recognition and acknowledgment of recognition come more readily than shock. And there is the trouble. The *Eroica* starts, or the Seventh, or even the Ninth, and for most listeners—or "listeners"—it means that the *Eroica* button is pressed (or the Seventh or Ninth button), and we respond as habit has taught us to respond to these pieces. We are apt, that is, to respond to the fact of the performance more than to the performance itself, to say nothing of the actual music. It is like driving a familiar freeway or counting off the stops on the Lexington Avenue IRT. The well-known markers go by, and that is very reassuring—which is the very thing it ought not to be.

For performers it is no less difficult. The most dedicated, responsible, and imaginative pianists and quartet players need to get away from the *Appassionata* and from Opus 131 once in a while—to get away and reconsider. For orchestra players it is especially hard to look at yet another *Eroica* as an exciting event, though there are conductors that can make it happen. Most Beethoven performances are, in a sense, automatic. They sound as though they have come about not as a response to fresh and searching study, but because we know that "that's how the piece goes." I am not saying we need eccentric performances or ones that seek originality for its own sake ("Have you heard my *Waldstein?*"), but we do want to come closer to the ideal of playing the classics as though they were new. Accents get blunted with the passage of years, and dynamics are flattened. How many conductors insist on and how many orchestras deliver a true, breath-stopping pianissimo? Most particularly, many of the traditional tempos—they too are responses largely to custom and convenience—need to be reconsidered in the light of what the scores imply and even what they actually say.

To his contemporaries, Beethoven was a shocking artist. Some of those contemporaries delighted in that quality; some resisted it from the beginning; some went along up to a point, only to lose contact and wax censorious a bit later. (The *Eroica* marked the parting of the ways for many of his early followers.) E. T. A. Hoffmann, that vital and original writer, musician, and artist, who, among other accomplishments, produced the first body of valuable Beethoven criticism, recognized the shocking newness of Beethoven's music; at the same time, however, he recognized Beethoven's "self-possession." (Hoffmann's word—and it occurs often in his essays on Beethoven—is *Besonnenheit*, a condition attained after *besinnen*, which means "call to mind," "reflect.") Hoffmann suggested to his colleagues in criticism that if they failed to see merit in what Beethoven was doing, the fault was most likely to be found in their own limited perceptions.

Imagine encountering the Fifth Symphony as a new piece and writing about it in these terms (the following is not by Hoffmann):

"The most recent Academy of the excellent orchestra of our Court Theater provided an opportunity to renew acquaintance with one of the two most recent symphonies from the genius-driven but sometimes unruly pen of Beethoven of Vienna. The work in question is the Symphony in C minor and major, first heard two years ago, and since made available in the form of orchestral parts clearly engraved by the esteemed firm of Breitkopf and Härtel in Leipzig.

"The passage of years has done its work in softening the shock of the encounter. That the execution was so much clearer this time—though certain passages will surely remain beyond the reach of all but some manner of Olympian ideal orchestra—made this experience less bewildering than that of the first rendering at Beethoven's Academy at the Theater-an-der-Wien; at the same time, the more confident and certain playing served to bring into sharper view the oddities, perversities even, and—dare one say?—the violences as well as the manifest beauties of this most extraordinary work.

"It is an exceedingly long work, though it must be admitted that the Master has not, in this respect, indulged himself quite so unstintingly as in the Heroic Symphony in E-flat that he presented some half-dozen years ago. It begins, even so, to emerge that quite consistently Herr van Beethoven's strokes of boldest individuality are those he conceives *in quaestio temporis*, in the matter of time—and we refer not only to absolute dimensions and to his penchant for reckless length, but also to his play with the flow of time, with the frenzied hurryings at one moment and the even more astonishing and disconcerting suspensions of movement at the next.

"This is manifest at the outset, for the first piece begins with three quick notes (of identical pitch) followed by a very long one a third lower, all announced with the greatest conceivable force. This idea is at once repeated a step lower and with the length of the last note exaggerated to an even greater degree. It is as though one had been twice encouraged to run and twice slammed hard and painfully into a wall of the most unyielding stone. It turns out that it is not the four notes that constitute the theme of this piece so much as the sum of the four notes and their instant reiteration. Indeed, the composer draws the most remarkable, the most unforeseeable combinations from his so persistent idea, and for a composition to be so dominated by, so saturated with a single idea—and that, so harsh—is unprecedented in our experience. It is almost as though Herr van Beethoven wished to make the statement that memorability is a more useful attribute in a theme than beauty.

"The composer's play with the notion of the sudden halt—that notion already so startlingly present in the second and fourth measures—returns more than once. Soon after the beginning, the violins stop on a long-held G as though frozen at the command of a magician's wand. At the corresponding spot in the third section of the movement, it is the oboe that not merely holds the G, but causes to emerge from it an unaccompanied cadence of a simple yet most touching expressiveness. Thus are pathos and beauty called to mitigate violence. Altogether, this is a composition of the most striking originality, and this claim can be made as confidently for its expressive power as for its ingenuities: here is music frightening in its ruthless economy and merciless force. After some hesitation—it was as though we had all been stunned—the public responded with heated and vociferous applause.

"The Andante serves to remind us of what we hope we may with impunity call Herr van Beethoven's more ordinary mastery; for here he presents a series of delightful variations—the kind where the figurations become ever quicker—on a melody as endowed in charm and grace as the first piece is devoid of those qualities. That we are in the presence of a work of Beethoven's is made clear not only by the delights of this melody—and with what pleasure one is reminded of the sweetness of his masterful Septet (and also perhaps of a less familiar but more demanding Sonata for the pianoforte in A-flat major)—but also by the surprising excursions into a distant and glaringly bright C major. This is strong stuff harmonically and not at once ingratiating, but it is masterfully arranged, not least because the key that seems so distant here is in fact home, as it were, to the symphony as a whole, and its final destination. Here, too, we find harshness, surprise, paradox, but for a purpose, and this is something to which we shall surely and gladly become accustomed.

"We are so far less convinced by those passages in which Herr van Beethoven, in preparation for the returns of his theme, spends lengths of time on a single chord (that of the fifth degree). They seem bizarre: it is almost as though the engravers had, in a moment of inattention, supplied too many repetitions of the same measure. Yet this strange effect, too, is consonant with the disconcerting halts in the first Allegro. Connections like this keep us from dismissing Herr van Beethoven's music as merely bizarre; even in his strangest music, the efforts of the discerning ear seem eventually always to be rewarded by the discovery of logic, clarity, consistency, the sense of purpose. It is merely that we sometimes wish that the Master would make the path to those rewards less thorny. Again, much applause, but of another flavor, warmly appreciative of secure and familiar mastery—thanks this time for the pleasures of the hearth as distinct from the excitement of adventure.

"With the third section, Herr van Beethoven once again leads us on ways so strange as virtually to constitute in themselves a guarantee of his authorship. He has in most of his earlier works disabused us of the notion that we might expect a true minuet, but never has he—nor indeed anyone—presented us with a parade of sinister spirits like the one that passes before us here. Basses and cellos dominate the scene. They creep in minor-mode unisons or, alternatively, they scrub in major with a frenzied jollity and at a speed really beyond the management of merely human fingers and bow-arms. And again, those strange stops—single notes dwelt upon in the midst of the flow of discourse, or, in the major-mode music for the sadly overtaxed basses, sudden rammings into brutally hard walls of silence. (At the first of the latter, there was an audible gasp from amid the public, many listeners assuming that something had gone seriously amiss in the execution.)

"But stranger things are to come. The movement does not stop. Rather, just when we expect it to do so, a false or deceptive cadence continues it artificially, with a long-held chord rendered restless by the insistent pulsing of the drums and by repeated attempts on the part of the violins to unstick themselves from this trap. All this is managed in a pianissimo that is the language of ghosts more than of flesh-and-blood human creatures, and the effect of this exceedingly drawn-out passage is compelling and bizarre in equal measure. Once again the idea of the disconcerting cessation of motion has seized the symphony and taken it over. Indeed, now it is as though this most astonishing music, the most extreme of all these halts, were the justification of the composer's passion for the device, and as though the previous instances of it in the symphony were merely preparations for this moment.

"This is the most crucial moment in the symphony. The violins' effort once again to set the music into motion, their persistence, is rewarded. The throbbing of the drums seems to draw closer until at last the veil is rent, and we emerge, dazzled, into the blazing daylight of C major. The finale has begun. It has begun, moreover, with the sound of trombones: church and theater have invaded the concert-room. Restraint of taste has never been characteristic of Herr van Beethoven, and this particular extravagance in scoring goes far. Extreme needs, however, call for extreme measures. The effect of the passage from darkness to light, from turmoil to victory, is so special and so new that one has a certain sympathy for the composer's desire to underline it with a new sound. One's sympathy is not, of course, free of apprehension: what is to stop the untrammeled Master from one day introducing Turkish music into a symphony or from carrying his borrowings from church and opera to the point of including the human voice itself?

"We used the word 'victory,' and the finale does seem to us a march of victory and of triumph. As the Andante is a familiar sort of music after the violent passions and compressions of the first Allegro, so is this march 'ordinary'—and we do not here intend this as abuse—after the eccentricities of the minuet. (The one most curious feature of this finale is, in fact, a brief return of the music of that minuet.) The very end of this exceedingly brilliant and difficult piece calls for comment. Never have we encountered so emphatic a reiteration of a single chord. One is reminded yet again of Herr van Beethoven's disinclination to let enough be enough. Yet, it must be admitted that if, abstractly, as it were, the chords of C major persist at incomprehensible length, in practice they are timed with perfect punctuality. They come out, one might say, 'just right,' and it is shrewd of the Master to give special finality to the last note by making it not one more chord but a bare and powerful unison.

"Connoisseurs brood over such things; amateurs can simply surrender to them. Herr van Beethoven's symphony presents us with a veritable thicket of puzzles, perhaps even offenses, as well as with countless manifestations of fiery genius. The enthusiasm the work aroused at this Academy seems to promise that we shall yet have many opportunities to come to terms with its extravagances as well as with its beauties. We may as well go so far as to express the hope that we shall never altogether cease to be to some degree shocked by what the willful but sure Master so clearly means to be shocking."

Well, that is a fake—with some intentional giveaways along with the involuntary ones; it is something that could be improvised for a workshop in reviewing new music. (Perhaps the American Musicological Society will some day establish an Anton Schindler Prize.) The imagined and smug reviewer knows a bit too much: he has, after all, known the Fifth Symphony for nearly 180 years. Of course he is also indebted to Hoffmann, but so should we all be. With his painstaking exposition of detail and his care for precise description, his susceptibility to poetic stimulation, his firm sense of the past that gives him so sharp a nose for the new, his delight in the manifestations of so original and untamed a personality, his sense at the same time for mastery and *Besonnenheit*, his intelligent and courteous notion that one will arrive at the most interesting and informative perceptions by beginning always with the assumption that the composer is right (or at least is doing whatever he is doing on purpose), his ability to tell one object from another, and his flexibility and personal confidence that allow him room for reservations about the work of an artist he intensely admires, Hoffmann is a virtually ideal critic of new music. How admirable it is that, in the musical cosmos which he so clearsightedly and receptively surveys, he finds room not only for evocation of a hitherto unexplored, unknown realm of the spirit, but also for discussion of the new practice of scoring for cellos undoubled by basses. How admirable also that, in his discussion of the *Egmont* music, he points to Beethoven's husbandry in the matter of ingenious compositional devices in a situation where the point is not only for the music to shine in its own cause and right, but also to say that the *Coriolan* Overture leads one to expect *Macbeth* at the very least, that it quite overwhelms poor Collin.

Most of the music criticism we meet in real life is as grudging and unloving, as automatic as the performances of which I complained before; it is profoundly unresponsive. The very activity is in disrepute. Yet the existence of a body of writings like Hoffmann's five essays in Beethoveniana rekindles our belief in words about music. There is plenty to be done. It will be better done and serve more vitally if there is more of a liaison between the worlds of criticism and scholarship. (I don't mean the musicological churnings that a distinguished performer has characterized as "intellectual welfare.") But critics will not be worse off for knowing what the most responsible and imaginative scholars are up to; indeed, one of their most useful tasks is the transmission—and, where necessary, translation—for the lay public of such work. At the same time, I wish it could go without saying that performers should be in direct touch with the world of scholarship. Avenues like the one opened by Rudolf Kolisch in his crucial study, "Tempo and Character in the Music of Beethoven," need far more extensive and intensive exploration. And surely we all need to keep returning to the scores themselves—to ask, as though it had never been asked before, what makes the Fifth Symphony a good piece; to ask new questions about, say, the Triple Concerto and *Consecration of the House*, problem pieces as intensely admired by some of us as they are despised by others; to look again, without prejudice, at a composition like *Wellington's Victory*, whose last three minutes are very good Beethoven by any standards, though one would not know it from the commentary.

Yes, too many of our responses as listeners are responses of habit and repetition, responses to a brand name and to an awesome cultural monument. We have come to be awfully comfortable with Beethoven—comfortable, unshocked, and unshockable. Often he traces for us the path from stress to victory, and the very idea that music might, without words, aspire to such a task is part of its newness. ("If only one knew what you had in mind in your music," said the dramatist and poet Franz Grillparzer to Beethoven. "After all, the censors can't touch a musician.") But the victory is diminished if we have not truly experienced the stress. That would surely provoke one of Beethoven's famous and terrifying rages. He would want to challenge us still, to jolt and unsettle us, in the end to make the reassurance the firmer and deeper for the jolting and the unsettling. To do that, he would have us *listen*—not overhear, not nod to familiar landmarks in pleased recognition, but listen as though for the first time and as though it might be the last.

Beethoven is of all composers the one who most insistently tells us that we cannot do without him. From that insistence—to which we respond so gladly—grows the paradox that the more time we spend in the presence of his music, the harder it is truly to hear it. That is the crux of his challenge to us all.

Music for Prague and Berlin: Beethoven's Concert Tour of 1796

Douglas Johnson

Beethoven talked loosely about concert tours on many occasions. A few times he seems to have made serious plans, but for one reason or another these plans never materialized. Health was a recurring problem, and towards the end of his life he could no longer think of performing other than as a conductor. But already after about 1800 his impaired hearing caused social difficulties, real or imagined, and his travel plans became dependent on others. Thus, for example, in one of his letters to Karl Amenda in 1801 he wrote:

> If after six months my disease proves to be incurable, then I shall claim your sympathy, then you must give up everything and come to me. I shall then travel (when I am playing and composing, my affliction hampers me least; it affects me most when I am in company) and you must be my companion. . . . My pianoforte playing has considerably improved; and I hope that our tour will perhaps enable you to make your fortune as well.[1]

Since Beethoven's deafness made him feel socially insecure, even in its early stages, it is perhaps not so surprising that his travel plans after 1800 usually came to nothing. His single extended concert tour occurred during the early years, in 1796. In that year he embarked on a journey which lasted five or six months and took him as far as Berlin; it was the farthest from Vienna he was ever to be after 1792.

Documentation of Beethoven's itinerary in 1796 is very skimpy. There are four nonmusical documents which bear directly on it. The first is a letter from Beethoven to his brother Johann, mailed from Prague on February 19, in which he says:

> So that you may know at any rate where I am and what I am doing, I really must write to you. First of all, I am well, very well. My art is winning me friends and renown, and what more do I want? And this time I shall make a good deal of money. I shall remain here for a few weeks longer and then travel to Dresden,

Leipzig, and Berlin. So it will certainly be six weeks at least before I return. . . .
Prince Lichnowsky will soon be on his way back to Vienna. He has already left
Prague.[2]

The second document, discovered recently in the archives of the Czech
Philharmonic, is a concert ticket in French which reads: "Ticket for the
concert of Louis van Beethoven in the Convict–Salle, Friday, March
11."[3] Although the year is not given, March 11 was a Friday in 1796,
and we cannot place Beethoven in Prague in any other year in which this
day and date coincide. The third document—or documents—is a pair of
letters from a man named von Schall to the Bonn Elector, Max Franz,
which were mailed from Dresden on April 24 and May 6.[4] From the
first we learn that Beethoven had arrived in Dresden on April 23 and
from the second that he left for Leipzig and Berlin after only eight days
there, having performed once for the Elector of Saxony. Finally we have
the record kept by Carl Friedrich Fasch of the meetings of the Berliner
Singakademie. Fasch noted that Beethoven was present at rehearsals on
June 21 and June 28, improvising for the group each time.[5]

Taken together, these four documents tell us that Beethoven
had traveled to Prague by early February, probably with Lichnowsky,
and that he remained in Prague at least two months before continuing in
late April without Lichnowsky to Dresden, where he stayed about a
week. We then find him in Berlin at the end of June. There is no record
of his visit to Leipzig or of his arrival in Berlin. We have it secondhand
from Ferdinand Ries that Beethoven also performed at the Berlin court
and from A. W. Thayer that the court dispersed to summer homes early
in July.[6]

The original documents say nothing of specific works; we do
not know the program of the March 11 concert in Prague or that of
Beethoven's performance at the court in Dresden. Ries tells us that the
principal works performed in Berlin were the two cello sonatas, Op. 5,
which were written by Beethoven expressly for the court cellist Jean
Louis Duport and himself, and which were subsequently dedicated to
Friedrich Wilhelm II.[7] All of our knowledge beyond this, however,
derives from the musical manuscripts themselves. Here the evidence has
accumulated very slowly.

There are two kinds of evidence associated directly with manuscripts used by Beethoven during his journey. The simpler is that provided by dedicatory inscriptions. Among the papers in Beethoven's *Nachlass* in 1827 was a copyist's score of the solo scene for soprano, *Ah! perfido*,

Op. 65. This copy has not survived, but one of its nineteenth-century owners, Aloys Fuchs, recorded the text of two inscriptions by Beethoven: "Une grande Scène mise en musique par L. v. Beethoven à Prague 1796" (first title page); and "Recitativo e Aria composta e dedicata alla Signora di Clari di L. v. Beethoven" (second title page). The lady of the dedication was the then eighteen-year-old Josephine de Clary, a gifted singer and player of the mandoline, who lived in Prague and who in 1797 married Count Christian von Clam-Gallas. At some point Beethoven changed his mind about the dedication; the first known public performance of the work was by Josepha Duschek, another Prague singer, in late 1796, and it was later published with no dedication.

Beethoven's brief association with Josephine extended beyond Op. 65, however. Early in this century several works for mandoline and piano (or harpsichord) turned up in the Clam-Gallas family collection.[8] Included were autographs of the two movements listed in Kinsky-Halm as WoO 43b and WoO 44b, each with a brief dedication from Beethoven to Josephine (initials taking the place of full names), and copies of three other movements. These copies have since been lost, but one of the movements—the C-major Allegro, WoO 44a—was published in 1912.[9] A draft of another inscription to Josephine, "pour Mademoiselle la Comtesse de Clari," is found at the bottom of a leaf in a Berlin miscellany containing sketches for *Ah! perfido* and several of the mandoline pieces.[10]

In addition to *Ah! perfido* and the mandoline pieces, WoO 43b, 44a, and 44b, all apparently written for Josephine de Clary, another work can also be assigned to Beethoven's Prague visit on the basis of an inscription. This is the set of six German dances for violin and piano, WoO 42. A copy of this work has been found in the Nationalbibliothek, Vienna, and the inscription on the title page is a humorous one:

> Deutsche für die zwei Comtessen Thun um andern Leuten danach auf dem Kopfe zu tanzen und dabey zu denken an ihren Sie verehrenden Ludwig van Beethoven Prague 1796[11]

> ("German Dances for the two Countesses Thun to tease other people with and thereby remember their respectful Ludwig van Beethoven, Prague, 1796")

The identity of the "Comtessen Thun" is uncertain. The daughters of the elderly Maria Wilhelmine can probably be excluded, since they had acquired new names through marriage (one of them was Princess Lichnowsky). It is more likely, given the nature of the inscription and the simple style of the pieces themselves, that Beethoven was referring to a third generation of Thun daughters in a related family.

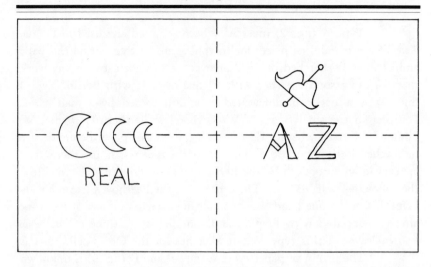

Fig. 1. Type X. Surviving sources: Prague, National Museum, bifolium (auto-graph of WoO 43b); Paris MS 79, bifolium (autograph fragment of Op.65; sketches for a song, *Heidenröslein*, and an unfinished symphony); Kafka miscellany, fol. 87 (autograph of WoO 43a); Kafka miscellany, fols. 104–6 (auto-graph of Op. 71 III; sketches for Op. 65, WoO 43b, WoO 44a, and Op. 49, no. 2); Fischhof miscellany, fol. 43 (sketches for WoO 43b, WoO 44a, Op. 65, and WoO 42).

On the basis of these inscriptions, then, we can add several Prague works to the cello sonatas, Op. 5, as the products of Beethoven's journey. But the list is still a sparse one for a tour of five months, especially when one considers the slight proportions of the dances and mandoline pieces. In order to extend it we must turn to a second kind of physical evidence, that provided by the paper of the manuscripts of this period.

Most of the music paper used in Vienna in the 1790s was manufactured in what is now northern Italy and is characterized by distinctive watermarks. Typically, these watermarks include three cres-cent moons opposite a set of initials, the latter often in combination with some device such as a crown, a crest, or a crossbow (type X; fig. 1). Among the papers used by Beethoven in these years, however, are four other non-Italian types with very different watermarks, types which can be assigned on the grounds of handwriting and musical content to the year 1796. Beethoven seems to have obtained them during his absence from Vienna.[12]

Type A (fig. 2) must have been acquired and used in Prague. Two of the mandoline pieces for Josephine are written out on this paper and another is sketched on it; moreover, it was not used for any works that we can associate earlier with Vienna or later with Berlin. Type B (fig. 3) is a paper manufactured at a mill owned by a man named Fournier in the small town of Wolfswinkel in northern Germany. We cannot be certain whether Beethoven acquired this paper before or after he reached Berlin, but we do know that the type was in use there, for it appears in an autograph by the Berlin composer Friedrich Himmel from the following year, 1797.[13] The contents of the Beethoven leaves are also helpful. On the one hand, they contain no sketches for any of the works already associated with Prague, and, on the other, three of the seven known leaves of this type contain sketches for the Op. 5 cello sonatas.

The origin of paper types C (fig. 4) and D (fig. 5) is unknown. But again we can make some judgments about their use on the basis of their musical contents. The sketches on type C *follow* those for the same works (Op. 5, Op. 16, and the symphony) on type B paper, so we may assume that Beethoven obtained paper of type C after type B—again, probably in Berlin. Type D presents a more complicated picture. The contents of leaves of this type indicate that it was probably the last paper that Beethoven obtained before his return to Vienna. In fact, several of the works that we find here can be associated with the period following the journey: the piano sonatas, Op. 7 and Op. 10, the variations, WoO 71, and even some Salieri studies that were done about five years later. But at least two sources of this paper—the autograph of the Handel variations for cello and piano, WoO 45, and the leaf with the cello fingerings—would seem to belong with the Berlin manuscripts.

The relatively small quantities of each of the four non-Italian papers which have survived suggest that these may represent the remnants of larger batches used by Beethoven for autograph scores which have not survived (for example, of Op. 5). In the particular case of type D, the several leaves that were used for sketching after the journey could have been left over from autographs such as that of WoO 45.

In addition to acquiring paper types A–D during his journey, Beethoven also took some paper with him when he left Vienna. This fact is easiest to demonstrate in the case of the Italian paper illustrated as type X. Beethoven had used large amounts of this paper in Vienna in 1793–95. But a few of the surviving leaves are devoted to works that we have associated with Prague: the German dances, *Ah! perfido*, and at

Fig. 2. Type A. Surviving sources: Berlin, Deutsche Staatsbibliothek, Gras-nick 25, fols. 8–11 (autograph of WoO 43b); Prague, National Museum (au-tograph of WoO 44b); Kafka miscellany, fol. 73 (sketches for WoO 43a and WoO 44b); Kafka miscellany, fols. 84–85 (sketches for an unfinished work in G for piano and winds); Vienna, Gesellschaft der Musikfreunde, A67, bifo-lium (sketches for *Erlkönig*, WoO 131, and *Rastlose Liebe*, Hess 149).

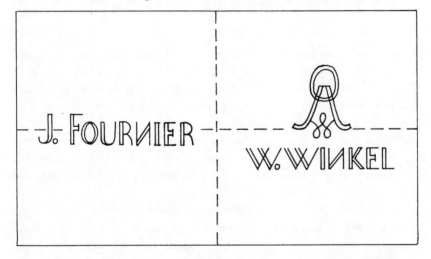

Fig. 3. Type B. Surviving sources: Kafka miscellany, fols. 48–49 (sketches for Op. 16, I–III); Kafka miscellany, fols. 81–82 (sketches for Op. 16, II; Op. 37, I; Op. 37, III; and Andante for an unfinished symphony); Kafka miscellany, fol. 83 (sketches for Op. 5, no. 1 and Op. 5, no. 2); Kafka miscellany, fol. 142 (sketches for Op. 5, no. 1); Bergamo, Donizetti Insti-tute, bifolium (sketches for Op. 5, no. 2 and for an unfinished symphony).

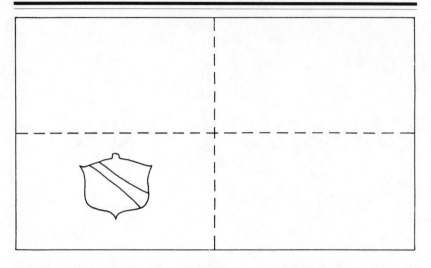

Fig. 4. Type C. Surviving sources: Kafka miscellany, fol. 119 (autograph of WoO 32 Minuet; sketches for Op. 5, no. 1, Op. 5. no. 2, Op. 16, and WoO 32 I); Fischhof miscellany, fol. 9 (sketches for an unfinished symphony); Fischhof miscellany, fols. 13–14 (sketches for Op. 5, no. 1, Op. 5, no. 2, Op 16, and an unfinished symphony); Fischhof miscellany, fols. 16–17 (sketches for an unfinished symphony).

least two of the mandoline pieces are sketched on paper of this type, and it was used for autographs of WoO 43a, WoO 43b, and *Ah! perfido* (a fragment only). Normally we might suggest that Beethoven did this work in Vienna and brought it to Prague. But in at least one case (WoO 43a), the autograph of a mandoline piece on type X follows sketches for the same piece on type A. This overlap in the use of Italian and Bohemian paper indicates that some of the former was used in Prague. It does not seem unreasonable to conclude that at least the mandoline pieces and the dances were written after Beethoven's arrival there.

Since the contents of the known leaves of types A–D and X are not confined to the works we have already associated with Beethoven's journey, we are now in a position to suggest some additions to that list. The contents of types A and X, the two papers that Beethoven used in Prague, are as follows:

> Sonatina in G, Op. 49, no. 2 (sketches)
> *Ah! perfido*, Op. 65 (sketches; autograph fragment)
> Wind Sextet, Op. 71, Minuet (autograph)

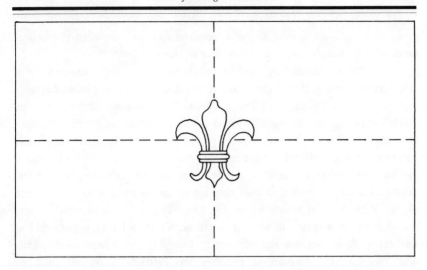

Fig. 5. Type D. Surviving sources: Vienna, Gesellschaft der Musikfreunde, A2, 15 fols. (autograph of WoO 45); Kafka miscellany, fol. 109 (cello fingerings in another hand); Kafka miscellany, fols. 110–11 (sketches for Op. 6); Kafka miscellany, fol. 155 (sketches for Op. 10, no. 3, Op. 37 I, and WoO 11); Kafka miscellany, fols. 156–57 (sketches for Op. 10, no. 3); Fischhof miscellany, fols. 27–29 (sketches for Op. 10, no. 1, WoO 53, WoO 71 [?], and Op. 10, no. 2[?]).

> German dances, WoO 42 (sketches)
> Sonatina in C minor for mandoline, WoO 43a (sketches; autograph)
> Adagio in E♭ for mandoline, WoO 43b (sketches; two autographs)
> Allegro in C for mandoline, WoO 44a (sketches)
> Variations in D for mandoline, WoO 44b (sketches; autograph)
> *Erlkönig*, WoO 131 (sketches)
> *Rastlose Liebe*, Hess 149 (sketches)
> *Heidenröslein*, Hess 150 (sketches)
> Quartet for piano and winds (sketches)
> Symphony in C (sketches)

The least surprising new entry here is an additional movement for mandoline, WoO 43a, the piece mentioned above that Beethoven sketched on Bohemian paper and wrote out on Italian paper. Although this is the only one of the four movements without some sort of inscription to

31

Josephine, it does appear to have been written for her with the others (and not, as Kinsky suggests, for Wenzel Krumpholz).[14]

Of the remaining works on these two papers, only two were completed. One of them, the wind sextet, Op. 71, cannot be exclusively associated with Beethoven's Prague visit. There are no sketches for the work on the leaves in question, and it can be shown from other sources that the finale was composed after the journey. On the other hand, the location of the Minuet autograph on the inner sides of the bifolium Kafka 104–5 does suggest that it was written out independently of the sextet as a whole, and that this could have taken place either in Prague or in Vienna. The Sonatina in G, Op. 49, no. 2 is somewhat less ambiguous. It was one of several works sketched in leftover space on the gathering that contains the Minuet of Op. 71; the others—*Ah! perfido* and two of the mandoline pieces—have already been assigned to Prague.[15] Thus it appears that the sonatina was also written there, probably at someone's request (though Op. 49, like *Ah! perfido*, was published in 1805 with no dedication).

The remaining Prague sources, Kafka 84–85 and Vienna A67, were devoted to works for which no finished versions exist, but the sketches are coherent enough to attract our curiosity. The bifolium A67 is filled completely by drafts of two songs on poems by Goethe. *Rastlose Liebe* occupies the first three pages and *Erlkönig* the fourth. The former is virtually complete; a draft of the entire song extends from the top of the first page through most of the second, and the remainder of the second page and most of the third were used for revisions. One suspects that there were earlier sketches, for the draft reflects a rather complex conception of the song: the first three of the four stanzas, sung twice, form the basis for a large binary structure ($E\flat \rightarrow B\flat \rightarrow G\flat \rightarrow E\flat$), with a large coda based on the contrasting fourth stanza. The *Erlkönig* draft on the last page is more tentative (fig. 6). The later stanzas, beginning with the first entry of the Erlkönig himself, are interrupted in several places by "usw." Beethoven indicates how a passage is to be set and then skips ahead; thus, for example, the entry of the Erlkönig is shown by a single measure, set off by a change of key from D minor to B$\flat$ major and a change of accompaniment, which Beethoven adds under the vocal line on the same staff (staff 4). What was to have been the closing ritornello is written out in full at the end of the draft.

These drafts have been variously dated. Reinhold Becker produced a version of *Erlkönig* based on the A67 draft in 1897—this is how

Fig. 6. Draft of *Erlkönig*, Vienna, Gesellschaft der Musikfreunde, A67, bifolium.
By permission of the Gesellschaft der Musikfreunde.

the work got into Kinsky-Halm as WoO 131—and he assigned the manuscript to the years 1805–10.[16] Nottebohm had first suggested 1800–1810, then 1800–1804.[17] And Jean Chantavoine, who published a transcription of the *Rastlose Liebe* draft in 1902, assigned it to 1792–96 on stylistic grounds.[18] This was the closest guess, as we can now see. The manuscript should be assigned tentatively to Beethoven's Prague visit in 1796. Indeed, these were not the only songs that he attempted there. On Paris MS 79, the bifolium containing the autograph fragment of *Ah! perfido*, he made sketches for another Goethe song, *Heidenröslein*. These sketches are even less thorough than the ones for *Erlkönig*, and it may have been inexperience with Beethoven's handwriting and sketch procedures that led a man named Henry Huss to make an edition of the song from them in 1898.[19] Ignoring the fact that a series of entries in the manuscript were probably intended as alternative versions of the opening phrase (they are marked "oder"), Huss strung the entries together as the successive phrases of the song.

How shall we account for these song sketches? They seem to have been prompted by some encounter in Prague. The fact that all three songs use texts by Goethe suggests that there had been some discussion of the poet or perhaps even of someone else's settings. J. F. Reichardt, for example, had published a collection of Goethe songs in 1794 that could have provided the basis for an informal evening's entertainment. We must also wonder whether or not Beethoven actually completed the songs. Had the Clam-Gallas collection not come to light in this century, we would be asking similar questions about two of the mandoline pieces, and indeed the loss of the Clam-Gallas copies probably means that certain other movements sketched in the Prague sources were actually finished. But in the case of the songs we must not be too optimistic. There are signs that Beethoven returned to the drafts much later with the idea of finishing and publishing them. Next to the sketches for *Heidenröslein*, for example, he added "4" and one further sketch, both in pencil and in a considerably later handwriting. The best guess is that this occurred in the early 1820s, when he looked through his early manuscripts again in search of bagatelles and songs for possible publication. This is how several early piano pieces got into Op. 119. *Heidenröslein* was apparently intended to be the fourth song in a similar collection.[20]

No similar numbers accompany the drafts of *Rastlose Liebe* and *Erlkönig*; they were perhaps too large in scope to fit comfortably in a set.

But there is one indication that Beethoven did contemplate publishing them at that time. In 1823 he wrote to Goethe, noting: "Soon perhaps several of your ever unique poems which I have set to music ought to be appearing and these will include *Rastlose Liebe*."[21] In view of the numerous other Goethe settings that Beethoven had published, it is difficult to imagine him withholding *Rastlose Liebe* and *Erlkönig* for twenty-five years. Still, we cannot be certain that completed versions of one or both had not been presented to someone in Prague in 1796. It does seem ironic that *Rastlose Liebe*, the one song of the three which is virtually complete melodically in the drafts, is the only one which has not been edited.

The sketches on Kafka 84–85 for a work for piano and winds are also of some interest.[22] In this case the interest derives less from the work itself than from its possible implications for another work—the Quintet for Piano and Winds, Op. 16. The sketches on Kafka 84–85, a bifolium of Bohemian paper, suggest that a group of wind players in Prague had given Beethoven the idea for such a work, perhaps after a performance of Mozart's quintet (although the latter was still unpublished). Significantly, the abandonment of these sketches appears to coincide more or less exactly with the conception of Op. 16. Beethoven's quintet has traditionally been assigned to the winter of 1796–97 on the basis of the earliest known performance in Vienna in April, 1797. But the sketches for the work, including all three movements, are found exclusively on paper types B and C, which Beethoven obtained and used in Germany. Thus the possibility emerges that Op. 16 was in fact completed in Berlin.

In this regard some interest attaches to a draft of a letter that Beethoven made in the margin of another Berlin leaf (fig. 7). The completed letter itself has not been found, and the intended recipient is not known, but the beginning of the draft reads: "I have the honor of sending you the quintet, and you will be doing me a great offence if you regard it as an unimportant gift. The only restriction that I must make is that you give it to no one else."[23] The rest is largely indecipherable because of damage to the leaf. Nottebohm, who misdated the leaf, assumed that Beethoven was referring to the Op. 4 string quintet.[24] But it appears from Artaria's plate numbers that Op. 4 had been given over for engraving *before* Beethoven left Vienna. His request that the gift remain private might have been intended to prevent pirating, of course, but then we must wonder why he would bother to send someone a copy of a work that was already in the process of publication. It seems more likely, given the location of the letter on a Berlin leaf and the contemporary sketches for Op. 16, that the work in question was in fact the Quintet for Piano and Winds—and, in view of the earlier sketches for a similar work on Bohemian paper, that the quintet was sent to someone in Prague.

In the course of this survey of the works that Beethoven sketched on papers obtained during his journey of 1796, a distinction has been gradually emerging between his compositional activity in Prague and in Berlin. The works written in Prague seem to reflect his assimilation into aristocratic circles there: dances for two young countesses, mandoline pieces for Josephine, a sonatina for someone else, and—in concept, at least—some Goethe songs. With the possible exception of *Ah! perfido*, which was also initially dedicated to Josephine, this is unpretentious music for private performance. It would appear that Beethoven had been accepted at once by Prague society, his entry undoubtedly eased by Prince Lichnowsky, whose in-laws (the Thun family) lived there.

As we know from Beethoven's letter to his brother, however, he continued the journey without Lichnowsky, and there is reason to suspect that his compositional activity in Berlin was more formal. The Berlin compositions seem designed not to flatter local friends, but to impress the court and the professional musicians associated with it. The major products, of course, were the cello sonatas that he performed with Duport. These were conceived to pass the scrutiny of a sort of cellists' Mafia, headed by Friedrich Wilhelm himself. That Beethoven escaped with a snuffbox full of gold pieces would seem to be a sign of approval. From our perspective, the Op. 5 sonatas were as royal in their proportions, if not in their taste, as anything he had written up to that time. And Beethoven may well have gilded his own offering with one or two sets of variations for cello and piano. The few existing sketches for the variations on Mozart's "Ein Mädchen oder Weibchen" (published later as Op. 66) were added to a leaf that Beethoven had used in Vienna in 1795 and taken along on the Berlin journey.[25] There has been some inclination to associate the variations on a theme from *Judas Maccabeus*, WoO 45, with the Viennese Handel enthusiast, Baron van Swieten. This is understandable, since van Swieten had organized a performance of *Judas Maccabeus* on April 15, 1794, and Beethoven's variations were actually dedicated to the hostess of that concert, Princess Lichnowsky.[26] But the

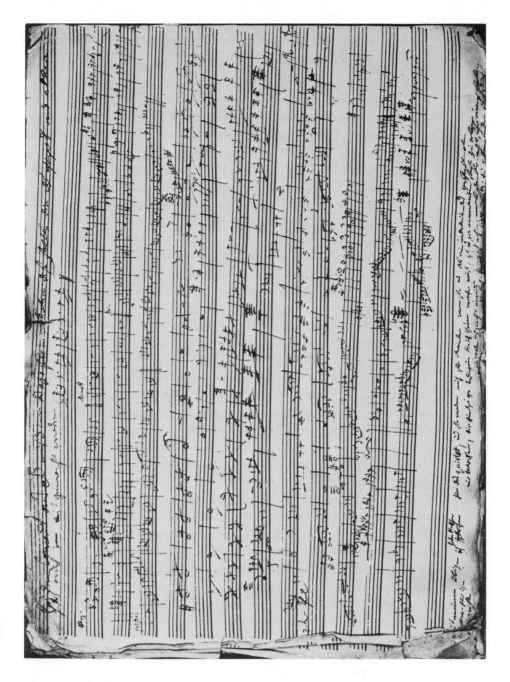

Fig. 7. Draft of the minuet (staves 3–4) and sketches for the coda (staves 6–10) and development (staves 11–14) of the first movement of the unfinished symphony in C major, Fischhof miscellany, fol. 16v.
By permission of the Staatsbibliothek Preussischer Kulturbesitz.

autograph of WoO 45 is on paper type D, which Beethoven obtained and used two years after the van Swieten performance. And there is an equally plausible connection of WoO 45 with Berlin, quite aside from the paper. *Judas Maccabeus* was the principal work rehearsed by the Berliner Singakademie throughout the winter of 1795–96.[27] Since Beethoven paid two visits to the Singakademie during his stay in Berlin, might he not have looked through the work with its members and then written (and played?) the variations as a memento of those visits?

A final indication of Beethoven's professional aspirations in Berlin is the extensive work that he did there on a symphony in C major. The sketches for the symphony have been dated variously from 1794 to 1800, but it can be shown that Beethoven conceived the work in Vienna in 1795 and took his preliminary sketches along to Berlin, where he made a series of elaborate drafts on paper of types B and C.[28] He must have contemplated the possibility of giving a concert of his music in Berlin, with the symphony as a centerpiece. But apparently the opportunity did not materialize, and the work was abandoned some time after his return to Vienna, to be taken up again four years later in connection with the First Symphony, Op. 21. It is the relationship of the first movement of the projected symphony to the finale of Op. 21 that has misled people about the nature of these sketches. A few thematic similarities aside, the movements have little in common. Furthermore, the first movement of the 1796 symphony is a very striking conception; it is more sophisticated in its handling of large-scale structure than the cello sonatas.

How far did Beethoven get with the work? For the first movement there are extensive drafts of a slow introduction (eight), the exposition (six), and the coda (three), and ideas for several parts of the development section. The last three introduction drafts, the last two exposition drafts, and two of the coda drafts were made in Berlin. Also on Berlin type B paper is a draft of an Andante in E major inscribed "zur Sinfonie," with a second inscription indicating a transposition to F. And on the same bifolium which contains the most advanced sketches for the first movement, Beethoven drafted a complete minuet and the first half of a trio. There is nothing for the finale beyond a few brief thematic ideas, however. Thus it seems unlikely that the work was actually completed, although it was far enough along that it could have been, had the opportunity for a performance arisen.

There are other aspects of Beethoven's journey about which one might also speculate, such as the program of that mysterious concert in Prague, the meaning of a few brief sketches for the C-minor Piano Concerto, Op. 37, which occur on the Berlin leaves, or the models for *Ah! perfido*. But identification and study of the manuscripts that Beethoven used have allowed us to see somewhat more clearly than before what he actually produced during the trip and to relate the works to the circumstances that prompted them. The sources suggest that most of his compositional activity was associated with the lengthy first and last stops in Prague and Berlin. (There is actually no direct confirmation of the planned appearance in Leipzig, and the Dresden visit lasted only a week.) He seems to have written nothing for his own use in Prague, devoting himself rather to the pleasures of a mostly amateur and mostly feminine circle. His own performances there and in Dresden must have involved works already written in Vienna. In Berlin, on the other hand, where the circle was professional, the same sort of attention to local tastes resulted in a series of more substantial works aimed at impressing rather than amusing his patrons. If the journey as a whole failed to produce the best of Beethoven's early work, it was nonetheless marked by the confidence, facility, and flexibility that we might expect from Beethoven at this stage of his career. "My art is winning me friends and renown," he wrote from Prague. The "friends" may seem to us to have been concentrated in Prague and the "renown" in Berlin. But Beethoven's rhetorical afterthought—"What more do I want?"—suggests a general satisfaction with the state of his art, which for a time at least seemed to be pleasing everyone.

Notes

1. Anderson 53.
2. Anderson 16.
3. Bohumil Plevka, *Beethoven a Praha* (Prague, 1975), p. 96.
4. Thayer-Forbes, p. 184.
5. Thayer-Deiters-Riemann, II^3:17–18.
6. Wegeler-Ries, p. 109; Thayer-Deiters-Riemann, II^3:18.
7. The sonatas were intended for Jean Louis Duport rather than his brother Jean Pierre, as has been assumed (Lewis Lockwood, "Beethoven's Early Works for Violoncello and Contemporary Violoncello Technique," paper read at a Beethoven symposium in Vienna in 1977).
8. The discovery was made (or published) by Arthur Chitz; the most easily accessible account of it is in Alexander Buchner, "Beethovens Kompositionen für Mandoline," *Beethoven-Jahrbuch* 3, Jg. 1957–58 (1959):38–50.

9. Arthur Chitz, "Beethovens Kompositionen für Mandoline. Mit einem unveröffent- lichten Sonatinen-Satz Beethovens," *Der Merker* 3 (1912):446–50 and Appendix.

10. StPK, Autograph 28, fol. 43r. See fig. 1.

11. ÖNB, S.M. 8977. The copy was described to me by Richard Kramer.

12. These are the papers classified as types II-A to II-D in the general survey of Beethoven's early manuscripts in my dissertation, "Beethoven's Early Sketches in the 'Fischhof' Miscellany: Berlin Autograph 28" (University of California at Berkeley, 1977). The handwriting evidence for dating these papers is also discussed there.

13. DStB, Mus. ms. aut. F. H. Himmel 5 (a *Musique champêtre* dated July 14, 1797).

14. We may speculate that a copy of WoO 43a was among the lost copies in the Clam-Gallas collection.

15. This list can be extended if we add the works sketched on Fischhof 43, the probable fourth leaf of a gathered sheet with Kafka 104–6.

16. Reinhold Becker, *Erlkönig. Nach einer Skizze von L. v. Beethoven.* (Leipzig: J. Schu- berth and Co., 1897).

17. The *Erlkönig* sketches are dated 1800–10 in N I:100–103, but in N II:575, the *Rastlose Liebe* sketches on the same bifolium are assigned to 1800–1804.

18. Jean Chantavoine, "Beethoveniana," *Revue musicale* 2 (1902):409–14.

19. It is reproduced in a review by Henry Krehbiel in the *New York Tribune Illustrated Supplement* of March 8, 1898. The edition was copyrighted by G. Schirmer.

20. Beethoven made several other sketches for *Heidenröslein* in the years around 1820.

21. Anderson 1136.

22. There is no specific indication of the complete intended scoring of the work; in his edition of the Kafka miscellany (London, 1970), Joseph Kerman tentatively asso- ciates these sketches with the inscription "quartett in g mit flauto oboe fagott" in the margin of another leaf of 1795–96 (Kafka 45v).

23. StPK, Autograph 28, fol. 16v. The German text is: "Ich [the word "schicke" is crossed out here] habe die Ehre ihnen hier das quintett, und sie werden mich sehr verbinden, wenn sie es als ein unbedeutendes geschenk von mir betrachten, die Einzige Bedingung, die ich ihnen machen muss, ist, es gar niemandem sonst zu geben." It is slightly garbled in N II:229.

24. N II:229.

25. Kafka 71; the verso of this leaf was used to begin a score of the symphony in C discussed below.

26. Reinhold Bernhardt, "Van Swieten und seine Judas Maccabeus-Bearbeitung," *Zeit- schrift für Musikwissenschaft* 17 (1935):541.

27. Martin Blumner, *Geschichte der Sing-Akademie zu Berlin* (Berlin, 1891), pp. 15–17.

28. The evidence is discussed at length in my dissertation, cited above.

Historical Problems
in Beethoven Performance

Panel discussion prepared by Sherwyn T. Carr

Moderator: *Owen Jander*; panelists; *Ilse von Alpenheim, Eva Badura-Skoda, Malcolm Bilson, John Hsu, Sonya Monosoff, Daniel Stepner, James Webster.*

Panelists frequently played musical examples during the discussion. The instruments referred to are a modern Steinway concert grand piano; a replica of a Viennese fortepiano by Anton Walter (early 1780s) made by Philip Belt of Stonington, Connecticut, in 1977; a Baroque violin by Joseph Klotz (1795); and a modernized Amati violin. The Baroque violin has been restored to its original proportions, with the neck at a lesser angle than on the modern instrument, and with a smaller sound post and bass bar; it has no chin rest. The Baroque bow is lighter than the modern Tourte-designed bow, and with less tension. The pitch of the old instruments used during the panel discussion was approximately a half-step lower than modern standard pitch.

[Owen Jander prefaced the discussion with a sketch of the background of Philip Belt's replica fortepianos and described the effect that the instrument owned by Wellesley College has had on ideas about performance practice at Wellesley and in the greater Boston area. He concluded: "We hear classical music differently now. We perform and study classical music differently. The presence of that instrument changes what we do in the classroom; it even changes the way we analyze classical music. It has become a powerful influence in our musical and educational thinking."]

Jander: We are here to talk about performance practice. These are the experts. At the outset, I'd like to talk about the problems of dynamics. When you come from the world of the late nineteenth and twentieth centuries into the world of eighteenth and early nineteenth-century performance practice you have to think very differently dynamically. When you start working with these instruments, you realize that there is no *ffff*; there is really no *fff*. There's very rarely even a *ppp*, and *f* and *p* become very important. There is no *mf* and no *mp* between *f* and *p*. Miss von Alpenheim recently had the experience of coming from the modern instrument and recording Haydn concerti on a replica fortepiano.

Von Alpenheim: It was my first experience with a fortepiano. I was asked by my recording company to play the concerti on it, and I accepted reluctantly. But then I had a look around and found a fortepiano, and I thought I'd go and record for three days and that would be it. The result was that I called the recording off, took the fortepiano home for three months, and learned to play it. It was very difficult both to learn the fortepiano and to go back to the modern piano. The fortepiano has a completely different touch, not to speak of dynamics.

Jander: How about bringing original instruments into combination with later instruments in performance? Is it feasible?

Monosoff: No, I think. When I first started playing the Baroque violin, we used to experiment with putting mutes on the modern instruments, and of course that's an entirely different sound, so it doesn't work at all. I think it's increasingly difficult to make that kind of combination of instruments, and of course the bow has much to do with the kind of articulation. If you use a modern bow, you really can't articulate as cleanly, clearly, and lightly as you can on the fortepiano. This would apply to harpsichord versus piano for continuo playing, too.

When I first started with the New York Pro Musica, we knew nothing whatsoever about the instruments. I remember one terrible moment when somebody came up to Noah Greenberg, the late director of the Pro Musica, and said, "Why doesn't your viola da gamba have frets?" We didn't know that it had to have frets—now we know. More and more young people are taking for granted the necessity of going back and using the old instruments for this kind of music; people don't try so much to make the kind of compromise which we all made a few years ago. Malcolm Bilson and I have experimented. The last time we did Beethoven's G-major Violin Sonata [Op. 30, no. 3], I used my modern violin tuned down. It didn't quite work for us.

Bilson: But we're not sure. I think it's important to say that.

Monosoff: What's interesting in terms of the violin is that it was just during Beethoven's period that the neck started to be pulled back more and more. The strings became more tightly wound—except the E string, which was always gut instead of wound steel until the twentieth century. And the bow was changing, because François Tourte [1747–1835, creator of the modern bow] was changing the whole balance and weight of it. So we don't know exactly what instruments were used. Maybe different instruments were used according to what was available in any particular place. We've had to do a lot of experimenting with this whole business.

Bilson: There were lots of different instruments and lots of different instruments were used. There are also big and little differences between instruments. A big difference, for instance, is between an Anton Walter fortepiano and a Steinway piano. A smaller difference would be between this Walter fortepiano and the almost contemporary Stein fortepiano, or between the Steinway and a Bechstein. But if we're dealing with the period from about 1775 to 1830, it's clear that everything was in transition. The bow was changing like crazy and different kinds of pianos were being built in different countries in different styles. But they all teach us different things.

Hsu: I think the question was whether it's right to combine, say, this fortepiano with modern strings to play a concerto.

Bilson: When we inaugurated the Wellesley Walter piano, we were supposed to get an orchestra of old instruments, and instead most of the musicians came with modern ones. The flutist brought her wooden flute, but when she saw what the bassoonist had, she put it away and got out her silver flute. What else could she do? But basically, when you have a pianist who is sitting at what should be a very light, delicate instrument, and he is pounding a little bit, and everybody else is sort of playing on tippy-toe, it isn't really an ideal situation. I wouldn't do it anymore.

Badura-Skoda: Isn't it fairly clear that no Tourte bow came to Vienna before 1825 or so? Anyway, not much before Beethoven's death. The other changes in the violin took place around 1800, but for the eighteenth century we should really think of the Baroque violin.

Monosoff: The words "Baroque violin" don't mean much. It was a transitional period. I've been told that when Stradivarius made some of his violins, there was a repairman around the corner, and people ran from Strad's workshop to the man around the corner to have the neck lowered. This is all so problematic, because there are no records that I know of. I've asked violin dealers who've been in business for a long time if there are any records of changes that have been made, and they don't have any until the end of the nineteenth century. I wonder about saying that the Tourte bow didn't get to Vienna, because in fact people were traveling around so much I can't imagine that somebody didn't appear in Vienna with one.

Badura-Skoda: But that bow was necessary only for the virtuosos, not the normal players.

Webster: This is an illustration of a rather important general point that bears on the question of historical performance practice and what the correct way of imitating is. There is a tremendous variety in virtually every aspect of performance in the eighteenth century—from place to place, from time to time, from type of music to type of music, even from period to period, or from genre to genre within a given composer's output. It's a simplification to say "the Mozart piano." It's certainly an oversimplification to speak of "the Viennese fortepiano," let alone "the eighteenth-century violin"; there's no such creature. These are little distinctions, in a way, but the more one gets into these subjects, the more important even these little distinctions seem to become.

Jander: When Beethoven was a young man, the prevailing instrument in Vienna was a five-octave instrument, the range of this fortepiano here. About 1805, the Viennese instrument became a six-octave instrument and virtually doubled in weight. Circa 1815, the Viennese piano expanded even beyond that, and went down from the low F which had been the prevailing bottom note for pianos and harpsichords for a century or more. It went down to contra C, half an octave below that, and again virtually doubled in weight. When you are talking about the three periods of Beethoven's piano music, you are talking about three different pianos. And a properly equipped music department of the future will want three pianos. This business of range is obvious when you are dealing with pianos. You can see how different the one is from the other just on the basis of the keyboard. It's not quite so obvious on the violin.

Monosoff: There are interesting examples in one of the Haydn quartets [F major, Op. 17, no. 2], where Haydn has *sopra una corda.* You go quite high on the G string, but by that time the G string was wound. It's only very early Baroque music where the G wasn't wound, and what's interesting is the other strings. The D, A, and E were gut strings until the beginning of the twentieth century, when the steel string became normal.

Stepner: At least for me, one of the important things about playing on a so-called original instrument is that one can light into it for the first time without worrying much about style. You can learn a great deal about the style, I think, from the instrument itself. When you play with a fortepiano, the great thing is that there's no balance problem. One is used to the pianist's having to mark an artificial *p* because the piano covers the violin, and so on. But whatever the discrepancy in dynamics between the violin and the fortepiano at a given time, there's still no problem. That's one of the great advantages. But even when one has the right instruments and has gotten used to them, there's still a great deal of mystery about Beethoven's dynamics. In a way, the problem of Beethoven's dynamics relates to the instruments and in a way it doesn't, because the dynamic gestures, the indications, are so radical in their changes from what came before.

Bilson: Philipp Emmanuel Bach uses, if not *mf,* at least more *f* than Beethoven, doesn't he? It is quite extraordinary how many different kinds of markings you find in his works.

Monosoff: I've always found it very disconcerting in Beethoven to have to make a tremendous crescendo, and then at the climax of a phrase suddenly have to play *subito piano.* It's a real problem in bow control. There's always a break. I remember one particular recording made with a modern instrument which I rather like, but you always wait for that break between the end of a crescendo and the *subito piano.* With original instruments, there's more of a contrast without so much fuss about it. You can really make the crescendo; you can do all the strange and violent dynamics which Beethoven asks for, but the control of the bow is not quite such a problem. Part of the reason is that you don't have to make so much sound altogether. You're not striving for the large, full-of-vibrato sound that you have to have on a modern instrument, and so you don't have to take so much time. Your reactions can be much quicker, and that's true on a fortepiano, too. The notes repeat more quickly; everything is more fleet; everything is lighter. Therefore, strange as it may seem, there's more dynamic contrast rather than less.

Von Alpenheim: But you still can't do a crescendo on the fortepiano on one chord leading to the next bar, which Beethoven sometimes writes. In the *Kreutzer* and the C-minor sonatas [Violin Sonata in A minor, Op. 47; Piano Sonata, Op. 13], he writes a chord and then crescendos into the next bar. There's nothing you can do to make that work—not on the fortepiano, not on the modern instrument.

Bilson: You could, I believe, on the new piano that Baldwin has made. It has no soundboard but electronic transducers. I'm not being facetious.

There is something else I'd like very much to bring up. You have said you think Beethoven would have preferred a modern piano.

Von Alpenheim: If he had known it.

Bilson: I don't think he would have. I'm perfectly happy to say that the modern piano is an improvement over the fortepiano. For one thing, it has a much longer tone. If I wanted to go to the Steinway basement and pick out a piano, I would pick the one that had the very longest tone. But this fortepiano has a very short tone life, and that is absolutely essential to playing the music that a composer like Beethoven wrote.

In order to put this into perspective: Bartók used the modern piano and the violin in such a masterful fashion that the pianist never has to hold back and the violinist is never clobbered. Part of the reason is that he rarely gives them the same music to play. If the piano part has *fff*, you can play *fff* without worrying about drowning out the violin. There's one place in the second movement of his second violin sonata [1922] where the piano plays a very loud chord, *ffz*, holding it while the violin plays a sort of cadenza passage, softer and softer and with a ritardando—this takes a certain amount of time—and then they both proceed *p*. Now if tone life is an ideal, then of course the modern piano has a far greater tone life than the fortepiano. I couldn't play the Bartók on a fortepiano; when Sonya made the diminuendo, it wouldn't work.

[Bilson then played an excerpt from Beethoven's *Pathétique* Sonata, Op. 13, first movement, on the fortepiano and then on the Steinway.]

Bilson: For me, the most important thing that happens on the fortepiano is the diminuendo.

Badura-Skoda: But you can do it on the modern piano—you can do it with the pedal.

Bilson: Can you do it that way? I don't think it's the same thing.

Von Alpenheim: It is.

[Von Alpenheim played the same passage on the Steinway.]

Bilson: We're playing a different instrument, and maybe it's just different. What you don't have on the modern piano is a feeling of the suddenness—it's a smooth collapsing instead. On the fortepiano you get a very sudden sound followed by rapid decay. There is another problem here; that area of the piano [below middle C] was not designed to play chords like that. And you won't find any composer that I know of in 1860 who writes a chord with all those low notes in there, whereas on a fortepiano like this it's perfectly all right.

Badura-Skoda: Yes, that's true.

Von Alpenheim: It is pretty true.

Bilson: This is just a small example. I like tone life, but it prevents me from playing the *Pathétique*, and that's the reason I'm interested in playing the fortepiano. It's not because I think it's better or because I think it sounds pretty; there are modern pianos which sound pretty too. It is much more because of this kind of thing: the *Tempest* Sonata [Op. 31, no. 2] is one which is, as far as I'm concerned, absolutely not possible to do on the modern piano. Carl Czerny wrote a book in 1842 on the proper performance of Beethoven's piano works in which he gives commentaries on all of them [*Klavierschule* (Op. 500), vol. 4, reprinted and annotated by Paul Badura-Skoda in 1963]. I happened to be learning the *Tempest* on a modern piano, and I looked up what Czerny, who was Beethoven's pupil, had to say about it. He had all kinds of pedaling in there. I tried to do those things and found that I simply couldn't do any of them. And now that I have this fortepiano, they all work fine. I think a lot of things that Czerny says, especially about the late sonatas which he maybe didn't understand very well, are probably not to be taken seriously. But this piece he did study with Beethoven, and Czerny has more specific things to say about it than about some of the other pieces. There is a pedal marking at the beginning of the piece.

[Bilson played the opening of the *Tempest*.]

Bilson: This is very interesting because it is an early example of a Beethoven passage which simply cannot be played without the pedal. There are passages one might play with or without the pedal in, let's say, Mozart, but the music doesn't necessarily change. This music is a totally different piece; so, therefore, Beethoven requires the pedal.

[Bilson played mm. 21–28 of the first movement of the *Tempest* on the fortepiano and then on the Steinway.]

Bilson: Czerny also says that Beethoven pedaled that passage, but that is an example of something one cannot possibly do on a modern piano. If the opening is the main theme of the piece and it is pedaled, then it makes perfect sense that the passage I just played is also pedaled.

Von Alpenheim: In this particular case, I have to agree.

[Webster raised the question of how much Czerny actually knew about Beethoven's intentions. Jander made the further point that by the time Czerny published his book, the piano Beethoven knew had been virtually forgotten. The discussion then returned to the issue of the characteristics of early and modern instruments.]

Stepner: The older violin is more resonant; the tone is longer within its narrower dynamic range. So one can make up chords (although they don't occur that often in Beethoven)—something that you can't really do on the modern violin. Perhaps it balances the fortepiano more in that respect, too. The opening of the *Kreutzer* Sonata can be very large sounding without being so loud if the fingers are kept down on the lower strings, which are sounded first, so those notes keep resonating.

[Stepner played the opening of Beethoven's *Kreutzer* Sonata, Op. 47, first on the modern and then on the Baroque violin.]

Stepner: I don't know if the difference projects, but I hear it.

Bilson: A lot of this has to do with how you're handling it, right? In other words, would you play on both violins the same way?

Stepner: There are so many variables it's hard to really know.

[Monosoff also illustrated the difference in articulation between the modern and the Baroque violin, concluding: "We simply can't play old instruments the way we play the modern ones. And therefore they make the kinds of small articulations which one finds even in the opening of the *Kreutzer* much clearer. And when you play with the fortepiano, you don't have to fight your way through the sounds of the modern piano."

The panelists discussed a variety of issues involved in the performing artist's approach to performance, including the questions of psychological set, audience expectations, and "atmosphere." The discussion then returned to the characteristics of original instruments; Badura-Skoda provided a tape recording of pieces of the late eighteenth and early nineteenth-century composers played on restored or reconstructed fortepianos. She also pointed out that J. F. von Schönfeld, in his *Jahrbuch der Tonkunst in Wein* (1796), provides a wealth of information about the builders, qualities, and geographical distribution of the instruments. Jander remarked: "It's very difficult to know how close a replica is to the way an instrument sounded when it was new; this is one of the great problems."]

Hsu: All this talk about the different characteristics of different pianos makes very good sense; that's the part we can learn to perceive very readily. But earlier in our discussion several of us mentioned the small dynamic range of the fortepiano, and I think that's misleading. There are historical descriptions referring to "the mighty bass" and so on. I think that's one aspect we can never recapture today, because we will always perceive the old instruments as having a small dynamic range.

Webster: There's another point: if you have once gotten used to a Stein replica, and then you suddenly hear a Walter, it *is* a huge sound. You've made a vast effort to get used to the tiny dynamic range of the Stein from the Steinway, and then all of a sudden you hear Walter, who's out here . . .

Monosoff: E. H. Gombrich, in *Art and Illusion*, talks about perception and the way a viewer sees according to the time in which he lives. I think this has exactly to do with what you're saying. One of the opening concerts at the now Avery Fisher Hall was by the Pro Musica, and the acoustics were terrible at that time. People couldn't hear, but as soon as they got used to the fact that they were listening to smaller sounds and that they had to hear in an entirely different way, they heard very well. We do have the perspective of the twentieth century, but since we're all involved with these early instruments, the question of loud and soft really is not a very important one. What is important is what Dan Stepner and I were talking about before. You don't expect the enormous kind of beautiful, lush, blossomy sound from a Baroque violin because you're achieving the sound in an entirely different way. You're not using so much vibrato. You're using more of a diminuendo in certain articulations. You're letting the sound die in just certain kinds of ways on this piano because that's what it does. I think it's the way we perceive the sound, and not really whether it's loud or soft.

Webster: It's possible for perceptions to change. If you once get used to a Stein and then you hear a Walter, you suddenly realize the range, the differentiation that's possible. You realize it's possible to have power in the bass even on a fortepiano with small-scale sound. It is in effect a fresh hearing of the music. It's possible that as we gain more experience with authentic performance practice we'll have more experiences of that kind. I think it's likely.

Bilson: Jim Webster has heard me play on my other piano, and this is the first time I've heard him say that he thinks the Walter is so much louder. This Walter is not one decibel louder than the Stein, but everybody says it's fuller—whatever that means.

Monosoff: I think the answer is that one listens or plays so differently on the different instruments. What interests me is that there's a greater range of passion, or anger—affections—expressed in these smaller instruments because everything is much clearer. The intention in this kind of music seems to be clear because you're not dealing with a large sound. Therefore, the means of expression is different from simply a large sound, as you would get in a Mahler symphony, for example.

Badura-Skoda: I would like to come back to the very first question, of modern instruments in combination with an old fortepiano. We all agree that this is very difficult, but those artists who have played old instruments have learned so much that they can handle a modern instrument so that it matches with an old one. We should try to stress in teaching that every good music school should have a replica fortepiano and a qualified teacher. One should teach students to play on it for a short period so that they can learn articulation and everything else on these old instruments. Then they can go on to larger instruments, bigger halls, but their whole attitude will have changed toward Mozart or Beethoven sonatas.

[Stepner remarked that he felt that the building of replicas should be encouraged because original instruments often cannot be successfully restored. He then returned to the issue of conditioned perceptions.]

Stepner: I want to mention the area of tempo, because I think it's the only one in which we can say anything definite. Presumably the time didn't go more slowly in Beethoven's Vienna; there were sixty seconds per minute. It's the only thing we can say anything about, and I think it affects how one plays greatly. It affects dynamics and articulation, and it seems to me that because of these instruments it's possible for the first time to take seriously some of Beethoven's tempi and implied tempi.

Jander: We at Wellesley are anticipating the arrival of a six-octave instrument such as Beethoven used about the time of the *Waldstein* Sonata. It's very important in Beethoven's middle period; it's the instrument that inspired him to the *Waldstein* and the *Appassionata* sonatas. Its new soft sounds were as important as its new loud sounds. But it's very important that we use that instrument in concerts only after audiences have heard the five-octave instrument, so that they come to it recognizing it for the big thing it was, and so that they don't hear it as a mini-Steinway.

Bilson: I would like to respond to something that Eva Badura-Skoda said. You believe that we can learn things from these old instruments and then transfer them to modern instruments?

Badura-Skoda: Many things, not everything.

Bilson: There is something of great importance, something that I would call, for want of a better expression, "tone of voice." Singers have different kinds of voices, and these different voices have a great deal to do with what kind of repertoire they sing. For instance, we don't imagine Birgit Nilsson and Elly Ameling interchanging roles. And if we don't want to listen to Elly Ameling sing Isolde, it's not because we think she isn't a good enough musician. I believe the same kind of situation prevails for these instruments.

Performance Conventions
in Beethoven's Early Works

Eva Badura-Skoda

Beethoven grew up in a world where it was still customary for a young musician to become a performer well before he started to compose music. Under normal circumstances, eighteenth-century composers remained performers throughout their lives, or, in rare instances, until their compositions had gained enough recognition for them to cease, if they wished, earning money through performance. Even those fully employed or acknowledged as composers continued to perform their own works because they were inclined to believe that musical notation was so insufficient that their own performing abilities were needed to convey their artistic intentions. In the case of opera or oratorio, their presence was especially indispensable.

As a young man, Beethoven placed great value on becoming an outstanding performer. Carl Czerny wrote:

> No one matched him in the speed of his scales, double trills, leaps, etc. (not even Hummel). His posture while playing was ideally calm, noble and good to look at, without the slightest grimace (though he did begin to bend forward as his deafness increased). His fingers were very powerful, not long, and flattened at the tips by much playing; because, as he told me, he had practiced prodigiously as a youngster, usually until well past midnight. [1]

C. L. Junker, a prolific writer on music, heard Beethoven in 1791 and reported in Bossler's *Correspondenz*:

> I also heard one of the greatest of pianists—the dear, good Bethofen. . . . I have heard Vogler upon the pianoforte . . . and never failed to wonder at his astonishing execution; but Bethofen, in addition to the execution, has greater clearness and weight of ideas, and more expression. [2]

When he came to Vienna, Beethoven soon impressed the important musical circles with his brilliant virtuosity. In 1796, a *Jahrbuch der Tonkunst von Wien und Prag,* which listed musicians in alphabetical order, described Beethoven: "Bethofen: a musical genius who has lived in Vienna for two years. He is generally admired for his outstanding velocity and the great ease with which he performs extraordinary difficulties."[3]

We can only speculate whether Beethoven would have spent more time practicing the piano over the years if his hearing problem had not gradually worsened and altered his entire view of life. At all events, he continued to conduct his own works in public as long as he considered it at all feasible. He continued to supervise performances of his own works as late as 1825–26, when his last string quartets were being rehearsed at his home and his deafness was virtually total.

Discussions of Beethoven's performance style today generally turn for guidance to the reports of Beethoven's pupils, including those of Czerny and of Anton Schindler, Beethoven's assistant and self-appointed friend during the composer's last years. These can be useful as long as we do not forget that Czerny was considerably more trustworthy than Schindler, and that these reports issued from musicians a whole generation younger than Beethoven. It was inevitable that they would arrive at maturity with general aesthetic views more "modern" than his. Furthermore, Beethoven was almost fifty when he met Schindler; by then he had changed some of his earlier ideas considerably and had developed such a strong personality that he could dominate the musical views of those around him. Beethoven doubtless brought with him to Vienna not only contemporary French and German views on philosophy and literature, but also some idiosyncratic musical notions. Nevertheless, Vienna's lively musical tradition, transmitted in lessons from Mozart, Haydn, Johann Schenk, Albrechtsberger, and Salieri, certainly made a vivid impression on him. Simply stated, Beethoven's early works belong firmly to the eighteenth century; we must at all costs avoid applying nineteenth-century performing habits to them, a temptation to which Schindler may have succumbed even more easily than we. Though it seems arbitrary, the usual rough division of Beethoven's creative output into three periods may still serve to differentiate his compositional styles and the performance conventions suitable to each of them.

What was musically valid for Mozart's generation was not necessarily valid for Beethoven's, even though there were only fourteen years between the births of Mozart and Beethoven and the same between Beethoven's and that of his pupil Ferdinand Ries (born in 1784). Further, if some of Ries's opinions differed from Schindler's, it was partly because he was considerably older and brought up in Bonn, whereas Schindler grew up in an Austrian crown country. Moreover, Ries was an excellent pianist and a successful composer; Schindler was neither. If performance attitudes among Beethoven's pupils differed, then, it was not only a question of the generation gap but of local and personal styles. As for Beethoven himself, it was above all his strong personality which became the main basis for stylistic differences with his contemporaries, even though those differences developed gradually. This essay proposes to illustrate the many dimensions of Beethoven's adherence to performance and notational conventions common to Bonn and Vienna before the turn of the century.

To discover what these performance practices were, we must rely to a great extent on the printed forms in which the tradition has been passed on. The major issues include *where, what, to what purpose,* and *how* music was performed. The how perhaps interests us most today, but we should strive to learn as much as possible about all of these conventions, knowledge of which is essential for interpreting the incomplete notation of Beethoven as faithfully as possible. A brief discussion of performance practices in Vienna during the 1790s is a prerequisite to the question of how the music was performed.

Church music continued to be performed almost exclusively in churches, with the exception of oratorios and cantatas on sacred texts. Chamber music was confined almost exclusively to private circles. Before the 1780s, there had been a species of chamber music related to the old church sonatas; these included the so-called solos for violin, oboe, or flute and accompaniment—usually sonatas, movements from concertos, or a single aria. Vocal numbers often included parodied texts, arranged not only from cantatas but from operatic arias as well. Pieces like these were heard in churches as well as in public concerts. During the second half of the eighteenth century, it became more and more the practice in Vienna to present public concerts in theaters or concert halls. Whether an *Akademie* during Lent or on a Friday, a benefit concert in a theater, or a subscription concert in a ballroom, any program not devoted to whole oratorios or similar large vocal works would commence with an overture or sinfonia, followed by operatic arias or scenes, and then by still more concertos or sinfonias. These concerts were frequently supplemented and enriched by improvisations in which Hummel, Beethoven, Cramer, Moscheles, and Liszt successively excelled, according to contemporary reports.

The first performance of most of Beethoven's works composed in Vienna before 1800 took place in the homes and palaces of the aristocracy, particularly as the majority of them were chamber works. Throughout Beethoven's lifetime, keyboard sonatas were also considered to be chamber music. Unwritten rules declared them unsuitable for larger halls, and this remained one of the few conventions that Beethoven followed like everyone else. In his later years, however, the composer did not hesitate to ignore the tradition of including at least some vocal music in every concert program. Perhaps he had good reason; Beethoven was no singer (Carl Czerny described his singing voice as deplorable), and although we know his studies with Salieri included Italian vocal style, his interest in this field was obviously rather limited. The concert aria *Ah! perfido* is one of the few fruits of assiduous tutelage under Salieri; Beethoven made few further attempts to comply with the conventional Viennese view that every good composer should be able to craft a model Italian aria.

When Beethoven arrived in Vienna, opportunities for a young and unknown musician to perform in public concerts were relatively rare. At all events, around 1793 Beethoven considered himself a student more eager to learn and absorb than to promote himself. Two years later, however, he had become so famous through playing in private circles that he was invited to participate in two public concerts of the "Tonkünstler-Societät"—an honor we may assume he happily accepted. In 1795 he also played in a benefit concert for Mozart's widow; he might well have performed Mozart's D-minor Concerto, for which he would then have composed his own cadenzas and perhaps also enriched the recurring subject of the Romanze (second movement) with some embellishments. From then on he performed frequently in public. In April, 1797, for example, he appeared in a Schuppanzigh benefit concert in Jahn's ballroom, playing his Quintet for Piano and Winds, Op. 16, a performance he repeated a year later in another concert of the "Tonkünstler-Societät." The minutes of the society for the meeting following that concert report: "The second day Mr. van Beethoven played a quintet and excelled in it through a fantasy." The event was more fully described by Ries:

> That same night Beethoven played his quintet for piano and wind instruments; the famous oboist Ramm from Munich also played and accompanied Beethoven in the quintet. In the last allegro a fermata occurs several times before the theme begins again. In one of these pauses Beethoven suddenly started improvising,

taking the rondo subject as his theme and entertaining himself and the others for quite some time. This was not the case with his accompanists, however; they were very annoyed and Mr. Ramm was even angry. It did indeed look rather droll to see these gentlemen, expecting to begin any moment, raising their instruments to their mouths incessantly and then quietly putting them down again. At last Beethoven was satisfied and returned to the rondo. The whole society was enchanted.[4]

It is not important whether Beethoven improvised this "fantasy" or "capriccio"—obviously a cadenza instead of a fermata embellishment—in the Rondo, or inserted a cadenza in the first movement, as has been suggested.[5] Both kinds of insertions were permissible as long as they were kept short enough—a rule which Beethoven certainly broke on this occasion.

A second report regarding the custom of cadenzas also stems from Ries. Here the work in question was Beethoven's C-minor Concerto:

I had asked Beethoven to compose a cadenza for me, which he refused to do, directing me to make one myself which he would then correct. Beethoven was highly satisfied with my composition and changed little. There was, however, one very brilliant and difficult passage which he liked but which seemed too daring, and he therefore instructed me to compose another one. Eight days before the performance he wished to hear the cadenza again. I played [the same one] and again smudged the passage; again, somewhat irritated, he told me to change it. [This time] I did, but the new one did not satisfy *me*. I therefore practiced the other one most assiduously, without being able to become absolutely certain of it. In the public concert. . . . I could not convince myself to choose the easier one; when I then launched brazenly into the more difficult one, Beethoven jerked violently in his chair. Nevertheless it worked perfectly and Beethoven was so overjoyed that he shouted loudly "bravo!" This electrified the entire audience and gave me instantly a position among the artists. Afterwards, as he expressed his satisfaction to me, he added: "But you are obstinate all the same. Had you missed that passage I would never have given you another lesson again."[6]

Ries's account of Beethoven's performance of Op. 16, as well as his second report that as late as 1803 the composer encouraged him to compose his own cadenza for the C-minor Concerto, suggest that Beethoven's attitude toward the conventional practice of virtuoso display in cadenzas, extemporized or prepared, must have changed considerably over the years. Around 1808–9, Beethoven composed a number of cadenzas for his earlier piano concertos and for Mozart's D-minor Concerto, perhaps at the request of his new student, the Archduke Rudolph, but perhaps—and this seems even more likely—because he was by then convinced that no one else could or would compose cadenzas worthy of either his or Mozart's concertos. Hence he began to regulate some of the traditional freedoms of the performer.

This regulation had begun as early as the oratorio *Christus am Oelberg*, Op. 85, where the cadenzas for both arias are written out.[7] But in the Violin Concerto, Op. 61, he once again left the composition of the cadenza to the soloist. However, in the finale of the G-major Piano Concerto, Beethoven demanded "la Cadenza sia corta" ("let the cadenza be short"), also writing down several different cadenzas for this concerto on separate sheets. The "Emperor" Concerto incorporates the two well-known written-out cadenzalike passages at the beginnings of the exposition and recapitulation in the first movement. At the point where the usual cadenza is to be inserted, Beethoven again wrote into the score his own short cadenza, leading to a fermata and the performance instruction "no si fa una cadenza" ("do not make a cadenza"). His most original cadenza is probably that for the first movement of the piano arrangement of his violin concerto, in which he employed the kettledrum.

In addition to cadenzas and fermata embellishments, eighteenth-century performers often showed their spontaneous creativity and virtuosity in extempore variations, in embellishing and ornamenting melodic lines and themes in repeats, or in da capo arias or rondo ritornellos. The closer to Italy a composer-performer grew up, the more likely he was to be interested in developing this skill. The geographical distance between Bonn and Italy was greater, of course, than that between Vienna and Italy; however, it should not be forgotten that an Austrian archduke whose *maestri di capella* were Italians ruled in Bonn. To the strong French-German tradition in Bonn the Italian influence must be added.

In 1796, a *Jahrbuch der Tonkunst von Wien und Prag* appeared in Vienna which contained some remarks devoted directly to the performance custom of embellishing melodies. Every performer who wants to be heard as a soloist, especially singers, this yearbook makes clear, must know how to ornament tastefully.

> From singers it is expected and demanded that they have a "method." By this one generally understands certain ornaments and graces which are inserted by the singer. To place these graces capably and suitably requires exceptional taste and feeling. Thus it happens that many singers insert too many runs and chromatic notes; their singing line often becomes too overloaded and obscured, so that the subjects and melodies become lost.[8]

The same source adds about instrumental ornamentation:

> There are places where it is advantageous to insert much ornamentation. This, however, must be done with care and consideration in such a way that the basic emotion does not suffer, but is enhanced. The adagio, which because of its simple melodic layout often becomes the playground of ornamentation, does not allow fast passage work and scales, but instead well-selected chromatic lines which sigh and languish and then die out.[9]

These ornamentation traditions were certainly known at Bonn in the 1780s and 1790s. C. G. Neefe's friend in Bonn, a minor composer and author of musical writings named d'Antoine, complained about the excessive melodic elaborations of the musicians at court, who added many small notes to the notated music. He regretted "the loss of this noble seriousness which the Germans had displayed in their music for so long," and he blamed the decline on the Italians, apparently referring to those who occupied the leading court positions in Bonn.[10] Neefe very probably shared d'Antoine's opinion, and it can be assumed that he implanted this attitude in his student Beethoven. These views differed, to be sure, from those on which most Viennese musicians had been raised and to which most of them probably still subscribed during Beethoven's lifetime—with the notable exception of old Haydn.

According to all contemporary reports except Czerny's, a contemporary pianist whom Beethoven admired greatly was Johann Baptist Cramer. Beethoven may have heard him as early as 1790 in Bonn, but certainly no later than 1796 in Vienna, when both artists were asked to play in a competition.[11] Some time later Moscheles met Cramer in London and entered some impressions in his diary: "Cramer sings on the piano in such a way that an Andante by Mozart is nearly changed into a vocal piece; I must complain that he feels free to insert his often rather petty embellishments into them."[12]

Cramer was not the only contemporary pianist who dared to embellish Mozart's works. Beethoven's most successful rival as a pianist in Vienna was Mozart's pupil Johann Nepomuk Hummel. He had once lived in Mozart's house, where Beethoven might have met him as early as 1787. Beethoven continued to encounter Hummel throughout his lifetime; he was even canvassed by Hummel on his deathbed to support the then novel notion of copyright laws for composers. In any case, Hummel performed, and later published, numerous embellished editions of Mozart's piano concertos. Ex. 1 illustrates Hummel's ornamentation of the second solo in the slow movement of Mozart's C-minor Concerto, K. 491. Twentieth-century listeners cannot help but be surprised that Hummel apparently was never accused by his contemporaries of showing lack of respect for Mozart's work, but we must remember that many other performers embellished with even more notes and less taste than he did.

Ex. 1 Second solo entry from Mozart's K.491/II, as ornamented by Hummel.

Not even Beethoven's piano concertos were exempt from the additions of virtuoso performers and publishers. Some of the textual problems in these works that still haunt us today were caused by Beethoven himself, who initially notated the solo parts of the earlier concertos only sketchily. Not only did he rely on his memory for the first performances, but he doubtless preferred to try some passages in several versions before settling eventually on the final reading. The autograph score of the B♭-major Concerto, Op. 19, thus remained incomplete, and only fragments of the first version of the piano solo part have been preserved in manuscript. These fragments differ widely from the final version. Only years later, when preparing the concerto for publication, did Beethoven write down a revised and completed solo part. The situation is similar with the C-minor Concerto, where the first print by Mollo seems to reflect Beethoven's final intentions more fully than did his initial writing down of the solo part. In these cases modern editors should pay more heed to the authentic first editions than to Beethoven's autographs.

The evaluation of sources is not always so straightforward. In the case of the other early concerto, that in C major, Op. 15, some of the added ornaments and slight alterations found in the first edition but not in the autograph are doubtless improvements. Others, however, are less convincing. For example, in Beethoven's autograph the main subject of the Largo is without the three-note grace which later, in both the autograph and print sources, embellishes the recurrence of the theme (ex. 2). But in the first edition, someone altered the theme to include that three-note figure (ex. 3). Without the grace notes in m. 6, the theme displays an initial simplicity which seems more convincing. Indeed, one might ask whether this added ornament represented Beethoven's final intention or that of his publisher. Likewise, the turns in mm. 100–101 of the first edition obscure both the double-dotted rhythm and the parallel with the same figure in the solo clarinet.

Ex. 2 Mm. 53–56 of Beethoven's Op. 15/II, as ornamented by Beethoven in both the autograph, and the first edition.

Ex. 3 Mm. 5–8 of Beethoven's Op. 15/II, as printed in the first edition (Mollo); the ornament that begins m. 6 is not in the autograph.

Unfortunately, the editors of the Eulenberg score of Op. 15 did not make clear that the many alternative versions they printed are of the most questionable authenticity. These doubtful embellishments are not found in the first edition by Mollo, but only in a later edition published by Haslinger in 1837. In most cases they are anything but "beautifications." The *ossia* version with added thirds in m. 99 of the second movement (ex. 4) is positively ugly. Equally questionable are doublings like those found in the first movement (ex. 5). One might well keep Ries's remarks in mind when assessing such passages.

> I remember only two occasions where Beethoven instructed me to add a few notes to his compositions—once in the Rondo of the Sonata Pathétique (Op. 13), and again in the theme of the Rondo of his first concerto in C major, where he specified several doublings to make it more brilliant. . . . In playing he would give now the right, now the left hand of a particular passage a beautiful but nonetheless inimitable expression; only in extremely rare cases would he add notes or ornamental decorations.[13]

There are good reasons to assume that occasionally Beethoven would have allowed performers of his early works to make use of the expanding range of the piano, particularly after the turn of the century. We can understand why many pianists, in the third movement of the C-major Concerto, play the higher octave in mm. 320ff., as recommended by Haslinger (ex. 6). It is noteworthy that Haslinger did not offer as many brilliant *ossia* alternatives in his edition of the C-minor Concerto (Op. 37) as he did in Op. 15. Only two *ossia* passages—both virtually unplayable and neither to be recommended—found their way into the Eulenburg score from the Haslinger edition. The most flagrant is illustrated in ex. 7. We can certainly hope that such accretions will soon disappear from this well-known score.

Czerny, who became a Beethoven pupil in 1801, played the same Op. 16 quintet in Beethoven's presence in 1816. His performance prompted an apologetic letter from the composer.

> Dear Z.,
>   I cannot see you today, but tomorrow I shall come to you myself in order to have a word with you. I burst out so yesterday and was sorry as soon as it had happened. But you must forgive a composer who would rather have heard his work performed exactly as it was written, however beautifully you played in other respects. I shall make this up to you very soon in the violoncello sonata.
>   Rest assured that as an artist I hold the greatest goodwill for you and that I shall always endeavor to make it manifest to you.
>   Your True Friend Beethoven[14]

It is astonishing that, in the fifteen years of his acquaintance with Beethoven, Czerny had not yet grasped the composer's resolute rejection of any additional ornamentation in his works. After this unhappy event he certainly must have. More than twenty-five years later, in his *Pianoforte Schule*, Czerny said that the performer of Beethoven's works must

Ex. 4 Mm. 99–100 of Beethoven's Op. 15/II, with Haslinger's *ossia*.

Ex. 5 Passage from Op. 15/I, with Haslinger's *ossia*.

Ex. 6 Mm. 314–30 of Beethoven's Op. 15/III, with the octave transposition recommended by Haslinger in mm. 320–30.

Ex. 7 Mm. 366–70 of Beethoven's Op. 37/I; Haslinger's *ossia* still survives in the Eulenburg score.

not tolerate any alteration of the music whatsoever. This fact provides us with some clues about the gradual change in Beethoven's attitude toward performance traditions and the rights of performers.

For ornaments that were indicated, Beethoven's notation was in many ways conventional. His understanding of these signs no doubt complied with common practice in Vienna—a practice which, unfortunately, does not always leave their execution clear and beyond doubt. Especially in Beethoven's earlier works, we encounter performance problems that also plague us in dealing with other Classical composers, such as the question of whether a trill should start on the main or upper note. The orthodox approach has been represented best by William Newman, who argues that both ways of executing trills can be defended before and after 1800, but that in later years Beethoven showed a preference for starting on the main note.[15] More recently, Robert Winter has introduced an old but in Beethoven studies novel idea that the issue is not one of main versus upper-note starts, but of strong-beat dissonance; the record of the primary sources lends considerable support to his hypothesis.[16] There is also sufficient but little-noted evidence that Beethoven's trills ended with an afterbeat if time permitted, as can be seen from comparing Beethoven's autograph of Op. 15 with the authentic Mollo edition, for which we may assume Beethoven read proofs (ex. 8).

Ex. 8 Passage from Mollo edition of Beethoven's Op. 15/II, showing afterbeats added to autograph trills.

Similarly, we cannot regard all problems involving appoggiaturas as solved. In Beethoven's early works we find short as well as long appoggiaturas notated with the same sign, just as in Mozart's works. It is sometimes difficult to choose the proper execution, but at least some of the rules valid in Mozart's mature works remain valid for Beethoven's.

For example, the figures ♩♪ ♫ or ♪♫♫ nearly always meant ♫♫♫ or ♫♫♫. That the young Beethoven followed these South German/Viennese conventions can be seen in the first movement of his Piano Sonata in D major, Op. 10, no. 3 (mm. 53ff.). Czerny reports that Beethoven always played these long appoggiaturas as equal eighth notes. It is also likely that he followed the Viennese custom (and not C. P. E. Bach's, as Franz Kullak suggests) of playing equal eighth notes in m. 54 (analogous to m. 4) of the second movement of the C-major Concerto. Beethoven's understanding of the Viennese notation of long accented appoggiaturas is verified in his cadenza to the first movement of Mozart's D-minor Concerto, where he correctly writes out a grace note as a long appoggiatura in quoting a Mozart theme.

Singers who wish to avoid violating performance rules still valid in Beethoven's time are not only allowed, but sometimes obliged, to alter notes at the end of recitative sentences or arias (or sections of arias). In certain cases vocal appoggiaturas must be sung. Even now it is not widely enough known that the vocal accent or appoggiatura was an expressive device that formed part of the musical language of opera for more than 200 years. From the times of Weber, Schubert, Rossini, and even as late as young Verdi, certain notes, especially in recitatives, were meant to be sung differently than they were notated. This convention derived from *stilo antico* rules which did not allow a dissonance on a strong beat. In Baroque operatic practice, on the other hand, it was felt to be desirable to set strong syllables (already normally set on strong beats) as dissonances. The solution to this paradox was a set of symbols which informed the initiated performer that he was indeed to create a dissonance on a strong beat, though it was not actually notated.

All theorists of the Baroque and Classical periods agreed that certain appoggiaturas were indispensable. G. B. Mancini, the singing master at the Viennese court for many decades and a friend of Salieri, wrote in 1774:

> All the excellence of the recitative depends on the knowledge of the proper use of the appoggiatura, or the musical accent, as it is generally called. This precious accent, in which is found all the grace of a cantilena, consists, in short, of a note at a pitch one step higher than written. This is practised especially when a word of several syllables is written with notes of the same pitch.[17]

A short time later, Vincenzo Manfredini expressed this customary demand even more bluntly:

Whereas an instrumentalist is not strictly required to perform appoggiaturas not indicated by the composer, this is not true for the singer, who, when he sees (especially in recitatives) two notes of the same value and pitch, must consider the first of these as an appoggiatura from above. That is, he must—particularly on a strong beat—perform it a tone or a semitone higher, according to the key in which the notes are written.[18]

Ignaz von Mosel, like Beethoven a pupil of Salieri during the 1790s, is best known today as the author of a book on the aesthetics of opera. He wrote:

That a recitative should be sung and spoken at the same time is incomprehensible to most singers, and the faulty manner in which virtuoso singers of today overload the recitative (which should approach speech or simple declamation) with embellishments proves clearly that they have little or no understanding of its nature. Incidentally, even if the composer commands the most complete knowledge of declamation and composes recitative according to the rules, the customary notation is insufficient for specifying the length of the notes or for bringing them into complete accordance with the proper declamation. The notation is also insufficient for indicating to the singer the nearly countless nuances of every dynamic or melodic accent which is called for by a word or often even a syllable; or to indicate every little pause which is necessary to set off an inserted phrase against the main part of a sentence, etc. It is impossible to indicate all this to the singer with such punctiliousness and precision that would allow him to follow his part mechanically. Therefore, the singer who takes upon himself the task of singing recitatives has to be a perfect reciter, so that in his execution he can supplement, according to his own judgment, whatever could not be written out because of the limitations of the notation.[19]

We also possess Nottebohm's full account of Beethoven's relationship to his teacher Salieri, including what he gleaned from the Italian master about vocal music. Toward the end of his life, Salieri wrote a "Scuola di Canto in versi e i versi in musica a 4 voci," verses explaining the basic rules of composition.[20] Since every musical example in them is a four-part canon, there are naturally no models of recitative. However, Salieri does refer to the problematic execution of the vocal appoggiatura: "A recitative has its rules, but these are a bit obscure; appoggiaturas, if they are not written out, are arbitrary and depend on [application of] the proper taste." Beethoven's notation of his vocal music confirms his concurrence with Salieri and Mosel.

The most striking example of different notational styles in instrumental versus vocal music remains the Finale of the Ninth Symphony, where both instruments and voices enter with the same recitative material. The string basses initiate the passage with the appoggiatura at the end written out in slurred notes on their literal pitches (ex. 9). The vocal part differs only notationally, of course, and it should be performed identically according to Italian and Viennese custom (ex. 10). It is even probable that the recitative passage in Beethoven's D-minor Piano Sonata, Op. 31, no. 2 (first movement, mm. 144ff.; ex. 11) would, if composed with underlying text, have been notated by Viennese composers as in ex. 12.

Ex. 9 Mm. 6–16 of Beethoven's Op. 125/IV.

Ex. 10 Mm. 213–20 of Beethoven's Op. 125/IV.

Ex. 11 Mm. 145–48 of Beethoven's Op. 31, No. 2/I.

Ex. 12 Mm. 145–48 of Beethoven's Op. 31, No. 2/I, notated for vocal performance.

Beethoven, who tended to write out more appoggiaturas than other composers in Vienna, might have notated the instrumental and vocal versions the same way in mm. 145 and 146, but probably not in m. 148. This at least is the impression the student of Beethoven's writing habits receives when studying his vocal works. Singers still must alter a number of notes in the oratorio *Christus am Oelberg*. At the beginning of the recitative *Ah! perfido*, Op. 65, many of the vocal appoggiaturas are not written out; later in this work they are often notated as grace notes. The recitative No. 11 from *Leonore* (later discarded) was set down as in ex. 13. The appoggiaturas notated with grace

Ex. 13 *Leonore*, recitative No. 11.

notes in mm. 5 and 15 of ex. 13 probably would not have been written by Italian composers, but Beethoven felt the need to do so. He did not, however, notate them at places where it must have been absolutely clear to both him and his contemporaries that every singer would automatically apply an appoggiatura: for example, the splitting of the one quarter note at "Herz" into two eighth notes in m. 6 and into two sixteenth notes in m. 16 was compulsory in Beethoven's time. (At all events, the rhythm in a recitative had to be "free" and could never be pinpointed by notation.) It might also be advisable to add an appoggiatura in m. 10 at the syllable "-tag-," or in m. 12 at the syllable "-trag-," but in both places the singer must be the final arbiter.

In practice many vocal appoggiaturas are indeed a matter of taste. But there are some appoggiaturas which must be applied if the singer wishes to avoid violating melodic rules that were known to every musical person in Vienna around 1800. Such an appoggiatura, for example, must be sung at the end of Leonore's aria No. 9 in *Fidelio*, where the accent falls on the syllable "lie-" of "Gattenliebe," and an F♯ must be sung instead of the written E (ex. 14). This appoggiatura is sung in most performances of *Fidelio*. At parallel places, however, it is often omitted, which requires further discussion of this ornament. Certainly the creation of a sharp dissonance by an appoggiatura ought never to disturb us; on the contrary, such graces were considered a beautiful and necessary seasoning.

Ex. 14 End of *Fidelio*, Leonore's aria No. 9.

Three examples of optional melodic accents and one compulsory accent at the end of the recitative are to be found in *Fidelio* in recitative No. 9 (ex. 15). Ignaz von Mosel's prescription was unambiguous: "The voice should never be suddenly lowered too much. . . . the recitative should move forward in small intervals . . . for it should be halfway between speech and singing and should be closer to the former than the latter." In judging recitatives, he goes on, one should proceed from the assumption that "they are more successful to the degree that they approach normal declamation; the laurels should go to whomever attains this imitation in such a high degree that one remains unsure whether he has heard declamation or singing."[21]

The general changes in aesthetic attitude which occurred during the second half of the eighteenth century are alluded to in the

Ex. 15 End of *Fidelio*, Leonore's recitative No. 9.

editor's preface to the revised fourth edition (Leipzig, 1804) of Leopold Mozart's *Violonschule* (first published in 1756):

> Although Mozart's Violonschule has kept its position throughout nearly fifty years . . . it is obvious that his book now displays the signs of age which make a large number of corrections necessary. . . . A distinguished person has taken over this difficult task with enthusiasm, and we hope that he has succeeded. . . . Doubtful or incorrect passages have been omitted or corrected; what was missing has been completed, and, finally, the last chapter—that concerning good execution—has been added in a completely new version.

The alterations—omissions as well as additions—are revealing indeed. Among the corrections considered most necessary were the removal of Leopold Mozart's assumption that nonlegato tone production marks the "normal onward movement" (this phrase originated with C. P. E. Bach) and the new importance assigned to the discussion of legato: "Everything cantabile needs slurred, bound and sustained notes; this is even more imperative in an Adagio than in an Allegro" (p. 67).

Whether through Neefe's teaching and his own study of J. S. Bach's *Wohltemperirte Clavier* or through organ playing, the young Beethoven apparently learned to play legato extraordinarily well. Czerny reported that "Beethoven's playing of adagio and legato in the sustained style had an almost bewitching effect on everyone who heard it; so far as I know it has yet to be excelled."[22] Comments like this should not lead us to assume that Beethoven was not equally capable and fond of crisp staccato playing. Otherwise his markings, especially in scherzos and fast movements, would be meaningless. But the Leipzig edition of Leopold Mozart's treatise suggests that it was not only Beethoven who showed a greater predilection for legato than earlier musical generations.[23] During Leopold's lifetime, and still around the turn of the century, a delicate clarity of sound was generally preferred to playing with any rough or harsh edges on it. Wolfgang's own aesthetic views in this regard are too well known to require repetition here, as is the criticism that Beethoven's playing tended to be less clear, or even sometimes harsh and muddy. It is significant that nearly all unreserved praise of Beethoven's playing stems from the period before 1800, while the more mixed or overtly critical reviews come from musicians like Cherubini or Clementi, who heard Beethoven after 1803.

Notational conventions taken for granted by every Viennese musician around 1800 included the knowledge of how to indicate legato and the meaning of slurs ending at bar lines. Before 1800, composers eschewed long slurs, preferring to end them at the bar line even when the lyrical sweep of a melody suggested its execution without a break in the middle. This notational habit stems from violin bowing, and it was retained for some time even in keyboard and wind parts. On the other hand, Viennese musicians distinguished clearly between two types of slurs. The first was the short slur over two or three notes, which required the player to shorten and detach the last note under the slur. The second was the slur found in cantilenas over several notes, which—regardless of whether it ended at the bar line or not—was simply indicated legato. Making these distinctions created no difficulties for eigh-teenth-century Viennese musicians,[24] though a modern musician can be vexed by such broken slurs, which are meaningless if performed literally.

The meaning of Beethoven's staccato markings has already been investigated (though even more comprehensive investigations are needed) by Nottebohm, who concluded that only after 1800 did Beetho-ven intend a distinction between dots and wedges. But this conclusion remains only a general ordering of very complex issues, and modern editors are usually left reading into signs what makes the most musical sense to them.

The *Leipziger Allgemeine Musikalische Zeitung* commenced its re-view of Beethoven's first self-arranged public concert in the Court Theater in 1800 with the remark that "Herr Beethoven was finally permitted to rent the theater and this was indeed the most interesting concert in a long time."[25] The program Beethoven chose was conven-tional: it began and ended with a symphony (the first one in this case was by Mozart), and included vocal works (an aria and a duet from Haydn's *Creation*) and the obligatory "improvisation" (a free fantasy performed by Beethoven on the fortepiano), as well as a piano concerto (probably Op. 15 in C major) and the Septet, Op. 20. The length of this program also was not unusual. What was unusual was the quality of the works; all were by Haydn, Mozart, or Beethoven.

Beethoven engaged the orchestra of the Italian opera for this concert, but the report in the Leipzig journal criticized the apparent lack of cooperation by the orchestral musicians. The musicians had their reasons. They preferred their Italian leader to the conductor appointed by Beethoven, Anton Wranitzky. They recoiled from the difficulties of the program, and doubtless also from Beethoven's demanding attitude. The Leipzig critic asserted that Beethoven's compositions were indeed difficult to play and that too many wind instruments were used in the C-major symphony; according to him, the symphony gave a stronger impression of music for a band than for an orchestra. Today the scoring of Beethoven's first symphony seems rather tame when compared to what he demanded in his later works.

How was the sound balanced among orchestral instruments in Beethoven's time? In the woodwind family, the oboes were still compar-atively louder and more penetrating than their modern counterparts. The clarinets were not necessarily softer than those of today, and could be rather more vital in tone. The same could be said of the bassoons. Only the all-wooden flute had a softer tone than its all-metal modern descendant. In relation to contemporary string instruments, the woodwinds (except the flute) had a louder, more piercing tone quality. Eighteenth-century horn players were still trained by trumpeters. But the sound of old horns could be soft and warm (the Viennese horns of today are still less crisp in sound than the French horns). The sound of historical trumpets is more familiar to us, and is characterized by a presence hard to duplicate on a modern instrument. The important consideration in late eighteenth-century balance, however, was that all string instruments were much softer in tone than the instruments of today. This was due to shorter necks (therefore lower string tension), thinner sound posts, gut strings, and bows constructed along slightly different lines. It is a challenging task to reconstruct the sound of a Beethoven orchestra, but perhaps it is possible. The results achieved in a few recent recordings have satisfied some experts.

At the first performance of the *Eroica* Symphony at the Palais Lobkowitz, fifteen wind players joined an orchestra of only fifteen string players. Even if we assume that the number of string players was enlarged for the next performance, the composite sound still must have resulted in a balance favoring the wind instruments, which perhaps at least partially explains the criticisms of the Leipzig critic. Considering these circumstances, we might well wonder how a fortepiano built by Walter, Schantz, or Stein could balance a whole orchestra. One is tempted to believe Czerny, who wrote in his *Pianoforte Schule*:

> With the present perfection of the pianoforte, which, in power and fullness of tone, vies with the instruments of the orchestra, the performance of a concerto is more easy and gratifying than at the time when Beethoven himself played his first concerto. . . . with regard to expression, we can also now count on much more accurate accompaniments by an orchestra than during the earlier period.[26]

Finally, Beethoven's use of the pedal makes a fitting close to this brief discussion of sound problems. A number of recent writers seem to believe that Beethoven indicated pedal markings every time he wanted the sustaining pedal to be used.[27] This, of course, is nonsense. The effect of lifting the dampers was surely invoked by Mozart on those numerous occasions when melting broken chords nearly cried out for this effect. In Mozart's time the dampers were usually raised by a knee lever, a device whose functioning Mozart praised enthusiastically when he visited Stein's workshop in Augsburg in 1777. Nearly all reports about Beethoven's piano playing mention his extensive use of the knee lever or pedal; Czerny, in particular, remarked: "He used a lot of pedal, much more than is indicated in his works."[28]

The question of pedal in Beethoven can also be turned around by asking whether the famous pedal markings in the C-major Piano Concerto; in the *Tempest* Sonata, Op. 31, no. 2; in the *Waldstein* Sonata, Op. 57; or in the A-major Sonata, Op. 101, can be played as written. William S. Newman and others have expressed the opinion that following Beethoven's instructions literally in these passages would lead to intolerable results.[29] I cannot share that view. Naturally, rendering these soft passages convincingly according to Beethoven's instructions is considerably easier on the fortepiano than on the modern instrument, with its longer sustaining tone. But it is possible on both. Here, as so often, Beethoven was not the great innovator; rather, he followed Haydn, who specified a similarly bold pedaling in his great C-major Sonata, Hob. XVI/50. A demonstration of all the relevant passages on instruments from the eighteenth century as well as on modern grand pianos would substantiate the statement that they can be played beautifully if the pianist has the finger and pedal control to create the piano-pianissimo necessary to avoid ugly blurring.

There are indeed sound effects in Beethoven's music which deserve to be called "romantic" or even "impressionistic." E. T. A. Hoffmann wrote of Beethoven's predecessors: "Mozart and Haydn, the creators of our present instrumental music, were the first to show us the art in its full glory; the man who then looked on it with all his love and penetrated its innermost being is—Beethoven! The instrumental compositions of these three masters breathe an identical romantic spirit—this is due to their similar intimate understanding of the specific nature of the art."[30] Who today would dare to call the compositions of Haydn, Mozart, and Beethoven "romantic?" But does our reluctance stem from a too narrow understanding of the term? Should we not allow ourselves to believe that Haydn and Beethoven knew what they wanted when notating their pedal instructions—that is, nearly impressionistic sound effects? These instructions should remind us once more of the wealth of creative ideas evinced by the great Classical composers, a wealth which every performer should feel a responsibility to attempt to recreate.

Notes

1. Carl Czerny, *On the Proper Performance of All Beethoven's Works for the Piano,* ed. and with a commentary by Paul Badura-Skoda (Vienna, 1963), p. 15.
2. Carl Ludwig Junker, in H. Ph. Bossler's *Musikalische Correspondenz,* November 23, 1791, quoted from Oscar Sonneck, *Beethoven: Impressions by His Contemporaries* (New York, 1926), p. 11.
3. J. F. v. Schönfeld, *Jahrbuch der Tonkunst von Wien und Prag* (Vienna, 1796; reprt. Munich, 1976), p. 7.
4. Wegeler-Ries, pp. 79–80.
5. The differences between cadenzas and fermata embellishments (called "Eingänge" by Mozart and Beethoven) are described in Eva and Paul Badura-Skoda, *Interpreting Mozart on the Keyboard* (London, 1960), chap. 11.
6. Wegeler-Ries, p. 114.
7. These were the aria of Jesus, "Meine Seele ist erschüttert" and that of the Seraph and the Chorus of Angels, "Erzittre Erde! Jehovas Sohn . . ."
8. Schönfeld, *Jahrbuch,* p. 176. (In the original the pagination of pp. 167–76 is erroneously doubled.)
9. Ibid., p. 167. (This page follows p. 176.)
10. Quoted from Ludwig Schiedermair, *Der junge Beethoven* (Leipzig, 1925), p. 62.
11. A document describing a meeting and competitive performance of Cramer and Beethoven is printed in Thea Schlesinger, *J. B. Cramer und seine Klavier Sonaten* (Munich, 1928), Appendix.
12. Charlotte Moscheles, ed., *Aus Moscheles Leben nach Briefen und Tagebücher* (Leipzig, 1872), I:53.
13. Wegeler-Ries, pp. 106–7.
14. Anderson 610.
15. William S. Newman, *Performance Practices in Beethoven's Piano Sonatas: An Introduction* (New York, 1971), p. 78.
16. Robert Winter, "Second Thoughts on the Performance of Beethoven's Trills," *MQ* 63 (1977):483–504.
17. G. B. Mancini, *Riflessioni Pratiche sul Canto Figurato,* 3d ed. (Milan, 1777), pp. 239–40.
18. Manfredini, quoted from Charles Mackerras, "Sense about the Appoggiatura," *Opera* (October, 1963), p. 672.
19. I. F. v. Mosel, *Versuch einer Ästhetik des dramatischen Tonsatzes* (Vienna, 1813), p. 61.
20. Copy in the archive of the GdM.
21. Mosel, *Versuch,* pp. 45, 47.
22. Czerny, *On the Proper Performance,* p. 16.
23. The trend toward an increased preference for legato is also clear from the following note in Muzio Clementi's *Vollständige Klavierschule* (Vienna, 1803): "If the composer leaves it to the performer to decide between staccato and legato, then the best rule is to play largely legato and to save the staccato for special passages."
24. See also chap. 38 of D. G. Türk's *Klavierschule* (Leipzig and Halle, 1789).
25. Thayer-Deiters-Reimann, II:172.
26. Czerny, *On the Proper Performance,* p. 97.
27. H. Grundmann and P. Mies, *Studien zum Klavierspiel Beethovens und seiner Zeitgenossen*

(Bonn, 1966), p. 12. Was it "sicher eine besondere Klangabsicht Beethovens" ("certainly a special sound intention of Beethoven's") that he did not write pedal markings in the theme of the variation movement of Op. 109 before the last chord? Some scholars are of a different opinion; see Franz Eibner, *Österreichische Musikzeitschrift* 20 (1965):190ff.

28. Czerny, *On the Proper Performance*, p. 22.
29. Newman, *Performance Practices*, pp. 63–64.
30. Quoted in Oliver Strunk, ed., *Source Readings in Music History* (New York, 1971), p. 771.

Concert Life
in Beethoven's Vienna

Otto Biba

Public concerts—musical performances announced publicly and to which anyone who purchased an admission ticket had access—began in Vienna in the last decades of the eighteenth century. (These public concerts may be contrasted both with performances in noble houses by retained musicians and with the "musical salons" of the middle class.) Vienna was blessed with a concert hall of its own only when the Gesellschaft der Musikfreunde, founded in 1812, opened its own building on November 4, 1831.[1] Before then, all public concerts had to be organized in theaters or in halls capable of serving multiple functions, most often including that of a restaurant.[2]

From 1774, as a result of an imperial decree, there were special "spielfreie Tage" in all theaters. The decree covered all church holidays and the evening before many of them, all days in Advent between December 16 and December 24, the entire five-week Lenten season preceding Easter, and the eve and anniversary of the day on which the most recently deceased imperial ruler had died. No theatrical or operatic performances were allowed on these days, although, except for during Lent, concerts could be given.[3] In Mozart's time these ordinances were observed very closely, but eventually theater managers allowed certain concessions. Since theatrical and operatic productions promised substantially better receipts than mere concerts, increasingly the rules were stretched to give preference to them. The Hoftheater (made up of the Burgtheater and the Kärntnertortheater) in particular had a tradition of amassing large deficits, and its managers were especially concerned with limiting the number of days with prohibitions. Likewise the private theaters—first and foremost the Theater-an-der-Wien—sought to limit the "spielfreie" days to as few as possible.

Both before and after 1800, however, the prohibitions were

followed almost without exception for the high feast and holy days and for the death-days of members of the royal family. Confirmation of the difficulties involved in renting theaters for concerts is provided by an unknown Viennese correspondent in the Leipzig *Allgemeine Musikalische Zeitung*.

> It is astonishing that in this munificent city of kaisers, where the passion for music is cultivated to the highest degree, there is no suitable concert hall at all, neither one which is acoustically favorable nor one which can accommodate a sizeable number of listeners. Until now the artist who wishes to display his wares has been limited to the theater [by which is meant the two wings of the Hoftheater], to the Redoutensaal, and to the Jahn Saal. The first two halls are very difficult to engage, and without the generous intercession of Baron Braun [Peter von Braun, the manager of the Hoftheater] virtually impossible. The reason for this I do not know.

That it was not at all easy to rent theaters for concerts we can also conclude from a report published in 1800 in the same journal, but the report implies that it was not difficult to rent concert halls. "Should an artist encounter difficulties in renting a theater, he is still not at a particular disadvantage. No less advantageous for a concert are the halls in the Augarten, that at Jahn's, or that in the Mehlgrube."[4]

The organizers of such concerts, whether in a theater or in another hall, were almost always the artists themselves—composers who wanted to present their own works to the public or virtuosos who wished to display their performing abilities. They rented the theater or hall, put the program together, took care of the publicity, set the admission prices, and assumed responsibility for the sale of tickets. Any financial gain or loss depended almost entirely on the receipts from the concert.

In the winter of 1781–82, the first subscription concerts (accompanied, inevitably, by the first concert impresario) were held in Vienna. A certain Philipp Jakob Martin organized a concert each Friday in the "Saal zur Mehlgrube" for which he both arranged the program and engaged the artists. Martin issued a subscription for this series, which resulted in a greatly lowered financial risk for any single concert. Wolfgang Amadeus Mozart was on friendly terms with Martin, and he performed a series of concerts as soloist in his own piano concertos.[5] Martin also strove to obtain the services of other important soloists.

The orchestra itself was composed of "dilettanti"; in his first year as an impresario Martin was accused of not being able to obtain the best of these. During the eighteenth and throughout most of the nineteenth century, a music dilettante was a trained musician who played his instrument perfectly, but for his own pleasure rather than for a living. A dilettante was simply a performer of professional caliber with amateur status. Of course, some dilettantes had more talent, more training, and more practical experience than others. But the unfavorable connotation which we are inclined to attach to this designation today was entirely unknown at the time.

We can trace Martin as an organizer of public concerts in Vienna until 1791. In the summers he arranged open-air concerts, and he sponsored not only concerts but balls as well. His contemporaries did not fail to take note of this phenomenon that appeared and relieved artists of the necessity of organizing their own performances. Nevertheless, when Martin suddenly vanished from the scene in 1791, no one stepped forward to replace him; composers and virtuoso performers reverted to their former practice.

In spite of his initially close relationship with Martin, Mozart himself organized six subscription concerts at his own risk during the Lenten season of 1785 in the hall "Zur Mehlgrube."[6] As Adalbert Gyrowetz reported in his autobiography, Mozart did something that up to then was quite unusual: he engaged a complete theater orchestra as his own ensemble for these concerts.[7] All indications suggest that it was the orchestra of the Burgtheater; that a concert series might defray the expenses of a professional orchestra was completely unheard of at the time. Orchestras in the theaters were used only for performances of opera and Singspiele, not for concerts. Whatever the orchestra, Leopold Mozart reported on its excellence in a letter describing Wolfgang's 1785 concerts.[8] The precedent, however, inspired little imitation. When, in 1808, Beethoven engaged the orchestra of the Theater-an-der-Wien for an "Akademie" at which the Fifth and Sixth symphonies were premiered, the result was a very unsatisfactory performance—even though only professional musicians were used.[9] Thereafter it again became the rule that orchestras for concerts were composed of dilettantes, or at the most some mixture of dilettantes and professional musicians.

From 1772 on, the regularly organized concerts of the so-called Tonkünstler-Societät occupied a special place in Vienna's concert life.[10] Its musical functions consisted of two large annual concerts, one during Advent and one at the end of Lent. Each concert was given twice, and the members took part without pay. The proceeds of these concerts were the largest source of income for the society, aside from membership fees. From this accrued wealth and the interest on it, the widows and orphans of deceased members received a subsidy. It amounted, then, to a very early form of pension insurance.

Soon the Tonkünstler-Societät could count many members. Consequently it could sponsor concerts that required large numbers of participants: Mozart's *"Davidde penitente"*, Haydn's *Seven Last Words*, *The Creation*, and *The Seasons*, and Beethoven's *Christus am Oelberg* are only the most celebrated works performed in this series. Virtually all of the repertory consisted of large oratorios. Each potential member was required to perform in one season's concerts on a trial basis. Nevertheless, all of the participants were professional musicians. In their essentials, then, these concerts were charity events which occurred only twice a year. They were, therefore, exceptions in Viennese concert life, even if celebrated ones.

At the end of the 1780s we uncover the first signs of "Musikfreunde" coming together as a special interest group to organize concerts whose programs featured works which the "friends" themselves wanted to hear. They no longer wished to leave to chance or to the decisions of artists which works they might have the opportunity to hear. Instead, they wished to choose democratically the musical fare to be offered, and at the same time participate actively in these concerts. Most of these friends of music were, therefore, dilettantes of the already familiar type.

As early as August, 1785, the *Wiener Zeitung* reported: "For the last few weeks in the morning, weather permitting, a society of worthy musicians and friends of music has been offering to an eager public in the garden of the Belvedere every variety of music in a public academy; each concert is imbued with the pleasant companionship of the enthralled listeners."[11] There were similar events in both the late 1780s and the 1790s, including concerts at the summer palace of Prince Liechtenstein.[12] All were free and open to everyone. Expenses were borne by the performers themselves, whose satisfaction derived from the opportunity to escape from "Hausmusik" and perform those larger works which pleased and challenged them. Unfortunately, we do not possess any more precise information about either the number of performers and listeners or the programs of these events.

The first really significant undertakings of this type were the concerts of the Associierten Cavaliers under the direction of Gottfried van Swieten.[13] Performances took place in the hall of Prince Schwarzenberg and included only oratorios, mostly by George Frideric Handel.

These loosely organized presentations commenced in 1788, reached a thoroughly organized form by 1793, and disappeared after 1801.

The next known attempt at this kind of democratization and organizational consolidation did not occur until 1807. In this year the Gesellschaft von Musikfreunden was formed, at the suggestion of Count Moriz of Dietrichstein and under the presidency of Prince Trautmanns- dorf. During the winter of 1807–8, the new society presented a series of twenty concerts in Vienna. Because Dietrichstein and Trautmannsdorf headed the fledgling organization, these concerts were entered into Viennese musical history as "aristocratic amateur concerts."[14] This des- ignation is, however, misleading. The middle class took part in the organization, execution, participation, and attendance just as much as the nobility.

The Napoleonic wars brought an abrupt halt to these concerts; for several seasons, Austria had other worries. However, after peace was again established in 1812, the Gesellschaft der Musikfreunde which still flourishes today was founded.[15] It specified the following areas of activ- ity: the organization of concerts, the founding of a conservatory for the training of dilettantes and professionals alike, and the establishment of a music archive to house an already budding music collection. The stat- utes also provided for "participating" and "supporting" members—that is, those who took part in performances and those who made such performances possible with their financial support. The governing board, which was selected every three years from among the members, proposed and agreed upon the concert programs. Perhaps the most fa- mous member of the board during the first half of the nineteenth cen- tury was Franz Schubert; Beethoven was never more than an honorary member of the Gesellschaft der Musikfreunde. Even after the founding of the Gesellschaft der Musikfreunde, however, most concerts organized in Vienna were still arranged by the artists for themselves. The programs were, almost without exception, potpourris of vocal and instrumental, orchestral and chamber music. Only one series, organized by Ignaz Schuppanzigh, concentrated on a single genre—that of chamber music—and largely on the string quartet.[16]

We may well wonder about the possibilities of income for an artist from a concert arranged by himself. On March 10, 1785, Mozart realized a profit of 559 gulden from a concert which he organized in the Burgtheater.[17] Johann Pezzl's *Sketches of Vienna*, which appeared in the same year, reported that an unmarried middle-class gentleman could reckon with an annual cost of living of 464 gulden, but that "with 500 or 550 gulden you can live quite comfortably."[18] Beethoven gave fewer of his own concerts than did Mozart. We know nothing about the receipts from his famous Akademien of 1800, with the premieres of the First Symphony and the Septet, Op. 20. On the other hand, the Akademie of April 5, 1803, which included the premieres of the Second Symphony, the Third Piano Concerto, and the oratorio *Christus am Oelberg*, realized the considerable profit of 1,300 gulden.[19] Even taking into account the increase in the cost of living since 1785, this sum from a single concert would have sufficed to enable Beethoven to live for two years without financial worry. Concerts appear to have allowed a healthy profit for the organizer, even when attendance was only average.

Any artist planning to sponsor a public concert in Vienna was required to obtain police approval.[20] We can assume that the necessary documents—the initial application and the final approval—would constitute an important source of information about Viennese concert life. Regrettably, a thoroughgoing search for these records has led me to conclude that they were destroyed in the 1927 fire that swept through the Palace of Justice in Vienna.

Other contemporary records that might have led to an overall picture of Viennese concert life have also vanished. We are forced to rely upon a more or less incidental series of documents. Concerts were neither reported upon nor reviewed regularly in contemporary newspapers, and only a tiny minority were announced in the papers beforehand. The modern style of review, containing discussions of both the works and their performance, begin to appear only in the second third of the nineteenth century. In the first third we encounter only brief reports (that a concert took place and that the artist enjoyed a greater or lesser success), and these only very infrequently.[21] Further, it was by no means understood that for each concert a printed program would be prepared. There was no central clearinghouse which assembled any such programs with an eye towards completeness. Those which survive do so fortuitously and are scattered among the various libraries and collections. For example, we do not possess a single program from the series presented by Philipp Jakob Martin or from that by Gottfried van Swieten, although we know for certain that both took place. It is impossible to determine whether none was printed or all have simply disappeared. A few other incidental reports of concerts can be found in letters, diaries, and memoirs.[22] We must not allow ourselves to forget that we have only fractional knowledge of Viennese concert life during Mozart and Beethoven's time.

We can, however, establish with some degree of completeness a list and the attributes of the major concert halls in the last quarter of the eighteenth and the first quarter of the nineteenth century.[23] The most important and distinguished was surely the Burgtheater.[24] Concerts were frequently given there on days when no theatrical productions or operas were scheduled. As its name implies, the theater was located in the complex of the Hofburg, where the emperor resided. He retained his own loge for performances. Unfortunately, the theater was demolished in 1888 to allow for expansion of the Hofburg. Only the old stage entrance has been preserved. The theater could accommodate, on evenings when it was "jam-packed" ("gedrangt voll"), some 1,800 spectators.[25]

Concerts were also given in the Theater-an-der-Wien, in the Kärntnertortheater, and in numerous small theaters in the suburbs. Not only *Fidelio*, but also Beethoven's Fifth and Sixth symphonies were premiered in the Theater-an-der-Wien. This colorful theater was opened in 1801 by Emmanuel Schikaneder; one of the entrances, adorned with Papageno and his entourage, survives today, along with much of the original layout.[26] The premiere of the Ninth Symphony and of three movements of the *Missa solemnis* took place in May, 1824, in the Kärntnertortheater, which remained in operation until 1869.[27] At these theater concerts the stage curtain was always closed. The orchestra occupied the same place as for a theatrical or operatic performance, sitting directly before the stage, but in the parterre and not in an orchestra pit, as is now customary. Around this time, orchestras holding concerts in halls gradually started using a platform, although considerable time elapsed before the practice became common. As early as 1782, a critic censured Philipp Martin for providing an orchestral platform in the concerts which he organized.[28]

After the theaters, the most important Viennese concert place was the so-called Zur Mehlgrube hall.[29] "At the sign of the flour shop" was, in fact, where all the bakers and grocers of Vienna purchased their flour. The ground floor housed a restaurant and the second floor a hall which, strictly speaking, also belonged to the restaurant. But not only banquets were celebrated there. The hall was also rented out for balls, concerts, and various other productions. Until about 1830, it was more important for concerts, and after that for balls. In 1866, the house was converted into a hotel; in 1897 it was demolished. We possess no good view of the outside of the structure and hardly any pictures of the hall itself. We do not even have accurate information about its seating capacity. According to one source, it could seat 150 to 200 people for concerts;[30] according to another source, six times that many people could cram themselves into the hall and its adjoining rooms, although the majority of them had to remain standing.[31]

Another important concert place for Mozart and many of his contemporaries was the so-called Trattnerhof.[32] This was a very large structure built for the book printer and publisher Johann Thomas Trattner. The building even had its own chapel. But when private chapels were forbidden in 1783 by an imperial order, the resourceful Trattner converted his into a festival hall and opened a cafe in the adjoining rooms. The hall was then rented for theatrical performances and concerts. It was torn down in 1911.

Another hall connected with a restaurant was located in the Himmelpfortegasse, right in the heart of the city. It was dubbed the "Jahnscher Saal," after its owner, Ignaz Jahn.[33] According to a description written in 1804, this hall, situated on the second floor, was narrow and not very high, but it could still accommodate 400 people. Numerous works of Beethoven were performed there, including the premiere of the Piano Quintet in E♭ major, Op. 16. The hall has long since been converted into apartments. Jahn also ran a summer eating establishment in the Augarten.[34] The Augarten was originally one of the emperor's private gardens, but it was opened to the public in 1775. Seven years later, Jahn opened his restaurant, which from the beginning he made available for concerts. During the warm seasons a great number of them were put on, sometimes inside the building and sometimes in front of it. It was at the Augarten in 1803 that Beethoven's *Kreutzer* Sonata was premiered. The building has been preserved and is today the site of a well-known china factory.

For very large concerts, it was possible to rent the Grossen Redoutensaal or the Winterreitschule in the imperial Hofburg. The Redoutensaal was actually built as a ballroom.[35] As it is preserved today, it contains some 600 seats, although it is reported to have held 1,000 in Beethoven's time. It was in this hall in 1824 that Beethoven repeated— with such disappointing receipts—the famous concert in which the Ninth Symphony was premiered. Particularly large concerts, however, took place in the Winterreitschule ("Winter Riding School") of the Hofburg. It was built in 1729–35 as the riding school for the kaiser. It

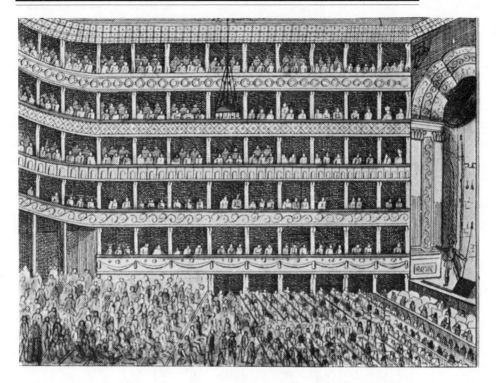

Inside the Kärntnertortheater, early nineteenth-century colored copper engraving. *By permission of the Historisches Museum der Stadt Wien.*

was also far and away the largest available hall in Vienna. Today this hall is still known as the home of the Spanish Riding School and is visited by countless tourists each year.

Since all the halls in Vienna which were available for concerts were, with the exception of theaters, relatively small, it was only a matter of time before an organization would seize upon the idea of sponsoring an event at the Winterreitschule. This could, however, happen only in a period when large ensembles had become part of the musical tradition. On November 29, 1812, the inaugural concert of the Gesellschaft der Musikfreunde was held there. More than 700 participants—mostly dilettantes, though supported by a smaller number of professional musicians—joined together in a mammoth production of Handel's oratorio *Timotheus, oder die Macht der Musik.* From then until 1848, the office of the kaiser frequently made the riding school available for oratorio performances of a similar kind. Large platforms had to be erected for both the performers and the listeners. We know of occasions when more than 800 participants were involved, and even then enough room remained for some 1,500 listeners! It was not the works of Beethoven, but the oratorios of George Frideric Handel, Joseph Haydn, and Maximilian Stadler which were presented, including Stadler's most successful work, *Die Befreiung von Jerusalem.*[36]

A survey of Viennese concert halls would not be complete without mention of the so-called Landständische Saal, even though we cannot document a single concert of Beethoven's music there.[37] This hall has been preserved and serves today as the meeting chamber of the lower Austrian regional government. It has served similar capacities since the sixteenth century, receiving its present form about the year 1710. It was rented for the first time as a concert hall in 1813. For the next fifteen years—until the opening of their own concert hall by the Gesellschaft der Musikfreunde—it remained a very popular location for concerts. Beethoven sought in both May, 1824, and February, 1825, to rent the Landständische Saal, but neither of these projected concerts took place. (The first event concerned the repeat of the Ninth Symphony concert, which eventually took place in the Redoutensaal.) The hall had excellent acoustics and was offered without rent to concert organizers. It had only one major disadvantage: it could not be heated. Today it seems hardly conceivable to us that concerts with 100 performers and 200 listeners could have taken place there, and in fact the last concerts were given around 1840.

Finally, a particularly important place for concerts was the festival hall of the university.[39] This hall has been preserved and is known now as the "Old University." The famous concerts of the Gesellschaft von Musikfreunden in the winter of 1807–8 were the first to take place there. These concerts included numerous works by Beethoven, and the last concert was a famous performance of Haydn's *Creation* at which the old composer was present. Balthasar Wigand captured this concert in a painting which reproduces the atmosphere more accurately than it documents the event.[39] Even so, we can see that the musicians performed on a platform and that the hall must have been capable of holding 1,300 subscribers, although they would have been very crowded and most of them would have had to stand. The acoustics must have benefited, however, for when empty the hall is quite resonant. This hall remained in regular use until 1840.

The nine halls already described were the most important in Viennese concert life during Beethoven's time. But the halls of at least three more restaurants deserve passing mention: "Zum römischen Kaiser" (Wien I, Freyung), "Müllerschen Gebäude" (Wien I, Rotenturmstrasse), and "Zum rothen Igel" (Wien I, Wildpretmarkt), where in their early years the Gesellschaft der Musikfreunde held smaller concerts. None of these establishments exists any longer.

Surprisingly, the price structure for Viennese concerts permitted even the least wealthy segments of society to attend in large numbers.[40] Occasionally the prices were raised for concerts by internationally celebrated virtuosos such as the singer Angelica Catalani. It is revealing that the unnamed correspondent of the *Leipzig Allgemeine Musikalische Zeitung* chastised Beethoven for doubling and even tripling the usual prices for his Akademie on April 5, 1803, at the Theater-an-der-Wien.[41] And just as the listening public was made up of persons from all walks and stations of Viennese life, so also were the chorus and orchestra of dilettantes. Ignaz von Mosel described this state of affairs in his memoirs: "Here one saw counts next to tradesmen, high officials next to civil servants, Ph.D.s next to students, and in the soprano and alto sections aristocratic ladies next to middle-class women—all took their place with the sole ambition of contributing to the success of the whole."[42]

The discussion thus far has touched only indirectly upon problems of performance practice. In closing I would like to offer the first results of my archival research into orchestral size and disposition during this period. Many will find the implications of the documentary evidence surprising and unsettling, but only because the conventional wisdom about performance forces has been founded upon the thinnest layer of historical fact. The picture presented here should broaden the basis for understanding.

For the subscription concerts in the winter of 1807–8 in the hall of the university, the following orchestra was employed: 13 first violins, 12 second violins, 7 violas, 6 violoncellos, 4 contrabasses, and a single complement of winds.[43] Orchestral works by Beethoven, including his first four symphonies, were played ten times in these performances. We must therefore assume that the composer approved of an orchestra of this size, with 55 musicians altogether. Recently I was able to locate in the private archive of a nobleman the list of names of the musicians who played in the orchestra for these concerts. Eighteen of the musicians were professionals and the rest dilettantes. This list is unquestionably the most authentic account of the makeup of an orchestra for the performance of Beethoven's works during his lifetime.

In 1813, Beethoven wrote to his friend and student Archduke Rudolph, stating: "For the symphonies [probably Nos. 4–6] I would like forces of at least four first violins, four second violins, four violas, two doublebasses and two violoncellos."[44] This letter has been cited much too often, and quite misleadingly, as evidence for the small size of the Beethoven orchestra. The composer used the word "probieren"—that is, to have a play-through rehearsal in order to become acquainted with a work. For such a session he required at least this minimum number of performers; Beethoven in no way suggests that these string forces were what he would wish for a concert performance. The most that can be drawn from his request is that any fewer strings would not be adequate even for a run-through.

Documents concerning the orchestra that played in the hall of Prince Schwarzenberg in Vienna in 1792 inform us of the orchestral forces for an Akademie in a noble house at the time of Beethoven's arrival in Vienna.[45] This ensemble did not belong to the prince, but consisted of hired musicians. It contained 34 men. The orchestra of the Tonkünstler-Societät was about the same size when there were no oratorios on the programs of their traditional concerts, as on April 15 and April 16, 1792. On these occasions there were 6 first and 6 second violins, 4 violas, 3 violoncellos, 3 contrabasses, and a single complement of winds, or 33 musicians in all.[46]

Inside the Theater-an-der-Wien, unsigned colored engraving, 1825.
By permission of the Historisches Museum der Stadt Wien.

Similar forces were engaged for the performance of dance music. The imperial court ball in the Redoutensaal in January, 1800—the period during which Beethoven wrote most of his dance music—employed an orchestra of 16 violins, 4 violoncellos and contrabasses, and a single complement of winds, or 35 musicians in all.[47] Hence we can infer that the 55 orchestral musicians for the concerts in the university hall during the winter of 1807–8 formed a well-manned ensemble, perhaps somewhat larger than usual. It must not be forgotten, however, that not only the string and wind families, but also the keyboard instruments of the time sounded significantly softer—and certainly different in timbre and character—than their modern counterparts. An orchestra of 35 to 55 musicians in Beethoven's time sounded completely different than an orchestra composed of an equal number and variety of modern instruments.

A tantalizing letter written by Beethoven (probably in 1816) to Vinzenz Hauschka suggests that the composer may have approved of an even larger orchestra on occasion. He writes to this organizer of the Gesellschaftskonzerten of the Gesellschaft der Musikfreunde that he is sending parts for "eight basses, four violas, six second violins and six first violins, and two parts for each wind instrument 'nebst zwei Harmonien.' "[48] If Beethoven indeed meant to sanction the use of doubled winds in tutti passages, then his postscript to the letter would seem to endorse even more strings: "N.B. You can still receive a number of handwritten parts from me." According to unpublished reminiscences written in 1842 by Johann Baptist Geissler, at that time archivist and librarian of the Gesellschaft, the strings used in the society-sponsored concerts consisted of 20 first and 20 second violins, 12 violas, 10 violoncellos, and 8 contrabasses. The winds were doubled "according to the needs of the composition," but the string complement always remained the same. Geissler also recorded another tantalizing bit of evidence concerning performance practice. For the concert on January 5, 1817, he notes: "At this concert for the first time an orchestral platform in oval form was used."[49] This disposition probably corresponded more closely to our modern seating arrangements than had yet become customary.

The concerts of the Tonkünstler-Societät involved particularly large instrumental forces. For a performance of *Christus am Oelberg* in 1817, the usual complement of instruments would have been 20 first and 20 second violins, 8 violas, 7 violoncellos, and 7 contrabasses. For the tuttis, the oboes, bassoons, and horns played with two or sometimes three on a part. This resulted in an orchestra of between 70 and 80 musicians.

In the chorus, where the soprano and alto parts were still sung by boys, there was an average of 15 singers on each part, or some 60 in the group.[50]

It will not be easy for modern performers sensitive to historical considerations to apply these findings from published and unpublished materials to their own work. That the material is not monolithic in its implications is hardly surprising, for a survey of performance conditions in Vienna or New York City today would doubtless produce similar results. But even though many of the lessons now emerge with new clarity, we are still wedded to instruments that have only an indirect relationship to those supplied for Beethoven by Archduke Rudolph. Indeed, until we intensify our efforts to recapture both these instruments and the skills necessary to perform on them, the work of the scholar can remain only partly fulfilled.

Notes

1. Carl F. Pohl, *Die Gesellschaft der Musikfreunde des österreichischen Kaiserstaates und ihr Conservatorium* (Vienna, 1871), pp. 19–21; Robert Hirschfield and Richard von Perger, *Geschichte des k.k. Gesellschaft der Musikfreunde in Wien* (Vienna, 1912), pp. 40–41.
2. Eduard Hanslick, *Geschichte des Concertwesens in Wien* (Vienna, 1869), pp. 69–70, 289–90.
3. *Theatralkalendar für Wien für das Jahr 1774* (Vienna, 1774), pp. 164–65.
4. *Allgemeine Musikalische Zeitung* 6 (Leipzig, 1803–4):470–71; 3 (Leipzig, 1800–1801):625–26.
5. Otto Erich Deutsch, ed., *Mozart. Die Dokumente seines Lebens* (Kassel, 1961), pp. 178, 182, 184, 187, 191; Erich Schenk, *Mozart, sein Leben, seine Welt* (Vienna, 1975), pp. 474–76, 488.
6. Deutsch, *Mozart*, pp. 209–13; Schenk, *Mozart*, p. 514.
7. *Adalbert Gyrowetz: Selbstbiographie*, in Alfred Einstein, ed., *Lebensläufe deutscher Musiker von ihnen selbst erzählt*, vol. 3 (Leipzig, 1915), p. 13.
8. Wilhelm A. Bauer and Otto Erich Deutsch, eds., *Mozart. Briefe und Aufzeichnungen*, vol. 3 (Kassel, 1963), p. 373.
9. Thayer-Deiters-Riemann, III:80–84.
10. Carl F. Pohl, *Denkschrift aus Anlass des hundertjährigen Bestehens der Tonkünstler-Societät* (Vienna, 1871). The programs for every concert sponsored by the Tonkünstler-Societät—alone among contemporary concert societies—are preserved today in the archive of the GdM.
11. *Wiener Zeitung*, 1785, no. 64.
12. Ignaz Edler von Mosel, *Die Tonkunst in Wien während der letzten fünf Dezenien*. Draft manuscript in the archive of the GdM (Sign. 1884/37), p. 27; Mosel, in *Allgemeine Wiener Musik-Zeitung*, vol. 3 (Vienna, 1843), p. 534.
13. R. Bernhardt, "Aus der Umwelt der Wiener Klassiker, Freiherr Gottfried van Swieten," *Der Bär: Jahrbuch von Breitkopf und Härtel*, 1929–30, pp. 74–166; Gerhard Croll, "Mitteilungen über die 'Schöpfung' und die 'Jahreszeiten' aus dem Schwarzenberg-Archiv," *Haydn-Studien*, vol. 3, no. 2 (1974), pp. 85–92.

14. Hanslick, *Geschichte,* pp. 75–79; Theophil Antonicek, "Musik im Festsaal der Österreichischen Akademie der Wissenschaften," *Oesterreichische Akademie der Wissenschaften, Veröffentlichungen der Kommission für Musikforschung* 14 (1972):31–40.

15. Cf. the literature cited in n. 1.

16. Hanslick, *Geschichte,* pp. 202–3.

17. Bauer-Deutsch, *Mozart,* III:378.

18. Johann Pezzl, *Skizze von Wien,* ed. Gustav Gugitz and Anton Schlosser (Graz, 1923), p. 345.

19. Thayer-Deiters-Riemann, II:385.

20. Oesterreichisches Staatsarchiv, Allgemeines Verwaltungsarchiv, Wien, Pergen-Akten, XVIII/A 1 H8.

21. The first detailed overview is provided by Clemens Höslinger, "Musik-Index zur Wiener Zeitschrift für Kunst, Literatur, Theater und Mode 1816–1848," *Publikationen der Sammlungen der Gesellschaft der Musikfreunde in Wien,* vol. 4 (Munich-Salzburg, 1980).

22. Of special importance is the Mozart family correspondence, even if it does not mention all of Wolfgang's concerts, or those in which his works were performed. Other sources include the diaries of Karl Graf von Zinzendorf (1739–1813) in the Haus-, Hof-, und Staatsarchiv, Vienna; the diaries of Wenzel Müller (1767–1835) in the Wiener Stadt- und Landesbibliothek; Mosel, *Tonkunst;* Johann Friedrich Reichhardt, *Vertraute Briefe geschrieben auf einer Reise nach Wien und den Oesterreichischen Staaten zu Ende des Jahres 1808 und zu Anfang 1809,* introduction and annotations by Gustav Gugitz, *Denkwürdigkeiten aus Alt-Oesterreich,* vol. 15 (Munich, 1915); Leopold von Sonnleithner, *Materialien zu einer Geschichte der Oper und des Balletts in Wien,* manuscript in the archive of the GdM.

23. There is as yet no definitive literature on this subject. In addition to Hanslick, *Geschichte,* see especially Hermann Ulrich, "Aus vormärzlichen Konzertsälen Wiens," *Jahrbuch des Vereines für Geschichte der Stadt Wien* 28 (1972):106–30; Rudolf Klein, "Traditionsstätten der Wiener Konzertpflege," *Österreichische Musikzeitschrift* 25 (1970):290–99; Klein, *Beethovenstätten in Oesterreich* (Vienna, 1970).

24. Harry Kühnel, *Die Hofburg,* Wiener Geschichtsbücher, vol. 5 (Vienna, 1971), p. 103; Eduard Wlassack, *Chronik des k.k. Hofburgtheater seit seiner Begründung* (Vienna, 1896); Richard Smekal, *Das alte Burgtheater 1776–1888* (Vienna, 1916); Otto Michtner, *Das alte Burgtheater als Opernbühne,* Theatergeschichte Österreichs, vol. 3, no. 1 (Vienna, 1970).

25. Margret Dietrich, ed., *Das Burgtheater und sein Publikum,* Veröffentlichungen des Instituts für Publikumsforschung, vol. 3 (Vienna, 1975), p. 238.

26. Raoul Biberhofer, *125 Jahre Theater an der Wien 1801–1926* (Vienna, 1926); Rudolf Klein, "Das zweite 'Wiedner' Theater," *Oesterreichische Musikzeitschrift* 17 (1962): 262–325; Dietrich, *Das Burgtheater.*

27. As this house was also a court theater, and was at times under the same direction as the Burgtheater, cf. the relevant literature in n. 24; see also Gustav Zechmeister, *Die Wiener Theater nächst der Burg und nächst dem Kärntnerthor von 1747 bis 1776,* Theatergeschichte Österreichs, vol. 3, no. 2 (Vienna, 1971); Dietrich, *Das Burgtheater.*

28. Schwarz, "Ueber das Wiener Dilektanten-Konzert" (Vienna, 1782), unpaginated (copy in the Vienna Stadt- und Landesbibliothek, sig. 10633A).

29. Felix Czeike, *Der Neue Markt,* Wiener Geschichtsbücher, vol. 4 (Vienna, 1970), pp. 67–76; Richard Groner, *Wien wie es war,* revised by Felix Czeike (Vienna, 1965), p. 377ff.

30. Leopold Mozart reported on February 16, 1785, that Wolfgang's concerts in the

Mehlgrube had been very well attended; on March 12, he spoke of more than 150 persons having subscribed to the series (Bauer-Deutsch, *Mozart*, III:373, 378).

31. The first concert of the Gesellschaft der Musikfreunde (the "Adelige Liebhaberkonzerte") in the winter of 1807–8, which took place on November 12, 1807, and for which 1,309 admission tickets were distributed, was held in the Mehlgrube; all other concerts in this series took place in the hall of the university (Graf Moriz Dietrichstein, "Entwurf zur Organisation des musicalischen Instituts," manuscript in the Archiv Schloss Waldstein, Steiermark. For the use of these materials as well as permission to publish from them, I am most indebted to His Highness Prince Heinrich Liechtenstein).

32. Hermine Cloeter, *Johann Thomas Trattner* (Graz, 1952), p. 89ff., 100; Groner, *Wien wie es war*, p. 609.

33. Cf. n. 4. See also Theodor Frimmel, *Beethoven-Handbuch* (Leipzig, 1926), I:237ff.; Groner, *Wien wie es war*, p. 256; Johann Ferdinand von Schönfeld, *Jahrbuch der Tonkunst von Wien und Prag*, Publikationen der Sammlungen der Gesellschaft der Musikfreunde in Wien, vol. 1 (Munich-Salzburg, 1976), p. 100, which characterizes the Jahnschen Saal, not as a concert hall, but as a dance hall for the nobility.

34. Hanslick, *Geschichte*, p. 70ff.; Frimmel, *Beethoven-Handbuch*, I:24ff.; Groner, *Wien wie es war*, p. 36ff.; Schönfeld, *Jahrbuch*, pp. 4, 52, 78, 98.

35. Hanslick, *Geschichte*, p. 361; Groner, *Wien wie es war*, p. 468; Kühnel, *Die Hofburg*, p. 80; Schönfeld, *Jahrbuch*, names this hall only as a ballroom (p. 100).

36. Groner, *Wien wie es war*, p. 664; Kühnel, *Die Hofburg*, p. 75ff.

37. Max Vancsa, "Ein Alt-Wiener Konzertsaal," in *Musikbuch aus Österreich*, ed. Richard Heuberger (Vienna, 1904), I:38–50; Hanslick, *Geschichte*, p. 187.

38. Antonicek, "Musik im Festsaal"; cf. n. 31.

39. Reproduced, among other places, in Antonicek, "Musik im Festsaal," and in László Somfai, *Joseph Haydn. Sein Leben in zeitgenössischen Bildern* (Kassel, 1966), p. 202. The original, whose last owner was the Historisches Museum der Stadt Wien, has been missing since 1945.

40. Ulrich, "Aus vormärzlichen," p. 122ff.

41. *Allgemeine Musikalische Zeitung* 4 (Leipzig, 1801–2):590.

42. Hanslick, *Geschichte*, p. 155.

43. Cf. n. 31.

44. Kastner-Kapp, *Beethovens sämtliche Briefe*, p. 248; Anderson 330.

45. Statniarchiv Český Krumlov, ČSSR, fasc. 26, no. 1/1, 1792, No. 517. For his generous assistance in the use of the Schwarzenberg family archive, where I found the documents concerning this orchestra, I would like to thank Dr. Jiri Zaloha.

46. Archiv der Stadt und des Landes Wien, Akten der Tonkünstler Societät.

47. Haus-, Hof-, und Staatsarchiv Wien, HMK IV, 1800, 12 January.

48. Pohl, *Die Gesellschaft*, p. 8ff. This "Gesellschafts-Konzerte" of the Gesellschaft der Musikfreunde took place in the Grossen Redoutensaal. Beethoven's letter is found in Theodor Frimmel, *Neue Beethoveniana* (Vienna, 1888), p. 101; Kastner-Kapp, *Beethovens sämtliche Briefe*, p. 396; Anderson 716.

49. "Die Gesellschafts-Concerte des Vereines der Musikfreunde des Oesterr. Kaiserstaates vom 3. Dezember 1815 bis 29. März 1840. dann vom 6. Dezember 1840 bis 13. März 1842, verzeichnet von Joh. Bapt. Geissler, Bibliothekar der Gesellschaft," manuscript in the Archive of the GdM (sig. 2712/47), pp. 3, 11.

50. Archiv der Stadt und des Landes Wien, Akten der Tonkünstler-Societät.

Traditional Elements in Beethoven's Middle-Period String Quartets

James Webster

The *Eroica* Symphony, composed mainly in 1803, marked Beethoven's irrevocable commitment to his "new way," a new music of unprecedented size, power, and expressive force.[1] Along with the *Eroica*, Alan Tyson groups a number of works from 1803 through early 1805, including the oratorio *Christus am Oelberge* and the opera *Leonore*, to form what he calls Beethoven's "heroic phase."[2] The notion seems appropriate not only for biographical reasons (chiefly Beethoven's decision to compensate for his deafness through his art), but because the vocal works deal with triumph over adversity. The connotations of the *Eroica*, symbolized by the planned dedication to Bonaparte and the very title, play a central role in this interpretation. But the concept of "heroic phase" would be hollow, were it not that the purely musical achievement of the *Eroica* strikes us as authentically heroic, as much or more than the biographical facts ever could.

In a larger historical and stylistic context, the *Eroica* definitively established what we call Beethoven's "second" or "middle" period. He then systematically exploited his "new way" in the other chief genres of instrumental music, creating for each a new style as the *Eroica* had done for the symphony. The *Waldstein* and *Appassionata* piano sonatas, the Triple Concerto, the G-major Piano Concerto, the Violin Concerto, the Fourth Symphony, and the three *Razumovsky* string quartets, Op. 59 fall between the *Eroica* and the end of 1806. These works are seen in terms of—one might almost say in the shadow of—the *Eroica*. When Joseph Kerman analyzes Op. 59, no. 1, and by implication all the middle quartets, under the heading "After the *Eroica*," he gives pointed form to a central tenet of Beethoven criticism.[3]

In particular, Op. 59, no. 1 in F major has often been interpreted as an "Eroica" for string quartet. Among the features cited are the size of the individual movements; the striving for orchestral sound; new and special effects such as pizzicato; the expanded tessitura; the use of register as a compositional resource (as at the beginning of the first movement); the reliance on sonata form in all four movements; the "through-composed" effect generated by the absence of internal repetitions in the first movement and the scherzo; the device Kerman calls "thematic completion," namely, reserving the most stable or the climactic version of a main theme for the final statement (first movement, m. 1 vs. m. 348); and the unprecedentedly original tone, style, and scoring of the Allegretto scherzando.

Despite its somewhat smaller outward dimensions, Op. 59, no. 2 in E minor is cited for the pregnant themes, the superlative logic, and the rich passion of the first movement; for the ethereal "starry sky and . . . music of the spheres"[4]—or, for those of different persuasions, the sonata form and tonic major—of the slow movement; for the sardonic minuet and the contrapuntal trio on the *thème russe*; and for the finale's insistence on beginning its main theme in the submediant C major.[5]

On the other hand, it is not easy to interpret Op. 59, no. 3 in C major or Op. 74 in E♭ major in terms of the stylistic norms implied by the *Eroica*. Despite its remarkable Andante and its triumphant contrapuntal finale, Op. 59, no. 3 as a whole seems more modest in scale and closer to tradition. It brings a minuet and trio in old-fashioned style in place of a scherzo, and its first movement exhibits obvious relations to earlier works, specifically to the first movement of Mozart's Quartet in C, K. 465. The "Harp" Quartet, Op. 74 is similarly modest in scale.

In fact, Op. 59, no. 3 has become something of an embarrassment to Beethoven criticism. (As the older German nickname of "Heldenquartett" implies, the nineteenth century took a rather different view, especially regarding the finale.) For some, its very modesty and closeness to tradition are disappointing. Thus Riemann wrote: "One searches in vain, even in the development [of the first movement], for passages of concentrated power with Beethovenian motivic work; it remains al fresco. . . . The movement brings no surprises. The entire quartet maintains this peculiar character of simplicity, exceptional in Beethoven, throughout all its movements" (pp. 73–74). Abraham criticizes the first movement for its "stiffness and formality," for lacking the "close reasoning" of the first movements of nos. 1 and 2; "one does not *feel* any inner logic" (p. 45); the minuet "emphasizes the general inferiority" of this work to its companions (p. 51); and the theme of the finale is "long and straggling and . . . not distinctive enough for effective polyphonic work-ing"; the "'fugal exposition' is rather skeletal . . . there is little poly-phonic flowering" (p. 54). Kerman views the work as unbalanced. The Allegro is "overshadowed" by the "restless" Andante and the introduction (p. 134); in the "elementary" minuet, only the codetta is interesting, and the trio is "perfunctory" (pp. 140–41); the "tub-thumping" finale (p. 119) is "brash" (p. 142), and its "operatic" crescendos and sequences "stretch . . . the material . . . unmercifully" (p. 142). Some writers also refer to the relative popularity of Op. 59, no. 3 when these quartets first became known, implying that by comparison with nos. 1 and 2 it is easy and superficial.[6] At another level, Tyson has interpreted aspects of the genesis of this work as support for the opinion that it is not completely successful.[7] Both of these points will be discussed later.

Whatever the intrinsic merits of Op. 59, no. 3, these recent critical attitudes regarding it seem not to have been articulated persua-sively. One reason may be a confusion about the role of tradition in Beethoven's music. Of course, the works of the first period, especially the Op. 18 quartets, are relatively well understood in this respect.[8] Recently, for example, Douglas Johnson has suggested that Beethoven's first compositional maturity, in the years 1794–95, resulted from his brief but intense study of Mozart's and Haydn's music in Vienna during 1792 and 1793 and perhaps especially from Haydn's tutelage in 1793.[9] It is curious that although Beethoven modeled several entire works or movements on Mozart, in each case in the same scoring and key,[10] he apparently never did this with a Haydn work. On the other hand he derived his rhythms, his thematic ideas, his inventive and ambiguous uses of tonality, his dynamic sense of process, and his techniques of motivic development more from Haydn than from Mozart.[11]

But the close contact between Beethoven's later instrumental music and the Classical tradition is not so well understood, or at any rate has never received comparable attention.[12] We can earn a fresh under-standing of this relationship by reexamining Beethoven's string quartets of the middle period.

Beethoven's large-scale instrumental music centers around genres that had reached maturity in the last decades of the eighteenth century: piano sonata, violin sonata, piano trio, string quartet (and trio and quintet), symphony, and concerto. In this most elementary sense, his entire career was based on tradition. But as Ludwig Finscher has argued, the string quartet had the most coherent identity and the most closely knit history of any of these genres.[13] In Vienna it had been cultivated continuously at least since 1780, when it suddenly flowered as a reaction to, and a stimulus for, two new aspects of Viennese musical life: the music publishing industry and the semipublic concert.[14] The cultivation of the string quartet depended on a free mixing of the social classes on the one hand, and of the musical professionals and amateurs on the other. A set of quartets might be commissioned by a noble or wealthy patron for his private use for a period of time preceding publication; or it might be composed on speculation, to be sold to a publisher on the open market, or circulated privately in hopes of finding a suitable patron. In either case, both private and public performances found composers, performers, connoisseurs, and amateur musicians joined together with the music-loving nobility in a peculiarly Viennese tradition of social music making.

Beethoven's chamber music originated within this tradition. This becomes clear when one compares his and Haydn's careers as composers of quartets and quintets between 1795 and 1803. In 1795, Count Apponyi solicited one or more quartets from Beethoven—a request the composer was unwilling or unable to fulfill.[15] But in that very year, Haydn's six quartets, Op. 71–74, which he had composed in 1793 while Beethoven was his pupil, appeared in print, dedicated to Apponyi.[16] We may infer that the count, now seeking a fresh recipient for his patronage, turned to the young lion of high pretensions. It is not unthinkable that Haydn recommended Beethoven to Apponyi—he had been impressed by Op. 1, and relations between Beethoven and Haydn were apparently good during much of this period—though of course Apponyi could have formed his own opinion in the matter.[17] We do not know whether Beethoven composed Op. 18 (1798–1800) on commission or on speculation, but its publication in 1801 proceeded under the patronage of Prince Lobkowitz.[18] But Lobkowitz was also the dedicatee of Haydn's Op. 77, composed in 1799 and published in 1802. And finally Beethoven's String Quintet, Op. 29 was composed in 1801 and published by Breitkopf and Härtel, with a dedication to Count Fries. In 1801, Haydn was reported to have promised a set of quintets to Fries; although nothing came of this promise, he may have begun the unfinished quartet Op. 103 in 1802. And this quartet did appear, published by Breitkopf and Härtel in 1806, with a dedication to Fries.[19] Thus as long as Haydn remained active, his and Beethoven's careers as quartet composers ran in parallel courses.

But Beethoven continued to follow these precedents after 1802. Count Razumovsky's initiative in the patronage of Op. 59, composed chiefly from May to December, 1806, is beyond dispute. Razumovsky himself played second fiddle in a respectable chamber ensemble, once again confirming the characteristic Viennese relation between composer and noble amateur. And of course Op. 59 is an "opus" in the traditional sense: that is, a group of three or six works, each complete in itself, written more or less at once and published as a set, but not constituting a "cycle."[20] The semipublic quartet parties organized by Schuppanzigh in the winter of 1804–5 differed little from the Viennese chamber music performance traditions going back to the 1780s.[21] It may have been such Schuppanzigh performances that stimulated Beethoven to consider composing quartets again after a pause of several years.

With Op. 74, to be sure, Beethoven abandoned the opus tradition. But in other respects the Eb-major Quartet recapitulates the history of Op. 18: we do not know of any external stimulus for its composition in 1809, but its publication ensued the following year under Lobkowitz's patronage. Thus, Op. 95 was Beethoven's first quartet to originate outside the traditional patronage and publication system: this work of 1810 was dedicated to his friend Nikolaus von Zmeskall, and did not appear in print for six years afterwards. It apparently marked Beethoven's only sentimental gesture as a composer of string quartets. In this respect he was perhaps less original than Mozart, whose first mature set of quartets was dedicated not to any patron, but to Haydn, his friend and colleague, and hence—by implication—to the musical public. (I leave out of account here the possibility that Mozart had previously tried and failed to find a conventional patron for these works.)

Furthermore, Beethoven's middle quartets maintain the inherent musical characteristics previously developed in the genre.[22] These include, first of all, the pretension to high art, the best and most serious writing of which the composer was capable. Quartets were usually large works, usually in four movements; the first movement, and often several others, were based on sonata form and adhered to "sonata style." Certain conventions governed the sequence of movements and the progressions from one movement to another: the outer movements were in fast tempo, the finale was "lighter" than the first movement, the inner movements comprised one in slower tempo and one minuet or scherzo, usually but not necessarily in that order. (Comparison with Beethoven's piano sonatas or Haydn's piano trios shows at a glance how much "stricter" and more uniform was the string quartet in these respects.) The scoring was paramount; the quartet was the locus of "pure" part-writing in instrumental music. Thus the quartet suggested learned or contrapuntal treatment;[23] many other passages were based on "thematic workings-out" (*thematische Arbeit*) or, in Beethoven's preferable phrase, "obbligato accompaniment." On the other hand, this "high" art was tempered by attractive, even popular features; the quartet was multifarious in its sources and styles. Despite all external differences, Op. 59 and Op. 74 perpetuate this tradition of the genre as clearly as Op. 18.

We may conclude that Beethoven's middle quartets maintained both the social and the musical traditions of the genre. We therefore have the necessary historical basis for inquiring into their relations to tradition in a specifically compositional sense.

Of course, many aspects of Beethoven's supposed originality in his middle period were not entirely original. His systematic use of register as a compositional resource, as in the expansion from the middle to extremes of high and low in the first nineteen bars of Op. 59, no. 1 and the introduction to Op. 59, no. 3, finds an antecedent as early as Haydn's Op. 20, no. 2 (ex. 1). The three quasi-fugal statements of the opening theme (mm. 1, 7, 15), all in middle registers, though moving upwards as a whole, are followed by a sudden downward extension in the cello (mm. 16–17) and an upward flight in the first violin (m. 18). This is as systematic as Op. 59, no. 1, if less single-minded than Beethoven's correlation of the registral expansion with other factors leading to the climax in m. 19. Haydn's abrupt change of register, in which the entire texture moves up or down so far that the melody of one passage is lower than the bass of the other, is as "dissociated" as anything in Beethoven's middle quartets; examples are m. 28 of the same movement, or the almost Webernlike passage at Op. 76/4/ii, 49–52 (ex. 2). The "orchestral" writing in the development of the "Harp" Quartet's first movement, or the brilliant first-violin passage-work in the coda, can hardly offend purists of quartet

Ex. 1(a) Haydn, Op. 20, No. 2/I, opening

Ex. 1(b) Beethoven, Op. 59, No. 1, opening

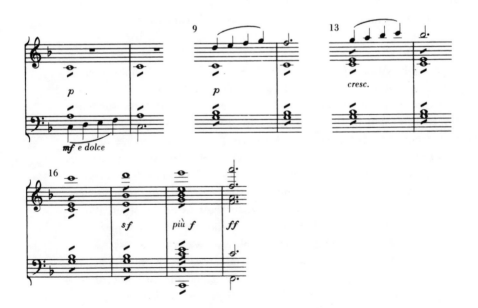

Ex. 2 Haydn, Op. 76, No. 4/II, 48–53

style more than Haydn's brilliant violin writing in Op. 17/5/i, 25–30, or the coda in Op. 74/2/iv, 213–71; the latter passage is actually more bizarre, because less clearly related to anything earlier in the movement.[24] The Scherzo of Op. 77, no. 1 persuades us that Haydn's rapid exploitation of registral shifts, reckless climaxes on the highest notes, and exuberant vitality are bolder and more self-assured than anything Beethoven wrote for this medium before 1806 and more than much that he wrote thereafter.

The placement of all four movements in the tonic, specifically the slow movement and the trio in the tonic major when the overall tonic is minor, as in Beethoven's Op. 59, no. 2, occurs in Haydn's Op. 20, no. 5, Op. 64, no. 2, and Op. 76, no. 2. Haydn also does the same with a major tonic in Op. 20, no. 2 and Op. 54, no. 2. The appearance of the theme of Op. 59, no. 2's finale in the submediant C major is an extension of Haydn's beginnings "off" the tonic or in tonally ambiguous fashion, of which the most familiar case is Op. 33, no. 1.[25] If one grants that the Allegretto scherzando of Op. 59, no. 1 is in sonata form,[26] then all four movements of that quartet are so constructed, and to be sure this is apparently unprecedented. But strictly speaking, no other middle-period Beethoven quartet has more than two such movements.[27] Hence Beethoven's middle quartets, as a whole, do not "advance" upon Mozart or Haydn in this respect, both of whom often bring three sonata-form movements out of four (Haydn, Op. 20, no. 1; Op. 74, no. 1; Op. 77, no. 1; Mozart, K. 499, K. 590, K. 593); the list is materially lengthened if Mozart's weighty sonata-without-development slow movements are included (K. 387, K. 458, K. 465, K. 515, K. 516).

Many of the individual movements within Op. 59 do not exceed the outward dimensions of Mozart's "Haydn" quartets and his string quintets. (Haydn, to be sure, always wrote on a smaller scale.) The first movement of Op. 59, no. 2, in 6/8, is 255 measures long; this is precisely the average length of the comparable first movements of Mozart's Quartet in Bb, K. 458, and Quintet in Eb, K. 614. The first movement of Op. 59, no. 3, without the introduction, is 235 bars; the average of Mozart's first movements in the same meter—the Quartets in G, K. 387; in Eb, K. 428; and in C, K. 465; and the Quintets in C, K. 515; in G minor, K. 516; and in D, K. 593 (without opening introductions)—is an almost identical 236 bars. Even the first movement of Op. 59, no. 1, at 400 bars, is but 9 percent longer than the first movement of K. 515, at 368 bars; and its finale, at 327 bars, is dwarfed by Mozart's gigantic 539-bar finale. Several other Mozart finales are as long or longer than that of Op. 59, no. 1. The movements in Op. 59 which are significantly longer than earlier movements of the same type are the Allegro and the Allegretto scherzando in no. 1, the finales in nos. 2 and 3, and—perhaps surprisingly—all three slow movements. Whatever new dynamic and expressive power resides in these quartets, then, must depend on factors other than sheer size or range.[28]

Finally, none of the middle-period quartets is, like the Fifth Symphony, clearly psychologically and musically "through-composed."[29] Beethoven goes no further in this direction than transitions between the third and fourth movements in Op. 59, nos. 1 and 3, and Op. 74, and the lead-in from the slow movement to the scherzo of Op. 95. But Haydn had gone quite as far in two striking quartets, Op. 20, no. 2 and Op. 54, no. 2. Like the Fifth Symphony, both are in C minor and major; both exhibit free-form slow movements which do not end, but break off and lead to the minuet; in Op. 20, no. 2, the trio likewise breaks off and leads back to the minuet *da capo* (as do other Haydn trios in this period); and each quartet culminates in a highly unusual finale which forms the climax of the whole. Likewise the "coherence of the total cyclic experience" which Kerman (p. 133) praises in Beethoven's Op. 59, no. 2 hardly represents an advance on Haydn's brusque and terse quartets in the minor, such as Op. 33, no. 1 and Op. 64, no. 2, both in the related key of B minor.

It took Beethoven until his late period to bring back a slow introduction later within a chamber music allegro, as Mozart had done in the Quintet in D, K. 593 (and Haydn in the "Drum Roll" Symphony, and Beethoven himself in several piano sonatas and the Piano Trio Op. 70, no. 2). In the middle quartets, only the "Quartetto Serioso," Op. 95 is as deeply felt throughout as Mozart's Quintet in G minor. In fact, the "Serioso" recalls Mozart's quintet in its unrelievedly earnest manner, its slow introduction to the finale (to be distinguished from the coda-transitions in Op. 59, no. 3 and Op. 74), and its inability to sustain the serious tone to the end of the work. Beethoven's inexplicable "buffa" coda is the emotional counterpart of Mozart's too determinedly cheerful finale. Each artist had worked himself into a position of not knowing, or not "feeling" (in Kerman's apt phrase about Beethoven[30]) how to end a wholly serious work.

All in all, the notion that Beethoven "emancipated" the string quartet in his middle period can be accepted only with reservations. In terms of size and range, it is true only for a few individual movements. Many of the ostensibly pathbreaking features in these works have ample precedent in the tradition. And as we shall now see, conventional features of that tradition inform Beethoven's middle quartets in rich measure.[31]

We may as well begin with Op. 59, no. 3. As has often been remarked, certain aspects of its first movement reflect Mozart's "Dissonant" Quartet in C, K. 465.[32] Both begin with a slow introduction, a rarity in the string quartet. Both introductions are in 3/4 and in C minor (curiously, neither notates C minor with a key signature); both lead eventually to a sprightly allegro in C major in 4/4 meter. Both introductions have been judged notorious—Mozart's for its dissonances and its cross relations, Beethoven's for its absence of thematic ideas and its systematic avoidance of clear resolution for its diminished sevenths until the very end—and both remain problematic today, Beethoven's perhaps more so than Mozart's.[33] But both are organized on the same structural principle: a steadily descending chromatic bass line (cf. ex. 3). Mozart's bass leads from the implied tonic in m. 1 to i^6 in m. 12, and again from the tonic in m. 14 to the structural dominant in m. 16; Beethoven's leads straight down the scale from f$^\sharp$ to his dominant,

Ex. 3(a) Mozart, K.465, Introduction

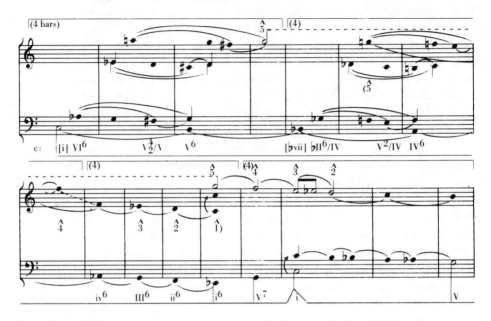

Ex. 3(b) Beethoven, Op. 59, No. 3, Introduction

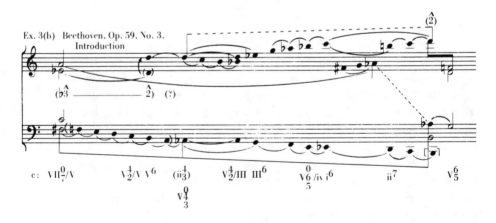

built on B rather than G. And both opening sonorities lie "off" the tonic—VI^6 and then $V^4_{20}ofV$ in Mozart, $V^0_{90}ofV$ in Beethoven. But whereas Mozart begins squarely on the tonic in the bass and ends squarely on the dominant, Beethoven (as Kerman has emphasized) uses diminished sevenths, which connect the leading-tones instead ($\sharp\hat{4}$ to $\sharp\hat{7}$); nor does his melodic progression (cf. ex. 3) reveal any clear prolongation based on the tonic triad.[34]

The similarity extends to certain points in the Allegros. In both, the particular C-major ambience has been called "sunny," though one suspects that this epithet expresses primarily the writer's relief at seeming to be on safe ground. (In fact, both Allegros contain chromatic and "difficult" passages: for example Mozart, mm. 107–21, 227–35; Beethoven, mm. 41–43, 65–68, 125–32.) As has often been noted, a theme in sixteenth notes late in Beethoven's first group—not the "bridge," as it is often called—uses a motive from the first theme in Mozart's second group (see ex. 4). An equally clear, hitherto unremarked similarity occurs within each second group: the same cadential figure, with the same disposition of material through all four parts, closes one paragraph (see ex. 5).

On the other hand, Beethoven's main theme perpetuates a different tradition of beginning a work in C major, which goes back at least as far as Haydn's Op. 33, no. 3 (see ex. 6a). The point is the statement of the main theme, *piano*, in sequence, first in the tonic, then in the supertonic D minor (mm. 1, 7). Haydn even begins a third time, in reverse sequence with the bass on B♭ (m. 13), but this statement swings round to V and then to I. (A typical subtlety is that the full cadence in m. 18 is timed to coincide with a new theme—the completion of a process.) Haydn never repeated this procedure, but Beethoven seems to have been almost compulsively fascinated by it. Its appearance in the First Symphony is well known, and it also appears in the finale of the String Quintet, Op. 29 (ex. 6b). But it also recurs in a C-major work from the so-called heroic years, the *Waldstein* Sonata (ex. 6c). Here Beethoven reverses the order of the two contrasting chords with respect to Haydn's Op. 33, no. 3: the first statement goes from C to B♭ (IV*of*IV), the second from C to D minor, preparing the transitional tonality A minor. The opening sequence in four-bar phrases on a descending bass, I—V^6, IV*of*IV—IV^6, also recalls the first two phrases in

Ex. 4(a) Mozart, K.465/I, 59–61

Ex. 4(b) Beethoven, Op. 59, No. 3/I, 59–64

Ex. 5(a) Mozart, K.465/I, 87–91

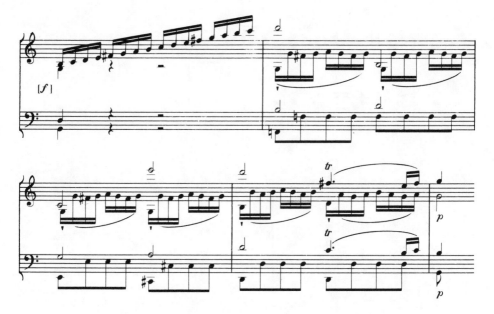

Ex. 5(b) Beethoven, Op. 59, No. 3/I, 88–91

Ex. 6(a) Haydn, Op. 33, No. 3, opening

Ex. 6(b) Beethoven, Quintet Op. 29, finale, opening

Ex. 6(c) Beethoven, "Waldstein" Sonata, opening

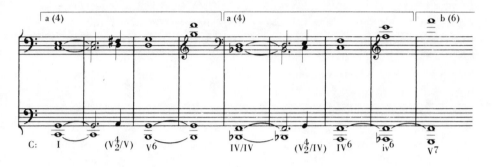

Ex. 6(d) Beethoven, Op. 59, No. 3/I, 30–43

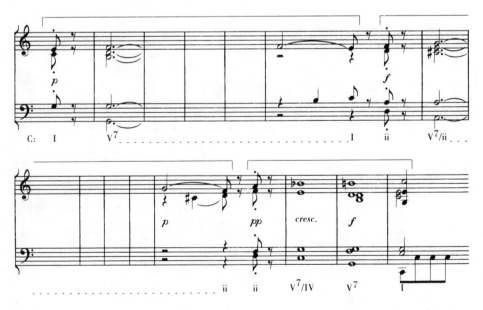

the introduction to the "Dissonant" Quartet (cf. ex. 3a). With all these precedents, it need hardly occasion surprise when we hear the sequence I—ii in Op. 59, no. 3 (ex. 6d). In contemporary works in the minor (the *Appassionata* and Op. 59, no. 2) and in later ones (the quartets Op. 95 and Op. 131) Beethoven transformed this diatonic sequence, I—ii, into his familiar expressive emphasis on the flat supertonic, I—IIᵇ. He never found an expressive version in the major.³⁵

The opening of the first movement of Beethoven's Op. 29 perpetuates still another C-major tradition which Haydn established in Op. 33, no. 3—the even, *piano*, homophonic, stepwise ductus, all in the lowest register, of the Scherzo (ex. 7a). (Haydn had already written something similar in the last eight bars of the minuet in Op. 20, no. 2,

Ex. 7(a) Haydn, Op. 33, No. 3, Scherzo, 1–10

also in C major.) Mozart had imitated this effect in the minuet of his
C-major Quintet, K. 515 (ex. 7b). Beethoven's opening (ex. 7c) not
only maintains this tradition, but also the sequential move to the supertonic described above—which, indeed, is also present in the Haydn and,
by implication, the Mozart examples. Beethoven's closeness to this tradition may be further documented, finally, by the appearance of a promi-

Ex. 7(b) Mozart, K.515, Minuet, 41–48

Ex. 7(c) Beethoven, Op. 29, opening

Ex. 8(a) Mozart, K.465/I, 23–26, 31–33

Ex. 8(b) Beethoven, sketch for Op. 59, No. 3

nent motive from Mozart's Allegro (m. 31) in an early sketch for several
C-major allegros within the context of Op. 59 (ex. 8),[36] and even in the
final version, the "sighing" appoggiatura resolution in mm. 34 and 40
(ex. 6d) may recall Mozart's similar figure from m. 24. (But Mozart's
motive, especially in its continuations, derives yet again from Op. 33,
no. 3: cf. ex. 6a, mm. 18ff.)

    Other aspects of Op. 59, no. 3 reflect still other dimensions of
tradition. In the development of the first movement, for example, a
pregnant motive in the bass creates an enharmonic modulation moving

by half-steps, recalling a modulation in the development of Haydn's Op. 77, no. 2—not only in the motive itself, but also in the prominence given to E minor (see ex. 9). Op. 59, no. 3 revives traditional movement types in the minuet and trio, and in the contrapuntal, pseudofugal finale.[37] The antecedent of this finale in the quartet literature is Mozart's Quartet in G, K. 387. But both its exuberance—which Kerman finds vulgar, and which Finscher interprets as a climax to the entire Op. 59—and the counterpoint's absorption in, and eventual submission to, triumphant sonata style in the coda also recall Haydn's fugal finales in Op. 20, especially no. 2 in C major.

Ex. 9(a) Haydn, Op. 77, No. 2/I, 89–96

The coda of Beethoven's finale borrows a striking feature of form from Mozart's *opera buffa* finales: for example, *Don Giovanni*, act 2, sextet; *Così fan tutte*, act 1,—and from that famous anticipation of those finales, the coda to the variation finale of the G-major Concerto, K. 453. A long passage which seems to have reached the climax breaks off, usually on the dominant, and leads back to a repetition of the entire passage. In Mozart's concerto, the passage in question is mm. 222–48, followed by the codettalike repetition of the theme in mm. 248–56; the

Ex. 9(b) Beethoven, Op. 59, No. 3/I, 125–133

repetition follows in mm. 273–306, with the altered codetta, following an interpolation, in mm. 331–42. In Op. 59, no. 3, the finale offers its tremendous buildup to the climax in mm. 361–85; the sudden halt then leads to the repetition in mm. 395–423, and thereby to the true climax. This repetition of a substantial coda section assumes added significance when we learn that as late as the autograph stage, Beethoven intended a similar and even longer repetition in the coda of the finale of Op. 59, no. 1, which he finally excised.[38] (The same feature recurs later: for example, in the finale of the A-minor Quartet, Op. 132.)

The last bars of this finale, on the other hand, clearly reflect the last bars of K. 515 (ex. 10). All four instruments move rapidly up and down the triad on pairs of repeated notes, in contrary motion, continually changing contour, but as a whole moving downwards until a halt on the antepenultimate bar prepares a massive V-I cadence on the final two downbeats—whose scoring is nearly identical. These passages look "conventional," but I know of no others quite like them.

It is thus clear that Op. 59, no. 3 is indebted to the tradition of Classical chamber music, and more particularly to several specific C-major antecedents within it. But this debt is clearly not described

Ex. 10(a) Mozart, K.515/IV, conclusion

Ex. 10(b) Beethoven, Op. 59/3/IV, conclusion

adequately by referring only to K. 465, or for that matter to any single theme or musical idea, nor even to any single type of relationship. Finscher's suggestion that Beethoven articulated these multiple and many-layered relationships to tradition self-consciously, and partly in a spirit of irony and parody, protests too much, to my mind; it seems sufficient to acknowledge that Op. 59, no. 3 is steeped in tradition.

What about the rest of Op. 59? Perhaps it is only a coincidence that the very first bars in no. 1 reflect a traditional texture for the beginning of a major chamber work: 4/4 time, the accompaniment in evenly pulsing eighth notes, the melody in the cello, and the tonic triad stated in ambiguous fashion (see ex. 1b). Each of these features, save the cello melody itself, appears (once again!) in Haydn's Op. 33, no. 3, which also, like Beethoven's Op. 59, no. 1, begins tentatively and reaches the first climax only later (cf. ex. 6a). An intermediate stage appears in Mozart's C-major Quintet, where the melody does appear in the cello; on the other hand Mozart, as always, begins squarely on the tonic, and he seems less interested in dynamic process than either Haydn or Beethoven.

Op. 59, no. 1 takes up different traditions in its sprightly, yet intellectual finale in 2/4 meter. An especially clear example occurs in the second group. The steady quarter-note motion, the harmony changing on every beat, the square phrasing, the background motive in faster note values, and especially the repetition of the theme in the minor, in canon, leading to the flat side and, through an augmented sixth chord, to the dominant—all this is based on Mozart's "purple patches" (as Tovey called them) in his second groups. Compare Beethoven's mm. 45–65 with, for example, the finale of the quartet K. 465, mm. 292–326, or the finale of the C-major Quintet, mm. 374–93.

The finale of Op. 59, no. 2 follows Mozart's common plan of moving from the development (in this case mm. 146–206, more or less) directly to the recapitulation of the second group in the tonic (mm. 216–51). Only afterwards does the main theme return, at once rounding off the main form and introducing the coda. On the other hand, Beethoven's fragmented upbeat-motive preparations for the returns of the main theme (mm. 89–106, 251–75) derive from Haydn's similar devices in finale reprises—most clearly, perhaps, in Symphony No. 102 (see ex. 11), but also in quartets: for example, Op. 76, no. 4, mm. 69–74.[39]

Beethoven's reprises of his theme always begin in C major, and the retransitions always prolong V of C, rather than the home dominant. This technique also derives from Haydn; a simple example is the role of B in the "Surprise" Symphony, first movement, mm. 148–58. But a much stronger influence on this finale must have been that of Beethoven's own G-major Concerto, Op. 58. Both finales are rondos, and both main themes begin in C major; in both, since the tonic is a key with one sharp, C major is (or implies) the subdominant. The reprises are always prepared by extended dominant preparations of C major. Both movements are sonata-rondos which move directly from the development to the reprise of the second group (as described above for the quartet). Both

Ex. 11(a) Haydn, Symphony No. 102/IV, 208–216

have lengthy codas. And finally, each movement brings the same stroke of genius (if this is not a paradox) at the very end. When the coda has apparently run its course and the end is in sight, the C-major theme suddenly returns more exuberantly than ever—not because we can possibly lose sight of the tonic any longer, but as proof that the vitality of the theme depends on this tonal contrast (quartet, m. 372; concerto, m. 568). Here we see Beethoven creating a finale tradition of his own in 1805 and 1806.

The repetition of *both* halves of the first movement of Op. 59, no. 2 has often been remarked. Naturally this also derives from tradition. Until Kerman (p. 121), it has been regarded less sympathetically than the apparently "forward-looking" absence of either repetition in the first movement of no. 1. Beethoven himself was uncertain about these large repeats. His last-minute decision to repeat the exposition in the first movement of the *Eroica* is well known; less familiar, however, are his changes of mind in Op. 59. In the first movement of no. 1, though apparently never considering a repetition of the exposition, he specified a repetition of the "second half" of the movement (the development and recapitulation) in the autograph. This is merely remarkable; it is

Ex. 11(b) Beethoven, Op. 59, No. 2/IV, 89–109

downright bewildering, however, to contemplate his intention to repeat mm. 155–393 of the Allegretto scherzando. And finally, in the *Waldstein* Sonata Beethoven also contemplated a repetition of the development and recapitulation of the first movement. In all these cases, his final decision was to omit the repeats.[40] But he retained comparable repetitions not only in the first movement of Op. 59, no. 2, but also in the development-recapitulation of the finale of the *Appassionata* Sonata. Here we may speak, perhaps, of a fictive tradition of expansive form—one which existed primarily in Beethoven's mind and which he admitted into finished compositions only twice.

Finally, the *thèmes russes* themselves perpetuate the long-standing practice in Viennese art music of using ethnic and pseudoethnic melodies. Like Haydn, Beethoven sublimates these melodies into true Classical themes, even in the slow movement of Op. 59, no. 3; an effect like Haydn's passionate gypsy lament in the slow movement of Op. 54, no. 2 remains foreign to him. On the other hand, the trio of Beethoven's E-minor Quartet, organized as a series of contrapuntal discussions of the theme without real episodes or contrasting sections, throwing the interest on the variety and ordering of the counterpoints themselves,[41] is a direct descendant of Haydn's beautiful trio to the E♭ Quartet, Op. 76, no. 6.

Like Op. 59, no. 3, the "Harp" Quartet in E♭, Op. 74, is modest in scale and expressive force. Only the first movement uses sonata form. The slow introduction, unlike that in Op. 59, no. 3, is motivically dense and, until the last measures, tonally stable (granting a certain subdominant orientation). Nevertheless, it is slightly surprising to hear a reminiscence from the slow introduction to the overture to Mozart's *Die Zauberflöte*—also in E♭ and in 4/4—based on the same interior tonic pedal, around which the motivic play in the outer parts creates similar sets of subdominant chords, connecting with the larger harmonic orientation (see exs. 12a and 12b). Possibly Mozart's subtly beautiful passage, based on the same chord and in the same key and meter, in the opening of his E♭ Quartet, K. 428, was also in Beethoven's imagination (cf. ex. 12c).

Some authorities have interpreted the subdominant placement of the slow movement of this work—which never happens in Op. 59—as a return to traditional tonal plans. The rollicking trio to the scherzo takes a bow in the direction of species counterpoint, both in substance and in notation. Is this why Beethoven refrained from notating this trio in 6/8 or 6/4? (Something suspiciously similar to Second Species had

Ex. 12(a) Mozart, Zauberflöte, Overture, 4–13

Ex. 12(b) Beethoven, Op. 74, Introduction

Ex. 12(c) Mozart, Quartet K.428/I, 5–9

already appeared in the finale of Op. 59, no. 3, mm. 210ff., and Fourth Species is unmistakable in the coda, mm. 345ff.) Perhaps this incident in Op. 74 was Beethoven's reaction to the drudgery of beating musical sense into the noble head of the Archduke Rudolph, who seems to have begun instruction with Beethoven in 1809.[42] In his own teaching, Beethoven used the Fuxian species, as had all Viennese composers before him, including Mozart, Haydn, and Albrechtsberger—the latter two in their instruction given to Beethoven himself.[43]

But the most obvious traditional feature in Op. 74 is its variation finale. Such finales were common in eighteenth-century quartets, not least in Mozart and Haydn, and this particular style of variation theme, in 2/4 meter, allegretto, in two equal halves, and motivically organized, was a common subspecies. Now and then Haydn avoided tonic and dominant cadences until the end, preferring third-related closes at the double bar: for example, on V*of*vi in Op. 33/5/iv, m. 8, or in iii in Op. 71/3/ii, m. 8. Likewise, Beethoven cadences on V*of*vi at the end of the first half of his theme and on V*of*iii midway through the second half. But the closest relationship is with a still later Haydn quartet theme, also in Eb, in 2/4, allegretto, and also the subject of variations: the theme which opens the first movement of Op. 76, no. 6. Both themes consist of continual repetitions of a motive; in each case this motive outlines a third, and its initial appearance connects the pitches g′ and bb′; each first half ends with a half cadence approached by contrary motion to an octave in the outer parts; both use dotted eighths and sixteenths (only implicitly in Haydn's first half, explicitly afterwards); in both, the motivic statements are detached from each other (obvious in Haydn, subtle but unmistakable in Beethoven); and in both, the harmonic structure of the first half is curiously nonfunctional, with various subdominants and tonics alternating in odd ways, and various chords placed unexpectedly in inversion rather than root position (see ex. 13).

Finally, both themes introduce masterly movements which glory in their consummate modesty—something attainable by only the most sophisticated and self-confident of artists. Beethoven does not attempt a compendium of all musical techniques, as in the variation finale of the *Eroica*, or a transcendent revelation, as in the finale of Op. 111. The "Harp" Quartet ends with a plain set of variations exquisitely poised, perfectly articulated. It thus recreates a traditional solution to the problem of ending a work in sonata style.

This remark returns us to our larger subject: Beethoven's relationship to tradition. His middle-period quartets exhibit obvious and manifold connections to the traditions of the Classical style, represented here by Haydn and Mozart. These relations are not restricted to the one work, Op. 59, no. 3, which has been extensively discussed in the literature, nor are they of the limited or limiting character which might legitimately suggest dependence or poverty of artistic resource. Every artist—this truism is worth recalling—works in and through tradition and occasionally against it, but never divorced from it. "Tradition" stands for many kinds of relationship: conscious purpose, social setting, means of dissemination, continuity within a genre, the idea behind a type of movement, compositional technique, form, uses of tonality, unconscious reminiscence, and specific thematic quotations. Beethoven's symphonies, concertos, and piano sonatas from these years doubtless exhibit nearly as many points of contact with tradition as we have seen in the quartets.

The modesty of scale and tone which we have seen in parts of Op. 59, no. 3 and Op. 74 also appears in other works of the middle period. The old-fashioned view that the Fourth and the Eighth symphonies are inferior to the others is long discredited. Within the quartets, in fact, the Haydnesque Op. 135 in F major now comes off well even in comparison to its formidable neighbors from the last years; I suspect the same is true of the piano sonatas Op. 54 in F and Op. 78 in F♯. Until criteria for making the distinction are developed, the argument that Beethoven creatively reinterpreted tradition in these works, but basely subjugated himself to it in Op. 59, no. 3, remains founded on a double standard.[44]

One further aspect of these "modest" works emerges from

Ex. 13(a) Haydn, Op. 76, No. 6/I, Theme

Ex. 13(b) Beethoven, Op. 74/IV, Theme

Beethoven's larger compositional rhythm. Within and independently of the three large periods, he seems to have alternated between phases of expansion into or exploration of new territory and phases of consolidation or repose. The heroic phase of 1803–5 obviously belongs to the former class; another such phase seems to be centered in 1807–8, when, as Tyson has noted, Beethoven's long-standing obsession with C minor reached a crisis, and eventually achieved a triumph, in the Overture to *Coriolan* (1807) and the Fifth Symphony (completed 1808).[45] On the other hand, many of the large instrumental works of 1804–6 make good sense viewed as a consolidation of the size, formal power, and expressive force of the *Eroica*. The G-major Piano Concerto, the Violin Concerto, the Fourth Symphony, and the *Waldstein* and *Appassionata* sonatas, like Op. 59, have neither the strain nor the exaltation of the *Eroica*, nor are they charged with comparable extramusical associations. Though larger than any previous works in their respective genres, they are markedly less gigantic than the *Eroica*, and their relations to Classical norms of form and procedure are clearer. The only obvious exceptions would be the size and pretension of the first two (or three) movements of Op. 59, no. 1, and the expressive intensity of the *Appassionata*.

Complementing the C-minor crisis of 1807–8, Beethoven achieved an even longer and more varied period of consolidation which includes the cello sonata Op. 69, the piano trios Op. 70, the "Emperor" Concerto and the "Harp" Quartet, and a series of piano sonatas including Op. 78 in F$^{\sharp}$ and *Les Adieux*. The "Harp" Quartet fits perfectly into this phase: like Op. 70, no. 2, the "Emperor," and *Les Adieux*, it is in E♭; more than this, it shares with Op. 70, no. 2 not only its relaxed tone, but the use of the same three keys—E♭ as tonic and A♭ and C minor in the middle movements.[46] It is especially significant that after the catharsis of the Fifth Symphony, C minor no longer awakens terror; it is merely the relative minor. There is nothing in the Scherzo of Op. 74 remotely comparable to the tension in that of the symphony; in Op. 70, the fearsome C major-C minor alternation provides the basis for a playful double variation movement à la Haydn. The contrast between these "consolidating" C-minor movements and the *Marcia funebre* in the *Eroica* (also in the relative minor with respect to E♭, and also containing a prominent C-major section) illustrates this change with equal cogency.

On a more detailed level, Beethoven's middle period often appears to exhibit pairs of individual works; in these pairs, the first work to be completed or published usually seems to be the bolder, larger, or more expressive, the second work the more modest, less pretentious, more Classical. This pattern holds for six of the symphonies: the Third and Fourth, the Fifth and Sixth, the Seventh and Eighth. It seems quite possible to read Op. 59 in the same manner. In terms of size, the first stage comprises the first three movements of no. 1 and the second movement of no. 2; in terms of intensity, one could add the first movement of the latter work. The gestures of consolidation then appear in no. 3, but they were already emerging in the Scherzo and finale of no. 2, and to some extent even in the finale of no. 1.

This distinction between expansion and consolidation, which also appears in Kerman, Solomon, and elsewhere, does not necessarily depend on clear chronological distinctions. To be sure, the three quartets of Op. 59 appear to have been composed more or less straight through in the order we now have them.[47] But in 1804 and early 1805, the latter stages of the heroic phase coincided with the earlier stages of the complementary phase of consolidation described here. In some cases, works of quite different character developed simultaneously. Discounting the largely irrelevant sketches for the Fifth Symphony in the *Eroica* sketchbook, the Fifth and Sixth were composed in complicated alternating periods from 1806 through early 1808; the Seventh and Eighth also originated during a single period. The Cello Sonata Op. 69 may also have originated in part simultaneously with the Fifth. In short, this concept of alternating phases describes primarily a psychological rhythm, indeed a fluctuating network of psychological and compositional attitudes, all of which were, perhaps, always potentially present. The concept remains valid even if the only clear basis for the distinctions is the contents of complete and discrete works or groups of works. By this view the heroic and the traditional in Beethoven's music—the expressive and the modest—are complementary, and necessarily so.

This sketch of Beethoven's relations to tradition in his middle quartets is, in itself, hardly a sufficient critical stance. And to describe Beethoven's relations to tradition in general is obviously not possible here. But the modern criticisms of Op. 59, no. 3 seem insufficiently grounded, and it may be useful to review the charges: (1) it exhibits inferior compositional technique; (2) it is not integrated as a cycle; (3) it quickly became relatively popular, suggesting a lack of substance in the work;[48] (4) it uses older material (Richard Kramer recently placed the theme of the minuet with an abandoned set of variations for piano dating from 1801); (5) Beethoven was uncertain about some aspects of the composition (early sketches show the minuet not in the tonic but in the subdominant F major, and the trio in its flat submediant D♭; and at one stage Beethoven contemplated a finale in C minor); and (6) it may have been written hastily.[49]

The latter three arguments are easily disposed of. Beethoven used older material throughout his life and in many of his greatest works. In fact, his original theme for an A-minor slow movement in Op. 59, no. 3 was soon abandoned, but it returned many years later in another great A-minor slow movement, that of the Seventh Symphony. If Beethoven once projected different keys for the minuet, or a finale in the minor, this is irrelevant to a critical evaluation of the finished work. In any case many Beethoven movements underwent changes of key during their evolution.[50] Finally, if Beethoven wrote this work in haste, we might consider the possibility that it is slight or superficial. But this does not necessarily follow. In fact, Beethoven apparently often composed "fiddle pieces"—a concept which seems appropriate for both the concertante texture of the first movement of Op. 59, no. 3 and its brilliant finale—in haste; other examples include the *Kreutzer* Sonata, the finale of the Violin Concerto, and perhaps the finale of the G-major Sonata, Op. 96.[51] These examples may suggest that haste produced some of Beethoven's most "effective" music, but hardly that it led to meretricious work.

Tyson must be right to interpret Beethoven's provisional plans for a C-minor finale in the context of his larger C minor-C major obsession, which came to the fore again in late 1806. But he continues: "It is probable that the curious coda to the minuet, with its inflections in the minor mode, was originally intended as a transition from the C-major minuet to a C-minor finale. Since it was later deprived of this function, the coda now appears a little aimless."[52] (More recently, he has related the imitative entries in this coda to Beethoven's projected coda for the abandoned piano variations in 1801.[53]) But Tyson offers no transcriptions to support his contention that this coda-transition was originally intended to lead to a finale in the minor. Nor is it accurate to speak of its minor-mode "inflections," or of its tendency to "wander from the tonic and make the tonality and modality . . . ambiguous."[54] It is clearly in C minor; the only modulations are cogent passing ones to the relative major E♭ and the subdominant F minor; and the final move to the dominant, colored in the last two bars by the major that is to come, is typical of introductions and transitions of this type. (Compare, for example, the introductions to Mozart's "Dissonant" Quartet, mm. 19–22, or to the finale of his G-minor Quintet, mm. 33–38; or mm. 34–35 in the slow movement of Haydn's Quartet Op. 54, no. 2.)

Beethoven's reasons for rejecting a minor-mode finale were undoubtedly good ones. This quartet was not the place to work through those obsessions. In the finished work the coda-transition provides an appropriate passing reference to C minor, a contrasting link between the (traditional) restrained minuet and the (in many respects traditional) exuberant contrapuntal finale. Moreover, as Kerman and Finscher have stressed, it refers back to the introduction, although its particular use of C minor and its tone have become clear, perhaps almost conventional, rather than "nebulous"—just as the fugal finale itself refers obliquely to the first Allegro. This view is supported by one of Beethoven's rejected versions of the last two bars of the transition, which constitute an almost literal quotation of the end of the first introduction.[55] Finally, the exuberance of the fugue theme itself seems to require some kind of preparation. Neither the rate of activity nor the triumphant tone could be effective following directly upon the minuet proper. Hence the transition is both appropriate in mood and creates relationships to other sections of the work which otherwise would be lacking. If in keeping it Beethoven also temporarily appeased his C-minor demon, so much the better for his psyche. But the only real basis for criticism, once again, would seem to be the finished work itself.

These remarks, coupled with the tenor of some recent work on Beethoven's sketches, suggest a general comment. The techniques of scholarship seem better suited to decipherment, transcription, reconstruction, classification, chronology, biography, and even psychohistory, than to analysis and criticism. Perhaps some of us also fear a confrontation with Beethoven the artist on his home grounds. Whatever the reasons, our justifiable fascination with the sketches and the compositional process ought not to supplant responsible analysis and criticism of Beethoven's compositions, the finished works of art whose power and beauty are the reason we care about sketches for them in the first place. Thus the grounds for criticism of Op. 59, no. 3 discussed above are at best supporting arguments, at worst rationalizations of the aesthetic position which holds that the quartet is not successful. Frank critical judgments are actually less likely to be misunderstood.

I do not urge that we raise Op. 59, no. 3 and the Fourth Symphony above Op. 59, no. 1 and the *Eroica*, in a new critical hierarchy of unpretentiousness. Various compositional and psychological modes alternated in Beethoven's music: some in concert with biographical events, others in response to inner urgings which not even the sketches reveal. Once in Vienna, the composer made the Classical style his own, and he never really abandoned it.[56] Besides animating his music from within, as in Op. 59, no. 1, from time to time this living tradition moved overtly onto the surface, as in Op. 59, no. 3. There is no basis for regarding works from the latter phases as "dependent" or compositionally insufficient. It would be worth while to investigate all of Beethoven's "traditional" works, including the potboilers, as representatives of specific types and functions and to ask, without feelings of defensiveness, what he did with them. For that matter one could, with equal profit, study the central role of tradition in virtually any class of Beethoven's works—not least in the "heroic" ones, and most certainly not excluding the *Eroica* itself. The concept of Beethoven's changing relations to tradition offers the opportunity for increased understanding of his lifelong development.[57]

Notes

1. A survey of the literature on the *Eroica* is in Lewis Lockwood, "*Eroica* Perspectives: Strategy and Design in the First Movement," delivered at the Beethoven Symposium at the University of North Carolina at Chapel Hill, April, 1977.
2. Alan Tyson, "Beethoven's Heroic Phase," *Musical Times* 110 (1969):139–41.
3. Joseph Kerman, *The Beethoven Quartets* (New York: Knopf, 1967), pp. 89–116, esp. pp. 90–93, 100–102, 105–6, 115–16; cf. also pp. 151–54.
4. In the famous assertion of Carl Czerny; quoted in Thayer-Forbes, pp. 408–9.
5. Considering their intrinsic and historical importance, sustained discussions of Beethoven's middle-period quartets are remarkably few. For this study, in addition to Kerman, I have consulted Theodor Helm, *Beethoven's Streichquartette*, 2d ed. (Leipzig: C. F. W. Siegel, 1910); Hugo Riemann, *Beethovens Streichquartette* (Berlin: Schlesinger, [1910]); Gerald Abraham, *Beethoven's Second-period Quartets* (London: Oxford University Press, 1942); Walther Vetter, "Das Stilproblem in Beethoven's Streichquartetten Op. 59" (1948), repr. in Vetter, *Mythos—Melos—Musica*, I (Leipzig: Deutscher Verlag für Musik, 1957), pp. 363–67; Philip Radcliffe, *Beethoven's String Quartets* (London: Hutchinson, 1965); Walter Salmen, "Zur Gestaltung der 'Thèmes russes' in Beethovens opus 59," in Ludwig Finscher and Christoph-Helmut Mahling, eds., *Festschrift für Walter Wiora* (Kassel: Bärenreiter, 1967), pp. 397–404;

Finscher, "Beethovens Streichquartett Opus 59,3: Versuch einer Interpretation," in Gerhard Schuhmacher, ed., *Zur musikalischen Analyse* (Darmstadt: Wissenschaftliche Buchhandlung, 1974), pp. 122–60.

6. On this point, see Thayer-Forbes, pp. 409–10.

7. "The Razumovsky Quartets: Some Aspects of the Sources," Beethoven Symposium, Chapel Hill. I am indebted to Alan Tyson for allowing me to consult this paper and for many helpful suggestions.

8. See Heinrich Jalowetz, "Beethovens Jugendwerken in ihren melodischen Beziehungen zu Mozart, Haydn, und Ph. E. Bach," *Sammelbände der Internationalen musikwissenschaftlichen Gesellschaft* 12 (1910):407–74; Hans Gál, "Die Stil-Eigentümlichkeiten des jungen Beethoven," *Studien zur Musikwissenschaft* 4 (1916):58–115; Reinhard Oppel, "Über Beziehungen Beethovens zu Mozart und zu Ph. E. Bach," *Zeitschrift für Musikwissenschaft* 5 (1922–23):30–39; Theodor von Frimmel, *Beethoven-Handbuch* (Leipzig: Breitkopf and Härtel, 1926), I:11–16 (with many references); Ludwig Schiedermair, *Der junge Beethoven*, 3d ed. (Bonn: Dummler, 1951), pp. 212–25, 290–94; J. Arthur Watson, "Beethoven's Debt to Mozart," *Music and Letters* 18 (1937):248–58; Hubert Unverricht, "Bemerkungen zum geschichtlichen Ort von Beethovens früher Kammermusik," *Beethoven-Jahrbuch* 9 (1973–77):501–29.

9. Douglas Johnson, "1794–1795: Decisive Years in Beethoven's Early Development," Beethoven Symposium, Chapel Hill.

10. For example, the Serenade, Op. 3 on K. 563, the Quintet for Piano and Winds, Op. 16 on K. 452, and the String Quartet, Op. 18, no. 5 on K. 464. These and other cases are described in the standard literature. See, for example, Donald Francis Tovey's discussion of Mozart's piano-wind quintet in *Essays in Musical Analysis: Chamber Music* (London: Oxford University Press, 1944), pp. 106–20.

11. A classic study is Gustav Becking, *Studien zu Beethovens Personalstil: Das Scherzothema* (Leipzig: Breitkopf and Härtel, 1921). A comprehensive recent survey is Georg Feder, "Stilelemente Haydns in Beethovens Werken," in Carl Dahlhaus et al., eds., *Bericht über den internationalen musikwissenschaftlichen Kongress, Bonn, 1970* (Kassel: Bärenreiter, [1971]), pp. 66–70.

12. The special case of the *Pastoral* Symphony is excepted. See Adolf Sandberger, "Zu den geschichtlichen Voraussetzungen der Pastoralsinfonie," *Forschungen, Studien, und Kritiken zu Beethoven und zur Beethovenliteratur*, Ausgewählte Aufsätze zur Musikgeschichte, II (Munich: Drei Masken Verlag, 1924), pp. 154–200; F. E. Kirby, "Beethoven's Pastoral Symphony as a *Sinfonia Caracteristica*," MQ 66 (1970):605–23.

13. Ludwig Finscher, *Studien zur Geschichte des Streichquartetts*, I (Kassel: Bärenreiter, 1974), esp. pp. 106–25, 129–36, 279–301.

14. On the absence of music publishing in Vienna before 1780 and its sudden rise around that time, see Hannelore Gericke, *Der Wiener Musikalienhandel von 1700 bis 1778* (Graz: Böhlau, 1960); Alexander Weinmann, *Wiener Musikverleger und Musikalienhändler von Mozarts Zeit bis gegen 1860* (Vienna: [Rohrer,] 1956). On Viennese concert life during Beethoven's time, see Otto Biba, "Concert Life in Beethoven's Vienna" in this volume. The conjunction of these social changes with changes in musical style around 1780 is outlined in James Webster, "Towards a History of Viennese Chamber Music in the Early Classical Period," *JAMS* 27 (1974):227–31, 241–42, 246–47.

15. Wegeler-Ries, as quoted in Thayer-Forbes, p. 262.

16. On Haydn's quartets from 1795 on, see Anthony van Hoboken, *Joseph Haydn: Chronologisch-thematisches Werkverzeichnis*, I (Mainz: Schott, 1957); his discussion of

these works, stemming from Haydn's last years and disseminated chiefly in printed editions, needs little correction.

17. It has recently become clear that the traditional picture of Beethoven's contempt for Haydn and his teaching is one-sided. See Alfred Mann, "Beethoven's Contrapuntal Studies with Haydn," *MQ* 56 (1970):711–26; Johnson, "1794–1795: Decisive Years"; Maynard Solomon, *Beethoven* (New York: Schirmer, 1977), ch. 7.

18. Unless otherwise indicated, biographical and documentary information on Beethoven and his music has been drawn from Thayer-Forbes and from Kinsky-Halm.

19. On the "quintets" for Fries, see Günter Thomas, "Griesingers Briefe über Haydn," *Haydn-Studien* 1 (1965–67):76. On the date of Op. 103, see James Webster, "The Chronology of Haydn's String Quartets," *MQ* 56 (1975):24–25.

20. The recent German tendency to interpret the whole of Op. 59 as a single cycle, represented for example by Vetter, Salmen, and Finscher (see n. 5) should be resisted. There is scant biographical or documentary evidence for this view, and precious little musical support either.

21. As in n. 14; cf. Thayer-Forbes, pp. 374, 409–10; Tyson, "Razumovsky Sources," at n. 1. There is little evidence for the common notion that either Beethoven or Schuppanzigh was consciously "founding" the public concert with Op. 59 or attempting to create "appropriate" music for that purpose.

22. See Finscher, *Streichquartett*, I.

23. On this subject the standard study remains Warren Kirkendale, *Fuge und Fugato in der Kammermusik des Rokoko und der Klassik* (Tutzing: Schneider, 1966).

24. Tovey loved to mock puritanical criticism of such "indiscreet" passages in string quartets. See, for example, "Haydn's Chamber Music," in *Cobbett's Cyclopedic Survey of Chamber Music* (London: Oxford University Press, 1929), I; reprt. *Essays and Lectures on Music* (London: Oxford University Press, 1949), pp. 37–38, 41; *Essays in Musical Analysis: Chamber Music*, pp. 12–13.

25. On this familiar example see Tovey, "Haydn's Chamber Music," pp. 49–50; Charles Rosen, *The Classical Style* (New York: Viking, 1971), pp. 112–16. At present, an accurate musical text of this quartet can be found only in the Haydn-Institut edition: *Joseph Haydn: Werke*, Ser. XII, vol. 3 (Munich and Duisburg: Henle, 1974).

26. This is a question that has bothered many writers on Beethoven. The best analysis of this movement in print, and unfamiliar to much Beethoven scholarship, is found in Erwin Ratz, *Einführung in die musikalische Formenlehre*, 3d ed. (Vienna: Universal, 1973), pp. 181–96.

27. The finale of Op. 59, no. 2 is a sonata-rondo, and although the slow movement in Op. 59, no. 3 has a second group, a development, and a reprise, as a whole it does not exhibit the essential characteristics of sonata form. Cf. Kerman, p. 150.

28. This point surfaces here and there in Tovey.

29. I thus agree with Kerman (pp. 151–52) when he finds Op. 59, no. 3 an unconvincing whole when viewed in these terms, and when he dissents from the traditional German view of it as an essay in culmination, centering around the finale. But there is no necessity to regard Op. 59, no. 3 in these terms.

30. Kerman, p. 183. Tovey chose to pass over Beethoven's coda when discussing the "inadequacy" of Mozart's G-minor Quintet finale, for example in *Beethoven* (London: Oxford University Press, 1944), pp. 59–60. Rey M. Longyear's interpretation of it as an example of Romantic irony, in "Beethoven and Romantic Irony," *MQ* 66 (1970):649, is at best one-sided.

31. The majority of the observations which follow are my own; others have been incorporated from the literature on Beethoven's relations to Haydn and Mozart, as cited

in nn. 8 and 11. I have assumed that, in Beethoven's view, Mozart and Haydn represented the most important and influential components of tradition. Studies of other parts of the Viennese chamber music repertory between 1790 and 1810 could always be undertaken; for one topic, the very brief slow introduction as in Haydn's Op. 71–74, see Finscher, "Beethovens Op. 59, 3," p. 127.

32. Helm, pp. 104–5; Abraham, pp. 42, 46; Radcliffe, pp. 72–74; Kerman, pp. 139–40; Finscher, "Beethovens Op. 59, 3," pp. 136, 139, 141; Tyson, "Razumovsky Sources," section 6.

33. Criticism creates its own amusing traditions. The metaphor of "groping" through "fog" in descriptions of this introduction appears in Helm, pp. 102–3 (in his turn paraphrasing A. B. Marx); Riemann, p. 71; Abraham, pp. 42, 46; Kerman, pp. 134–35; and doubtless elsewhere. Perhaps the repeated denigrations of this quartet among the critics quoted in the first section of this essay represent merely a larger-scale example of criticism thus feeding on itself.

34. Some evidence in the sketches which can be interpreted as support for these hypothetical relationships is presented in Tyson, "Razumovsky Sources," exs. 2 and 3. For analyses of the "Dissonant" introduction, see A. E. Cherbuliez, "Zur harmonischen Analyse der Einleitung von Mozarts C-Dur Streichquartett (K. V. 465)," in Erich Schenk, ed., *Bericht über die musikwissenschaftliche Tagung der Internationalen Stiftung Mozarteum in Salzburg* (Leipzig: Breitkopf and Härtel, 1931), pp. 103–10; Heinrich Schenker, *Der freie Satz*, 2d ed. (Vienna: Universal, 1956), supplementary volume of examples, figure 99.3. Abraham, p. 46, first drew attention to the relationship of the chromatically descending bass lines; cf. Kerman, pp. 139–40; Finscher, "Beethovens Op. 59,3," pp. 136–37.

35. Many of these I—ii sequences are noted in Feder, "Stilelemente Haydns," p. 67, but he does not mention Op. 59, no. 3 nor the other C-major traditions noted here, nor the Neapolitan analogue in the minor. Tovey wrote extensively on these passages; see, for example, *Beethoven*, pp. 23–24, 30–33; cf. Kerman, pp. 126–27.

36. Ex. 8b is taken from N II, p. 86; cf. Tyson, "Razumovsky Sources," ex. 1.

37. On the contrapuntal aspects of this finale, see especially Ludwig Misch, "Das Finale des C-Dur Quartetts: Eine Formstudie," in Misch, *Beethoven-Studien* (Berlin: Walter de Gruyter, 1950), pp. 36–41; Kirkendale, *Fuge und Fugato,* pp. 271–77; Finscher, "Beethovens Op. 59,3," pp. 151–59. For other related movements in Beethoven, cf. Kerman, p. 144.

38. Tyson, "Razumovsky Sources," ex. 11.

39. This point appears in Helm, p. 99; Kerman, p. 132; Feder, pp. 65–66.

40. On these projected repetitions, see Emil Platen, "Beethovens Autographen als Ausgangspunkt morphologischer Untersuchungen," *Kongress Bonn 1970*, pp. 535–36; Tyson, "Razumovsky Sources," section 8; Barry Cooper, "The Evolution of the First Movement of the 'Waldstein' Sonata," *Music and Letters* 58 (1977):188.

41. See Kirkendale, pp. 273–75; Finscher, "Beethovens Op. 59, 3," pp. 132–34.

42. Thayer-Forbes, p. 467; N I, pp. 171, 177–96.

43. The standard account is Nottebohm, *Beethovens Studien* (Leipzig and Winterthur: Rieter-Biedermann, 1873); see also the citations in n. 17.

44. Kerman (pp. 49, 355) compares Op. 135 favorably to Op. 18, no. 2, but he attempts no similar comparison with Op. 59, no. 3 or Op. 74.

45. Alan Tyson, "The Problem of Beethoven's 'First' *Leonore* Overture," *JAMS* 28 (1975):325–31.

46. Cf. Kerman, p. 185. The rondo of the "Emperor" Concerto is based on the same tonal plan in its development, with C major substituting for C minor.

47. See Tyson, "Razumovsky Sources." On the general point of this paragraph see particularly Maynard Solomon, "The Creative Periods of Beethoven," *Music Review* 34 (1973):36–37.
48. Riemann, pp. 73–74; Abraham, p. 45; Radcliffe, p. 72; Finscher, "Beethovens Op. 59,3," pp. 123–24.
49. On the last three points, see Tyson, "Razumovsky Sources," and the references given there.
50. See, for example, the convenient assembly of examples drawn from Nottebohm, with amplifying comments based on letters and on Thayer, in Paul Mies, *Die Bedeutung der Skizzen Beethovens zur Erkenntnis seines Stils* (Leipzig: Breitkopf and Härtel, 1925), transl. Doris L. Mackinnon, *Beethoven's Sketches: An Analysis of His Style Based on a Study of His Sketch-Books* (London: Oxford University Press, 1929; rprt. New York, Dover, 1974), pp. 174–82.
51. I owe these suggestions to a private communication from Alan Tyson.
52. Tyson "*Leonore* Overture," p. 326, with transcriptions on p. 327.
53. Tyson, "Razumovsky Sources," section 7.
54. Ibid., end of section 7.
55. On these points, see Kerman, pp. 141–43, although he does not like the transition; and Finscher, "Beethovens Op. 59,3," pp. 150–51, with transcriptions on p. 152.
56. This view motivates all of Tovey's writings. For the early works, see also Johnson's article cited in n. 9; for the later years, see Rosen, *Classical Style*, pp. 380–87, and passim through the rest of the chapter.
57. For a brilliant and thorough exposition of this topic on quite a different subject, see Warren Kirkendale, "New Roads to Old Ideas in Beethoven's *Missa Solemnis*," *MQ* 66 (1970):665–701.

Future Directions
in Sketch Research

Panel discussion prepared by Sherwyn T. Carr

Moderator: *Robert Winter;* panelists: *Sieghard Brandenburg, D. Kern Holoman, Douglas Johnson, Joseph Kerman, Robert Marshall, Howard Serwer, Alan Tyson, James Webster.*

[Winter opened the discussion with a summary of the historical background to the Beethoven sketches, pointing out that Beethoven left a significantly larger amount of such materials than many composers and emphasizing that the disposition of them after Beethoven's death in March, 1827, created formidable problems for modern researchers. The sketchbooks were sold at auction in November, 1827; many were subsequently dismembered by buyers whose interest in them was more that of the souvenir hunter than of the musician or musicologist. He then asked Alan Tyson to explain the methods by which a researcher attempts to reconstruct the original form of a sketchbook.]

Tyson: The work that has been carried out in the last ten or fifteen years has been to look at the sketchbooks in the various libraries and decide whether any are in the same condition as when they were auctioned. The Kessler Sketchbook in the Gesellschaft der Musikfreunde seems still to have ninety-six leaves, which was the number it had when Beethoven used it, but possibly all other sketchbooks have had leaves removed. We have developed a series of techniques for locating damage and trying to trace the leaves or sections of the sketchbooks that have been removed. Some of this detection is very simple. If you leaf through many sketchbooks, you'll find stubs where leaves have been torn out. In other cases one has to look at the way the sketchbook has been put together as a book. If you find that there are only seven leaves instead of eight, for instance, you'll guess the leaf has been removed. Or you may find that somebody has numbered the leaves and there's a gap in the numbering—then something is gone there.

You can look around in the places where sketchbooks and sketchleaves are preserved, and perhaps find leaves that would appropriately fit into the gaps.

Some of us have been occupied in making a sort of profile or fingerprint of missing leaves, so that if one turns up we can identify it straight away. That would mean identifying what sketch it is likely to be a lost leaf of, and perhaps the number of staves on the page. We assume that the number would be the same as on the leaves that remain. Watermarks and the way the staves are ruled are also important. In these ways one can build up a good description of a wanted leaf and perhaps find it.

Winter: Let me ask Douglas Johnson how close we are today to having the sources for Beethoven's sketches back in their original condition.

Johnson: We're fairly close. Most of the surviving sketches are in just a few libraries. A few of us have seen virtually everything and traced almost every watermark. We have nearly "computerized" the possible association of loose leaves with sketchbooks that have gaps. I think it's relatively unlikely that large numbers of presently unanswerable questions are going to be answered in the future, unless large numbers of sketches suddenly turn up—as, for example, the lost manuscripts from World War II have in Poland recently. But I think we've come a long way, at least on paper, toward matching up loose leaves, either with their own signatures in libraries or with sketchbooks that they might have come from. Not all of them came from sketchbooks, obviously.

Beethoven seems to have used three kinds of materials on which to make sketches. Sometimes he simply bought loose sheets of paper, had them ruled, and cut them down to a manageable size. Usually he bought sheets that would make four leaves. At other times he bought actual notebooks, which were forty-eight, sixty-four, or ninety-six leaves, and sewed them together (rather crudely at times), ending up with homemade sketchbooks. These homemade ones are more difficult to deal with, because there's no way to predict what kinds of gatherings Beethoven was using. He sometimes took single leaves of paper, sometimes bifolia, sometimes groups of leaves stuck inside each other. When you have a case like that, it's more difficult to tell where the gaps are on the basis of bibliographical information.

Tyson: There were a great many mills producing paper that was used in Vienna in Beethoven's time, so when he went out and bought paper it was usually different from the paper that he bought before. When he went to Berlin and Prague, he bought paper which we can recognize as being typically Prague paper or typically Berlin paper.

Holoman: Beethoven was working right at the end of handmade paper, and by the next generation of nineteenth-century composers, paper was factory made. I wouldn't advise everybody to get excited about the possibilities of watermark research two decades later. It's not easy.

[Winter asked Marshall to compare the evidence of Beethoven's sketchbooks with the available evidence for Johann Sebastian Bach's practices. Marshall began by observing that there is very little to suggest that Bach made sketches. Rather, "Bach did all his composition in score throughout his life." Marshall felt that the fact that Bach did not make preliminary designs for his compositions might be traced to his extraordinary technical facility and to his need to produce music as quickly as possible. Furthermore, Bach composed within a musical environment that was comparatively stable stylistically.]

Marshall: Bach wrote the great majority of his cantatas at the rate of one per week during his first three years in Leipzig. This means that Bach wrote just about every piece in maybe three days. He would probably have begun to write a cantata on Monday morning and be done with it at the latest on Wednesday, so that he could spend a day having the parts copied out. And then maybe a day or two at rehearsals before the performance on Sunday; then next Monday the process started over again. When you're writing music at that rate of speed, you're not going to have the luxury of time, as Beethoven had, to do a lot of sketching. We really don't have sketches in the Beethovenian sense at all from Bach's hand, but rather just little marginal notations, perhaps of a thematic idea, of what he wanted to do in a later movement of the composition with which he was concerned at the moment.

When he's writing out a "composing score," as I would call these documents, one knows that they are composing scores because they are full of changes and corrections. They aren't beautiful examples of musical calligraphy, though Bach could, when he wanted to, write out a very handsome manuscript. I think that was also the mentality at the time. At some point we have to talk about the psychology of Bach and Beethoven—Bach probably felt much more secure about the very process of putting music down on the page.

Serwer: Handel is, of course, an exact contemporary of J. S. Bach, composing under very different conditions of employment, but essentially the same kind of music. We have every indication that the first compositional writing down in most cases for Handel is the autograph score. They're not pretty, but they have perhaps fewer corrections than Bach's autograph scores. There are entire pieces written out with virtually no corrections. Sometimes one will see an error in a Handel autograph, and one has the impression that he had stopped paying attention for the moment, or he was getting even more rushed because the curtain was going to go up on the opera in twenty-four hours and he was still only halfway through. The pressure at times for Handel was perhaps even greater than for Bach, although it was not as constant.

Handel's autographs present a situation that is practically unique. Most are not only in one institution, but in one room in one bookcase: in the Royal Music Library at the British Library. A second set of materials is also together in a single institution (with one major exception). This is the set of conducting scores that were copied for performances by Handel's assistant. Then there are what I call "floor sweepings," most of them in the Fitzwilliam Museum in Cambridge. These are individual leaves of works, or sometimes things torn out of the autographs because Handel didn't need that piece anymore. Or a leaf that was written out on a separate piece of paper that has gotten away from others—discarded materials. Handel's principal assistant, John Christopher Smith, Sr., survived Handel by a few years, and apparently inherited all his materials. Except for a few items, he preserved them carefully and passed them on to his son. Smith, Jr. gave the autographs to the British Library. The conducting scores were almost destroyed but were rescued in the nineteenth century. A lot of other materials passed in a way I don't understand yet to the Fitzwilliam Museum—these floor sweepings seem to have been kept together.

[As an example of Handel's "sketchlike" materials, Serwer described a draft for a second revision of a chorus written some years earlier. Returning to the example of Beethoven's sketches, he concluded: "There is virtually nothing like them from Handel—only an occasional instance where he tried a revision for a revival and succeeded in messing up his own clean score by attempting to write over it. He was writing brand-new music on the same place."]

Webster: Haydn, of course, as a composer stands somewhere between Bach and Handel on the one hand and Beethoven on the other, not merely chronologically, but in terms of the way he composed. There are not many surviving sketches by Haydn, and there's absolutely no indication that Haydn ever used volumes of paper for sketching in the way that Beethoven did. There are a couple of contemporary accounts allegedly based on conversations with Haydn as to how he composed. One says he ate breakfast at eight o'clock and immediately thereafter went to the piano and began to fantasize and diddle around—if we may interpret here, for however long it took for him to find a suitable idea. When he found it, he immediately went to the desk and wrote it down on paper; in this way he wrote the first drafts of his compositions. He went again to the desk at four o'clock in the afternoon, took the drafts that he had written that morning, and wrote them out in score, using three or four hours for this activity every day.

Another man says that Haydn always began by getting ideas at the piano, and he always wrote a composition or part of a composition at one time. For each movement he sketched out the melody and the main voices rapidly, without showing all of the detail. Afterwards, in the second process, he took this dry skeleton and breathed life into it through "artfully composed inner parts and artful transitions." This is a precise description of Haydn's compositional process, and I think it would be fair to say that the rather small number of surviving sketch-leaves on the whole substantiate it. They are drafts; they are not sketches in the Beethovenian sense. They are almost always drafts of a whole movement or of a large section of a movement. They most often agree quite closely with the finished work as we know it, though there are interpolations and changes of mind and so on. Furthermore, Haydn's autographs are usually very close to being fair copies; there is a quite small proportion of corrections and alterations.

In general, it seems reasonable to suppose that Haydn made only one set of drafts for a piece of music, first laying out the main melody parts, the melody and the bass, and then the inner parts. Afterwards, he used this draft as the basis for writing an autograph. The only known exception to this procedure is the fairly large number of sketches for the "Chaos" movement which begins *The Creation*—which is entirely reasonable, given the nature of that movement and the rather complicated kind of musical process that takes place there. So, though this is an oversimplification, I think the general picture that we have of the way Haydn composed music is reasonably clear-cut.

[Following some comments in response to questions from the audience, the discussion returned to Beethoven's sketches.]

Kerman: What interests me is the whole matter of whether Beethoven added sketches later to earlier sheets. That's a very vexed question. If you're trying to trace the entire course of a composition through a sketchbook, you go to considerable trouble to get the sketchbook put together again. The basic assumption is that the book was written in the order in which the pages, once they've been reconstructed, stand. That's not necessarily the case, because there's nothing to stop a composer from going back to an old book and writing on it when he chooses to. I know that when I started working on sketch studies as a student, there was a great deal of nervousness—indeed, extending to paralysis—as to how we could ever say anything about the succession of two sketches on a page. Maybe Beethoven came back the next morning or the next year and made a revised statement. It seems to me that one of the striking new assumptions that has allowed sketch research to go forward as it has in the last ten years is that the sketchbooks were indeed written pretty much in order, and that there's not a great deal of crossing of sketches from one to the next. Of course there is some, but these cases are exceptions. On the whole, what we now believe is that the time when Beethoven bought paper of a certain watermark was, roughly speaking, the time when he wrote the sketches on it. And also, very broadly speaking, one can proceed on the assumption that things were written in order, unless there is some reason to believe otherwise.

[A member of the audience asked if researchers ever found it necessary to use chemical processes to facilitate reading watermarks, and if such a procedure was potentially harmful to the manuscripts. Panelists generally agreed that the difficulty of reading watermarks differed with the times and composers involved. Two other questions also concerned the physical preservation of the sketchbooks and sketchleaves. Tyson responded that they were on the whole well preserved, and that some of the visible damage may have occurred while they were still in Beethoven's possession. Some panelists complained about the handling of materials by individual libraries, but they agreed that the manuscripts were in no particular danger of further deterioration.

In response to another question from the audience, the discussion turned to consideration of Mozart's compositional practices.]

Tyson: I haven't looked at many Mozart sketchleaves or sketches yet. I think that once again we get onto the problem of the different characters and personalities of the composers in question. One characteristic way that Mozart seems to have worked was to start a full score of a piece and write the bits he felt sure of. Say, for example, he'd write the first violin part for twenty bars and the base line for twenty bars, and put in one or two instrumental parts (I'm thinking of an orchestral work, but the same thing applies to chamber works), filling in some bits fully scored, very neatly without crossings out. Perhaps bars eight to ten will be fully scored, and then there'll be that *Hauptstimme* or main melodic pattern passing from one instrument to another for another fifteen bars or so, and then perhaps breaking off. The first violin goes on a few more bars before tailing off. We wouldn't call that a sketch; perhaps we'd call it a draft or a fragment or something like that. But I think that all of Mozart's completed scores went through that stage, except he added more notes when he finished them. This is much more like Bach's practice than like Beethoven's.

There are some Mozart items that are more like Beethoven sketches, and they seem to be particularly contrapuntal passages. Fugal passages, contrapuntal passages, imitative passages in which a melodic fragment went from one instrument to another. He'd write them out in what was really a short score, and in much smaller writing, usually.

[Winter asked Sieghard Brandenburg, as general editor of the Beethovenhaus edition of the Beethoven sketches, if he could justify the time and expense of that project.]

Brandenburg: This complete edition started more than twenty years ago, and the situation was quite different then. People at that time thought that it would be good to make the sketches available through print; today one might think print is not necessary. Photocopies are much less expensive. But there are other reasons for the Beethovenhaus to bring out such an edition. Beethoven sketches are normally not very easy to read, and therefore it is useful to publish them in a transcription which will be easier to read for scholars who are not so well acquainted with Beethoven's way of sketching.

I think it's quite another question whether it is better to have only several sketchleaves or sketchbooks published instead of a complete edition. Some of the sketches, I think, are not very important. Others are more important; we are more interested in them. For instance, it would be interesting for us to have the *Eroica* sketchbook edited, because it contains virtually all of the sketches for that symphony. But it would not be so interesting to have all the stuff published which Beethoven wrote before 1800.

Kerman: I think the interest of the sketches really is that one sees an earlier draft of the piece that one knows and loves from hearing it performed. The interest of the sketches for the Third Symphony is that you see the first version that Beethoven wrote for this work—or not actually a version, because one has just a line, and it usually takes interpretation. Just the main melodic line will be sketched out. In a good case, such as the Third Symphony, you can trace the growth of the conception of the work stage by stage, through four, five, six, seven, eight, nine drafts. Now to musicians of a certain frame of mind, this is a fascinating procedure. I think there is a prima facie case for publication of a photocopy so that you can really see what the original transcription looks like. I think it also requires another stage, namely an analytical article or essay, or some kind of a chart so that one can see what the real conclusions are: how Beethoven strengthened this cadence, how he made this tune more beautiful, whatever.

[In response to a question from the audience, Kerman returned to the issue of similarities between the compositional practices of contemporaneous composers.]

Kerman: Did all or most composers of Handel's and Bach's day sketch in more or less the same way, and did all composers of Beethoven's day sketch in his way? The answer, of course, is no. I think I'm right in saying that composers sketched more in the nineteenth century than they did in the eighteenth or seventeenth because music had gotten to be a different sort of thing. It's more *problematic*, to use a term from the twentieth century. Composition becomes more problematic for Beethoven, for Schumann, for Wagner, than it was for Mozart or for Bach. Bach didn't have the leisure, as Professor Marshall says, to experience problems. He had to get on with the job. But the point about Beethoven, and the reason the Beethoven sketches have had so much attention, is that he was a very special composer. He had a strange commitment to the act of writing—he just liked to write. Haydn apparently would get up in the morning and fantasize at the piano and then write something down; Beethoven, it seems, did his fantasy work with a pen. He liked to doodle, as it were; he needed to get the creative juices going. He needed to write, and he sometimes wrote down little jottings that seem nonsensical when you first look at them, but then they get to seem less so. I believe we have sketches by all the nineteenth-century composers, and these are being studied more and more: Berlioz, Schumann, Brahms, Wagner, Richard Strauss. But they didn't sketch in the same comprehensive way that Beethoven did. They didn't have the same kind of psychology of getting the work going and getting it down.

Winter: There's a certain irony, of course, that Beethoven, the great improviser, preferred to write, and that Haydn, who was not known as a keyboard virtuoso, preferred to doodle at the piano rather than to write.

Serwer: I'd like to say something else about the use of sketches. The material Handel rejected for a revival are terribly interesting when we find them. There isn't much, relative to the total volume of his music, but they give insight into Handel's compositional process. They allow us to look over the man's shoulder for a little bit and follow his thought processes. And sometimes there is even a little extra dividend. We get a better understanding of how the final product goes because we understand what might have been deemed unsuitable for a revival. We see the new piece being reworked, and we understand why it was better, perhaps. It leads us occasionally even to insights in performance. Can this be said on occasion of Beethoven's sketches as well?

Tyson: There was a controversy—perhaps there still is—about a particular reading in one of the Diabelli variations [no. 15]. There's a general agreement that in the second part of this variation there should be some matching of the first part, in which the left hand is more or less high for eight bars and then more or less low for eight bars. The second part also starts with the left hand high and ends with the left hand low. But there doesn't seem to be any particular way for the left hand to come down from about middle C to about the G or F$^\sharp$ right at the bottom of the bass clef. The question is whether you insert a bass clef at some point or not. It seems to me that whatever you do doesn't quite work out. Siegfried Kross in Bonn tried to use some sketches, which are in fact rather hard to work out, to try to decide on the final reading for this variation. I'm not sure how far it's legitimate to do this, but I can imagine there are cases in which you use sketches to see how things went wrong. You could see the development—Beethoven sketching something and then perhaps miscopying, and that's why you get a final version which is hard to take in some way. I don't think that it was possible to prove it in this particular case. My own view is that in a certain sense Beethoven didn't complete this variation, because when he wrote it down there was a sort of ambiguity in the notation. He partly imagined a treble clef, and he partly imagined a bass clef. And therefore it escaped him that he'd forgotten to write a little passage getting the left hand from the roughly middle C register down to the bass. That variation was never completed, although he certainly printed a form that *sounds* very acceptable. We hear it that way until somebody points out that maybe it ought to be in bass clef; then what one has gotten used to doesn't sound quite so acceptable. And if one puts in a bass clef, one produces something very clumsy. I ended up by deciding that the variation hadn't ever been completed by Beethoven, though we have something we can play. In fact, we have two versions we can play. The question is whether either of them is by Beethoven.

Webster: I have a slightly polemical comment. The case of Beethoven sketches is unique in the conjunction of a composer of the greatest significance and a very large body of sketch material which is clearly extremely important and very interesting. For most composers you don't have anything like this kind or quantity of material to deal with. Virtually all that needs to be said about Haydn's sketches, for example, has been said in a single excellent article by George Feder, the head of the Haydn Institute in Cologne ["Bemerkungen zu Haydns Skizzen," *Beethoven-Jahrbuch* 9 (1973–77):69–86]. If you're going to deal with Haydn's music, you have to deal with the music—you can't depend on the sketches, for there aren't enough to provide insight into the music.

I think that in the case of Beethoven, especially recently, there has been a danger of allowing the fascination with the compositional process to draw our attention away from the music as music, from analysis and criticism of the music. I have the impression that up to World War II the sketches were understood mainly as a way of understanding the music better, and the interest in the compositional process was secondary, a means to an end. Recently the interest seems to have been more in the compositional process as a process. This is good; I'm the last person to think that we should not concern ourselves with the sketches. But I think it's well to keep a perspective on the ultimate aim of the whole operation, which is Beethoven's music as individual works of art.

[Winter asked Marshall to comment on how he understood "compositional process" in his study of Bach's vocal music.]

Marshall: I think that investigation of the compositional process is much closer to biography than it is to musical analysis. Sketch research helps to answer the questions of how the man went about his work and when he wrote a piece—or even whether he wrote one, as in the case of Beethoven's "Tenth Symphony." These are all biographical questions. But even the questions that might at first glance be taken as being much more analytical are ultimately biographical. What kinds of music or genres gave the composer the most difficulty? What line in the music did he write first? Did he start with the bass or the melody? There are composers that preferred one or the other. We've always been interested in the biographies of great men, and I think that is in itself a justification for this kind of work. I think also that sketch research does illuminate our comprehension of the composition itself. From that point of view, it belongs to the realm of analysis.

I would like to turn more directly now to the actual question, which I think asked for my definition of the compositional process. It's to some extent a play on words. I was thinking whether to call my book "Bach's Compositional Procedure," or "Creative Process," or "Compositional Process." I decided on *The Compositional Process of J. S. Bach* because it avoids the connotation of a mechanistic or mechanical act of writing. You could ask yourself why he wrote down the first thing, seeing that it was ultimately rejected, but it also must have had some kind of compositional motivation. Then you ask yourself, "Why did he remove it?," once you've found a good musical reason for putting it there in the first place. Why did he replace it specifically with what he did? In this sense I'm describing what I like to call "the internal history of a composition," the compositional process. This study becomes the biography for the composition, as distinct from the biography of the composer. But I think sketch studies or studies of corrections really illuminate both.

Kerman: One of the things I find most useful about sketches is that they give you the simple possibility of seeing something that the composer rejected. You see him making a decision and your attention is focused on what was obviously in some sense a trouble spot. It's true that we should be able just to look at the final work of art, the final beautiful artifact. We listen to it, and we should say: "Oh, I can hear it. That's a marvelous place; that's a funny place; that's a mistaken place." But the truth is, our ears are not as good as that. Sketch studies or biographical studies focus our attention on the key points, the points that the composer really worried about, and therefore the points which perhaps were most important and where he succeeded most triumphantly when he finally got it right.

Winter: I would like to ask Douglas Johnson to summarize his perception of the value of sketches.

Johnson: My conclusions are similar to Professor Marshall's. That is, the basic value of the early Beethoven sketches that I've been working with tends to be biographical in a number of different senses, up to and including the sense of the compositional process, which I also regard as essentially biographical in interest. I've been hampered because I've been working with Beethoven's early period, in which a lot of sketches have bee.1 lost, but I've never been able to persuade myself that I knew more about the work, from an analytical point of view, after I studied the sketches than I did before I began.

Kerman: One of the things you've been doing is working with important projects which Beethoven never finished. We've learned in the most recent flush of enthusiasm for Beethoven studies about a large number of very important projects that Beethoven worked on and developed to a considerable extent. Sometimes he started a complete score and then abandoned it. This is again of biographical interest, but it does have a special cachet. There's a huge sixth piano concerto which he got going in 1814; there was a piano trio that would have been the seventh, in F minor, which also was begun in score. There's a big symphony in C major, a very momentous work for a young composer to begin. If he had ever completed it, it would have been bigger than the First Symphony and probably bigger than the Second Symphony, judging by the first movement. There was a big duo concertante, and there must have been other potentially important works too. This is a large dimension of Beethoven's work that one only gets to know by looking at the sketchbooks.

Winter: I want to ask Professor Holoman to give another view of the meaning of "compositional process."

Holoman: I think one's inevitable conclusion, the more one tries to justify sketch research as being anything more than biographical, is something equivalent to what Professor Webster said. Yet if we believe that the two principal goals of a professional music historian are to explain musical compositions through analysis and to describe how they came to be, then I think we cannot fail to be excited by the point at which these goals seem to coincide. We watch, through the documents, a composer fashioning his works.

I have two cases that strike me as interesting. Some of you will know act 4 of *Les Troyens*, which ends with one of Berlioz's most extraordinary passages, the "Nuit d'ivresse, nuit d'extase" love duet, based on the beginning of act 5 of *The Merchant of Venice*. This is the most extensively sketched work that Berlioz ever wrote, as far as we know, and yet it was all sketched in F major. At the very last stage, when he was putting together *Les Troyens* as a grand opera, Berlioz transposed it into G♭, the key of all good nineteenth-century love duets. He revised the whole scene, so that as the love duet begins, the progression moves from F major into G♭, a very drastic rise of a half step. That we can document this development strikes me as a very great insight into what the composer was trying to show there, although of course you can hear it whether you know the compositional process or not.

The other example is the religioso coda of the first movement of the *Symphonie fantastique*, which can be documented to have been sketched and tacked on at the end. Frankly, I can never hear that passage without seeing the seam in my mind. I regard that as a flaw of that work. I think this reaction may be the other side of the possibilities of sketch research.

Marshall: What sketches do is draw our attention to a detail that we hadn't noticed before; we begin to think about how the piece could have gone otherwise than it does. In general, I think sketch studies are fascinating because, number one, everybody likes before-and-after comparisons. Number two, it is something of a success story, in which the success is the ultimate great work, and you follow the vicissitudes that the work had to go through in order to reach its successful conclusion. To some extent, I think this is the same fascination that history has for us. We are interested in knowing how great battles were planned by those in charge of designing them. I think it's the same kind of human curiosity that we indulge in when we look at these worksheets of the great composers.

The Conversation Books:
Aspects of a New Picture of Beethoven

Karl-Heinz Köhler

Probably few composers have left such a wealth of biographical material as Ludwig van Beethoven. Letters, memorandums, reports, notices, and legal documents afford us a penetrating view, not only of the man, but of his working habits and—although all too rarely—his creative process as well. Indeed, so plentiful are these sources that it is hard to imagine either major new discoveries or interpretations; yet the Beethoven research of today underscores the need both for investigation of hitherto untapped material and for fresh interpretation of the long familiar.

Beethoven's conversation books, those remarkable documents on which the composer was almost fully dependent in his last years, occupy a unique position in this ongoing research. After all other means had failed, these diminutive volumes became his only means of communication with others. The question of whether the 138 surviving conversation books can offer us any real insights suggests a modern analogy. Not infrequently, we find ourselves in the position of overhearing a telephone conversation. We can generally draw inferences from what we hear, even though we cannot hear one of the partners in the conversation at all. Often we can piece together the context of the conversation and even the views of the partner who is not present by using the clues provided by the speaker whom we can hear. Beethoven's conversation books preserve such a dialogue in written form: it is in this unique form that conversations with Beethoven have come down to us, conversations in which visitors and friends used wax tablets or paper folded into booklets to carry on their part of the conversations. Beethoven's answers are usually not recorded because he answered orally. The composer also occasionally used the booklets for more general notations, and next to the recorded conversations we can find unrelated entries that prove to be unusually significant.

Anton Schindler, Beethoven's secretary and confidant for many years, passed on only 138, about three-eighths of the original number of conversation books; in 1846 he sold these to the Königliche Bibliothek in Berlin (today the Deutsche Staatsbibliothek). The adventures of these little volumes since that time, the partial attempts at transcription and publication, as well as the only partial success in interpreting them, need not concern us here. A three-member team of musicologists in the Deutsche Staatsbibliothek has labored for well over a decade to prepare an edition which is both philologically sound and thoroughly annotated; a good half has either already appeared from the Deutscher Verlag für Musik or is in advanced stages of preparation. (A translation of this edition into English is being contemplated by a press in the United States.)

Faithful documentary transcription of the conversation books is very important, but adequate annotation is also essential. An edition lacking thorough annotation would prove to be of little use to the uninitiated. The subjects of discussion change too rapidly, the trivial follows the important too abruptly, the gaps are too great, and too often the comprehension of a passage depends on the consultation of other sources. Only a systematic exposition of the contents of the conversations enables us to pinpoint their dramatic kernel—and what has been transmitted to us is dramatic in the richest and best senses of the word. For example, the climax of the proceedings toward the guardianship of Beethoven's nephew Karl in 1819–20 becomes comprehensible. We read of interesting meetings and decisions in the documents from 1823, the principal year of composition for the Ninth Symphony, and of the controversy swirling around the first performance of this work in the spring of 1824; we experience much concerning the genesis and first performances of the late quartets in 1825–26; we witness the tragic suicide attempt of "son" (no longer "nephew") Karl; and finally we read the moving entries from the months of Beethoven's terminal illness.

Almost all of the books span a wide range of topics in addition to such biographical ones. Numerous notations of book titles illuminate Beethoven's literary interests. Art, poetry, music, the great and controversial figures of the day, politics, and contemporary history are encountered frequently. Everything of significance, indeed all events influencing the flow of history, are reflected in the conversation books. Beethoven was not only the contemporary of the campaigns and eventual downfall of Napoleon, but he was also the contemporary of Metternich, the witness to liberal uprisings in Spain, southern Italy, Hungary, Russia, and Portugal, and to the overthrow by South American colonies of their mother countries. Finally, we find musical entries scattered throughout the conversation books, always of special interest for our understanding of compositional processes. All of these entries—supported and supplemented by other documents—paint a picture of the composer that in many of its contours is surprisingly new. In the remainder of this essay I would like to recount a few of these aspects.

The legal proceedings surrounding Beethoven's struggle with his sister-in-law Johanna over the guardianship of his nephew Karl have been described frequently in recent times, yet with less than unanimity in the interpretation of many details. The maneuvers are shot through with contradictions and often appear to conflict morally—relying for the moment on contemporary standards—with Beethoven's transcendent spiritual creations, particularly the *Missa solemnis*. The battle began on November 15, 1815, with the death of Beethoven's brother Karl, proceeded through four separate judicial reviews, and ended only five years later, in September, 1820. In a codicil to his will dated April 12, 1813, the bank official Karl van Beethoven had declared his brother to be the sole guardian of his only son; on his deathbed, however, he altered this provision in favor of a guardianship divided between the child's natural mother and his uncle. This arrangement was soon rescinded at the insistence of the uncle and then reinstated once more at the insistence of the mother. After prolonged negotiations, Beethoven was offered a joint guardianship which excluded the mother, but he neither accepted nor attempted to implement such an arrangement. Finally, on January 9, 1816, he received a judgment from the Nieder Österreichische Landrecht which awarded him the sole guardianship while transferring young Karl's education to the boarding school of Giannastasio del Rio, an institution where predominantly noble children were instructed.

Two decrees followed shortly: Johanna, the sister-in-law despised by Beethoven, might visit her child only once a month and only in the presence of witnesses; and second, she must participate financially in the raising of her son by contributing a generous portion of her late husband's estate. Why Beethoven therefore had Karl removed from school and set up with a private tutor in the composer's own quarters remains a mystery. But from this period date the first surviving conversation books (February–March, 1818). These contain, in essence, only answers from a twelve-year-old on inconsequential matters of comportment set out by his uncle—on, for example, the correct way to eat a sausage!

In the fall of 1818, Johanna van Beethoven struck back quite sharply, and understandably so. First, she challenged the jurisdiction of the court, a tribunal which was supposed to mediate conflicts only among the nobility. The Dutch prefix "van" was not recognized as proof of aristocratic title, and on November 15, the whole affair was transferred to the Wiener Magistrat. Beethoven was advised to surrender the guardianship in favor of someone stipulated by the courts. But by the end of June, 1819, we find the city councillor Mathias Tuscher dissolving this guardianship and reappointing Beethoven after a short interval. The struggle, however, suddenly took an almost ludicrous turn: Johanna was reinstated as the guardian, working jointly with a court-appointed coguardian, a municipal employee named Leopold Nussböck. Beethoven fought on stubbornly and finally received, before the Viennese appellate court on April 8, 1820, a ruling reinstating him once more as the guardian, with Privy Councillor Karl Peters, a leading pedagogue of his time, as coguardian. Johanna van Beethoven's final appeal against this judgment proved to be in vain, for on September 8, 1820, her suit was rejected in favor of the composer.

Although most of these generally accessible facts are well known, the first sixteen conversation books of 1819–20 clarify for the first time essential portions of this melodrama. Friends and visitors give sound tips as to how Beethoven might best present himself in this or that phase of the proceedings. At the beginning of book 4 we can follow the progress of a hearing before the Viennese municipal court on December 7, 1819. Beethoven understood nothing, and because he was someplace where he feared his loud voice might be overheard, he shoved the booklet to Peters, who wrote: "About the annual outlay for the child. Now we must await the decision. The council favors the inclusion of the mother and said that her earlier transgressions, which I noted as having been very disruptive, were now a thing of the past." A particularly angry retort may have followed, for Peters soothes Beethoven: "The councillor also mentioned the beautiful clothes which you gave the nephew, and about which the mother made an appreciative remark." This contradictory legal process, scarcely comprehensible to us today but very painful for the participants, remains in the foreground in the conversation books, and it illuminates certain aspects of Beethoven's character still worthy of our consideration.

The question as to why Beethoven led a crusade for this child at all can be illuminated only from a psychological standpoint. The provider role which the composer was forced to assume early on toward his two brothers probably led him to claim parental authority over their choice of professions and spouses, an authority which, at least in the choice of spouses, was rejected by both brothers. Since it was not granted to Beethoven—and his deafness may have played an important part in this—to found his own family, his interest in the affairs of his brothers' families may have been intensified. He found both a substitute for a child of his own and a fulfillment of his youthful role of substitute parent in his relationship with Karl.

The extremes to which the proceedings led seem to have provoked a kind of equilibrium in Beethoven in the form of a creative catharsis. Personal difficulties seem to have stimulated him to composition, and we should not dismiss out of hand the notion that we owe at least in part the composition of the B♭ Piano Sonata, Op. 106 (composed in 1817–18) to such a catharsis. As Beethoven himself expressed it in a letter to Ferdinand Ries, the work was written "under miserable conditions." Of course, we need not assume a literal correspondence between external and internal events. For one thing, the legal proceedings raise the well-known issue of the nobility, about which Schindler reported that Beethoven "regarded it as the greatest insult and as an unjustifiable humiliation and degradation to the artist." He declared before the court that his nobility was "here and there," pointing to his head and heart, "for such nobility there was neither in Austria nor in any other state the proper judicial authority." We can be sure from an entry in the conversation books that at least in this instance Schindler was not guilty of exaggeration. "Shall I speak of the nonnobility?" wrote Beethoven, and exhibited the letter of January, 1819, to Archduke Rudolph in which he declared: "A horrifying incident has occurred recently in my family affairs, so that for a time I have lost all my senses." This pretension to nobility of an artist who was accustomed to mingling with highly cultured aristocracy has of course not the slightest thing to do with occasional and less important feelings of belonging to a privileged segment of society, or with certain political concepts held by the Austrian aristocracy of this period.

Nevertheless, Beethoven's own volatile artistic life marked the boundary between a tightly knit yet fading order of feudal patronage— in which he participated extensively—and the impetus towards artistic independence. A growing public concert life provided artists with a new opportunity to free themselves from dependence on patrons, but it would not for some time to come provide enough economic security to assure this freedom. The problems which arose in this border area could not have failed to leave their mark on Beethoven. They are made perhaps especially clear in the conversations from 1823, the year of the Ninth Symphony. On the one hand, enormous works like the *Missa solemnis* and the Ninth Symphony were distributed by subscription to various European courts; the sale of only ten copies of the former—nine of them to kings, princes, and grand dukes—realized the considerable sum of 500 ducats. On the other hand, large-scale distribution was undertaken by printing houses or furthered through public concerts (the so-called academies). Beethoven's net receipts from the concert which included the premiere of the Ninth Symphony were so meager that they would have paid his rent for only five months.

There is more peripheral discourse in the conversation books regarding the origins of these two works than there is information about the creative process which produced them. Nevertheless, a few of the conversations indicate clearly some of the more important compositional decisions. The *Missa solemnis* was completed in the late autumn of 1822. Sales were regulated through private copies, and Beethoven was expected to be casting about for a suitable new work. His friends were perfectly aware of the break in musical projects, and some pressed the composer, after the successful revision of *Fidelio*, to undertake a second opera. Count Moritz Lichnowsky succeeded in interesting the poet Franz Grillparzer in drafting a suitable libretto, and that led to contact and conversations between Grillparzer and Beethoven.

Several such discussions are preserved in the conversation books, although these admittedly offer more information about Grillparzer's personal circumstances and points of view than about the romantic operatic theme of "Die schöne Melusine." In spite of successive and very friendly conversations between the two men, Beethoven simply did not take to the material. He favored instead a project which he had carried with him since his youth: the musical setting of Schiller's "Ode to Joy," which by then he had connected with a symphonic plan of enormous scope. The operatic plan was more than a mild biographical episode in Beethoven's life; from the wealth of details, particularly in the conversation books, about the discussions with Grillparzer, and from the evidence which the most recent sketch research has provided us, we now know that Beethoven com-

menced serious work on the symphony only after he had studied Grillparzer's proposed libretto. In the course of his considerations Beethoven
was constantly faced with the dilemma of symphony versus opera, the
expression of the Classical aesthetic versus projection of his era's Romantic
leanings.

We shall have occasion to speak later of the conversation books
as vehicles for musical sketches, but a small entry from November,
1823, for the still developing "Freude" theme, as well as a series of
notations from the fall of 1826 for the metronome markings to all
movements, round out the picture which these volumes give us of the
compositional process in the Ninth Symphony. We read less about the
actual composing than about the sometimes difficult circumstances
which surrounded it. The preparations for the first performance were no
less dramatic, and the conversation books transmit a few hitherto unknown details. Beethoven's friends participated actively in the arrange-
ments. They assisted in negotiations with theater managements, with
the shape of the program, with the copying of performance parts, with
the choice of soloists, with both the organization of and assistance at
rehearsals—and thereby earned the enmity of the composer, who frequently found himself only in the way. "The eagerness with which
everyone offers to help is astonishing," reflected Beethoven's nephew. "It
would be a shame if it were all in vain."

The preparations dragged on and on. On April 19, 1824, the
first performance was delayed until April 22. This date also proved to be
untenable, and the premiere was rescheduled for "not later than the 3rd
or 4th of May." The results of the first dress rehearsal on May 2 were
nearly catastrophic. The parts for the scherzo were missing, and Ignaz
Schuppanzigh remarked nervously, "The singers don't know their parts
at all." The performance was postponed once more, for three days. At
the orchestral rehearsal on May 4, the entire ensemble was not present,
as "no one had informed them." The bass soloist, Joseph Preisinger,
withdrew at short notice, and the alto Caroline Unger "sat home with a
sore throat." There was quarreling over the text for the poster announc-
ing the concert, with the participants screaming back and forth at each
other. Yet all this turmoil was followed by the greatest artistic triumph
of Beethoven's life. Schindler summarized the impact of the concert:
"Never in my life have I heard such furious and yet heartfelt applause as
today. The second movement of the symphony was entirely interrupted
once by applause and should have been repeated. The reception was

more than royal, for the crowd broke loose four times, and 'Vivat' was shouted the last time. [During the performances] peace reigned—not the slightest disturbance could be heard. When the parterre began to applaud for a fifth time, the police commissioner shouted 'Quiet!' "

Beethoven, however, was disappointed and embittered over the receipts from the concert. Unjustly, he accused the very friends who had helped him. Entries made during a noon meal in the Prater on May 9, 1824, document a heated argument between Beethoven on the one side and Schindler, Ignaz Umlauf, and Schuppanzigh on the other, all provoked by Beethoven's unwarranted mistrust. Soon, however, the atmosphere was calm again, and a repeat of the initial concert—with an altered program to be sure—was set for May 23. No detailed reports of that second performance have survived, but nephew Karl wrote, "It was not full because many people are already in the country." Hence the shining hour of music history in which the Ninth Symphony began its victorious march around the globe came amid summer lightning storms of hypersensitivity, misunderstandings, and pettiness.

After the premiere performance of the Ninth, Beethoven afforded himself only a short break. He was soon moved by new creative stirrings. A commission from the Russian prince, Nikolas Boris Galitzin, already offered in November, 1822, was the initial impetus for the writing of the late quartets. The first of these, the Eb-major Quartet, Op. 127, was completed in the spring of 1825. Practical questions about the performance of the new work are discussed in the conversation books. It is apparent that the first performance (by Schuppanzigh's quartet) was something of a fiasco. Karl Holz, Beethoven's friend from his last years, wrote laconically of Schuppanzigh's attempt that it "had not yet finished baking." A serious falling out between Beethoven and Schuppanzigh surfaces once more in the conversation books. Only the assistance of the young Hungarian violinist Joseph Böhm enabled a satisfactory performance to take place on March 23. "In everything there was a mood," remarked Beethoven's brother Johann, "that exists in no other quartet. The interweaving [of voices] is so rich that one is fully occupied just observing a single voice; therefore each wished that he could hear the quartet four times."

Four weeks later Beethoven fell prey to a severe intestinal illness. The ensuing interchange with Anton Braunhofer, his doctor, can be followed almost completely in the conversation books. The physician was partial to natural means of healing, which he commended fervently to Beethoven: "Instead of all medicines you must follow a well-ordered diet with moderate exercise. . . . You must not try to pamper nature and forever be swallowing pills. . . . Cast off your prejudices against drinking milk for nourishment in the country. . . . Be patient for a little while." At the beginning of May, once again in full possession of his powers, Beethoven's lofty, dry humor also returned. In a conversation book he set down the following triple pun: "My doctor helped me, for I could not write a note [*Note*] more, but now I write notes [*Noten*] which helped me out of my need [*Nöthen*]."

Shortly afterwards the first sketches for the A-minor Quartet appear, including Beethoven's "Heiliger Dankgesang" as the second movement, but also the B-A-C-H related opening of the first movement. This homage seems to have fascinated Beethoven throughout 1825; for example, in the almost fully recorded conversations of an outing with Friedrich Kuhlau on September 2, 1825, the two composers exchanged a pair of comical canons on this famous motive, which included the punning words "Kühl, nicht lau" ("chilly, not tepid"). We read of negotiations with the publisher Moritz Schlesinger, who expresses great interest in Beethoven's new quartets. Schlesinger's farewell meal, the first performance of the A-minor Quartet, and the rehearsals leading up to the premiere are all reflected in the conversation books.

The richest material from a biographical point of view—and largely unknown even today—is contained in the volumes from 1826 to 1827, with their narrative of the tragic events leading to Karl's suicide attempt and Beethoven's final illness. It becomes clear that the picture of a slovenly and debauched nephew who created nothing but problems for his uncle, a picture transmitted largely by Schindler, is entirely false. Quite the contrary, Karl shows himself to be an obliging young man who relieves his uncle of numerous responsibilities, smooths over the chronic conflicts with the hired help, and remains touchingly concerned about the composer.

The tragedy of the uncle-nephew relationship had its roots above all in Beethoven's well-meaning intention of pushing the boy along an educational path for which he was not suited, and on which he ultimately was sure to run aground. The stages of deterioration are evident from the preserved conversations. Initially, Karl studied ancient languages at the University of Vienna, but failed the exam at the end of the first year. Angrily, Beethoven demanded that he repeat the curriculum. Karl's teacher, however, counseled strongly against his continuation of language studies. Beethoven then chose a new profession and place of study: Karl would become a merchant and attend the Polytechnic Institute. Again Karl had no academic success. He lacked both the ability to learn easily and the necessary endurance. His failure as a student on the one hand, and his dependence on his mistrustful and easily provoked uncle on the other, led first to resignation and finally to despair. On July 30, 1826, Karl attempted suicide by shooting himself in the head.

Almost every detail of the eventful hours that followed, including the search for and discovery of the wounded youth, is documented in the conversation books. Against almost all of the advice offered to him by friends who showed virtually no understanding of his nephew's action, Beethoven confronted the mistakes he had made in raising Karl with compassion and insight. He visited his nephew in the hospital as frequently as he could; he finally surrendered to Karl's own wishes for a military career and made arrange-ments for the youth's future with uncharacteristic tact.

Two problems had to be solved. First, Karl's suicide attempt was a criminal act, and the threat of imprisonment was real; and second, a position as a cadet in a regiment had to be found. Even Beethoven could not prevent Karl's transfer to police headquarters after his recovery. But contrary to all versions of the story that have come down to us, the conversation books reveal that Karl remained there only a single night, even though the law clearly mandated "six weeks of religious instruction under the supervision of the police authorities." After this period a priest was required to interrogate the potential suicide carefully to determine if any danger existed that he might repeat the act. However, the priest's certificate was issued only a few hours—and without any discussion—after Karl had been delivered to headquarters, and one can only surmise what kinds of measures were taken at Beethoven's instigation.

Nevertheless, it is clear that part of the agreement was for Beethoven and Karl to leave Vienna for a while upon Karl's release. This fact clarifies for the first time why Beethoven set out for his brother's estate in Gneixendorf at such an unusual time of year. The very name of the village, as Beethoven wrote when recalling that eventful summer, had for him the sound of a "cracked axle." The return trip on December 2, 1826, brought on a cold which led to the serious illness that eventually caused Beethoven's death on March 26, 1827.

The last fourteen conversation books bear witness to these months. The stream of doctors, their prescriptions, and the treatments and puncturings will probably interest historians of medicine more than historians of music. All the while Beethoven's spirit remained bright, and the conversation books teem with spirited discussions about art, music, and literature. With a conversation on March 5, 1827, about the meaning of new editions of Shakespeare's works, the circle of the conversation books closes for good, some three weeks before the composer's death.

Besides reflecting the biographical drama, a common thread of the conversation books is the wide variety of topics discussed throughout them. Beethoven's literary interests are especially instructive. In the surviving volumes he takes note of 178 titles he found in the daily press. Some of these books served to further a general education (language books, for example); some offered assistance in the practical exigencies of life (illness, household organization); some encouraged further musical development; and some deepened the knowledge of philosophy and the natural sciences. (Of special interest was the then fashionable study of astronomy.) He was also drawn to notable works of world literature, especially those of Shakespeare, Goethe, and Schiller. Finally, we find in the realm of his interests edifying religious books with a tendency to pantheism. The insights into Beethoven's mind these titles afford are supplemented by what we can learn from the impassioned underlinings of poetry and prose in the ten books handed down from his library. They also reveal what aroused his enthusiasms as well as the significant sources of his musical inspiration. There are excerpts which touch the ethical-human-social circle, verses in which suffering and the surmounting of suffering are represented, passages reflecting Beethoven's strong ties to nature, and verses about love (especially from Goethe's "West-Östlicher Divan").

Beethoven's admiration of Goethe went very deep: some seventeen of Beethoven's works are drawn from his older contemporary. The conversation books offer even more information. Verses from Goethe were frequently recited by memory—although not always entirely correctly—by visitors. Goethe's works were recommended, and Karl was urged to acquaint himself with Goethe's poems. In the fall of 1823, Karl wrote: "I have already read much of Goethe; it is splendid." And a month later, in another volume, Beethoven wrote: "I do not compose only that which I would most like to, but that which I must for the sake of money; once this period has passed, I hope finally to write what is the highest to me and my art: Faust."

Scarcely any of Beethoven's great artistic contemporaries—with the exception of the eleven-year-old Franz Liszt in 1823 and Franz Grillparzer—are represented as discussion partners in the conversation books. Simple mentions of great personages are much more common, and here tradition plays an important role. Mozart, for example, furnished a frequent theme of discussion. In more than 80 entries, he was always spoken of with the greatest esteem. Haydn was mentioned in some 30 entries, usually with great respect, but there was also an occasional critical remark. Doubtless such remarks mirrored memories of a less than perfect student-teacher relationship.

Just as Beethoven sought out his predecessors, so younger composers looked to him. One was Carl Maria von Weber, who visited Beethoven on the occasion of the premiere of *Euryanthe* in October, 1823. The recorded postmortem remarks about this meeting are a rich source of material about the relationship between Classic and Romantic. They reach their summit in Schuppanzigh's bon mot: "Weber speaks as God wishes; Beethoven speaks as Beethoven wishes," to which later was added, "Rossini speaks as the Viennese wish."

Of Franz Schubert we hear little. In June, 1823, Karl remarked, "Schubert is praised very much." The premiere performance of *Rosamunde* was noted. On April 6, 1826, Karl Holz wrote: "Schubert was just with him [an unidentified companion]; they read from a Handel score. For songs he has great understanding. Do you know the 'Erlkönig'? He always spoke very mystically." Beethoven's implied acquaintance here with at least a small number of Schubert's songs is congruent with Schindler's claim that Beethoven praised Schubert's genius in the last weeks of his life. Remarks such as these are invaluable aids in clearing away biographical misconceptions.

No less fascinating are the more than sixty-five entries in the conversation books which reflect contemporary events. We would scarcely have expected reminiscences in 1823 of a conversation between Beethoven and General Bernadotte in February, 1798; twenty years later Bernadotte ascended the throne as King Karl XIV of Sweden. Beethoven is supposed to have offered him a copy of the *Missa solemnis*, "as he stood on such friendly terms with him." There was bitter disappointment over the developments following the Congress of Vienna; the conversations were laced with criticism and sarcasm. Beethoven and his friends were clearly partisans of the deprived and the oppressed, never of the representatives of authority. The Karlsbad Accords of August, 1819, were greeted with similar contempt. Frequent mentions were made of the liberal Spanish uprising of 1820. The sudden attack in April, 1823, on the Holy Alliance aroused indignation. Similar condemnation greets developments in the Latin American colonies. In order to quell their aspirations towards independence, the European powers had already agreed at the end of 1822 to intervene militarily in the Spanish colonies. To be sure, they thereby overextended themselves, for the plans were successfully opposed by Great Britain and the United States. Less successful was the uprising of the carbonari in southern Italy, crushed by Austrian troops in the spring of 1821. In September, 1820, the conversation books recorded: "The Neapolitans will defend themselves as well as the Spaniards. . . . The carbonari have their sabres and weapons blessed at the image of Mary in order to use them against the enemies of their freedom." The continuations of these conversations in the spring of 1821 are missing, possibly because Schindler may have found their contents politically dangerous and destroyed the rest of the year's books.

Even the Decembrist revolt of 1825 in Russia receives mention. The disappointing political developments led to a reassessment of Napoleon. Already in 1820 an acquaintance of Beethoven's had written, "If Napoleon were to return again now, he would be accorded a better reception in Europe. He understood the spirit of the times and knew how to keep a firm hold on the reins. . . . He had a sense for art and science and hated darkness. . . . The children of the revolution and the spirit of the times demanded such an iron disposition." Hardly less far-reaching were discussions in which, for example, themes such as the relationship between private rights and society were debated.

This brief overview of Beethoven's conversational world illuminates the many facets of the composer's interests, and at the same time permits us to trace the contours of a new Beethoven picture more precisely than ever before. In concluding, however, permit me to mention two further dimensions. The first concerns that which interests us most about a composer—his music; the second involves a recent discovery that affects our evaluation of the conversation books.

Earlier I mentioned that Beethoven used these books not only for discourse, but also for sketching. No fewer than fifty-eight such sketch entries are found among thirty-seven different books. Aside from 1821 (the volumes are missing altogether) and 1827 (the year of Beethoven's death), there are musical notations for every year in Beethoven's life after 1817. Eleven of the sketches still cannot be associated with any specific works. In general they cluster in three main works or groups: the *Missa solemnis* (1819–20); the Ninth Symphony (1822–23); and the last quartets (1825–26). There are also entries for the E-major Piano Sonata, Op. 109; the "Abendlied unter gestirntem Himmel," WoO 150; the "Opferlied," Op. 121b; and finally for the Bagatelle in G major, Op. 126, no. 5. This last sketch was entered into a conversation book on May 7, 1824, the day after the premiere performance of the Ninth Symphony.

There are other notations which are not compositional in the strict sense, but instead transmit directions for a copyist or performer. A special class includes those which were never intended for any projected work, but which test certain principles of composition. One instance is a contrapuntal exercise on a Dorian scale; others involve cadences, rhythmic figurations, or chords. The existence of these special exercises within the conversation books offer extensive evidence—largely untapped—concerning Beethoven's sketching habits.

The second, recently uncovered, dimension of the conversation books deserves special mention. In March, 1977, two of my coeditors on the complete edition, Frau Grita Herre and Frau Dagmar Beck, made public at the Berlin Beethoven Congress the results of their careful investigations into a large complex of entries by Anton Schindler. They were able to show that Schindler had appropriated empty pages to simulate parts of conversations. Unfortunately, these findings were greeted in both the popular and scholarly press as something of a criminal sensation, out of which has grown the widespread notion that the entire corpus of conversation books is so contaminated with plagarisms that their value is greatly diminished. It cannot be emphasized sufficiently that this is not the case, particularly since only some 150 such entries are found in 138 books.

We are left to explain why Schindler saw fit to supplement these books at all. His principal motive may well have been to present a forceful picture of himself to posterity as a special friend of Beethoven. All in all, these entries seem to me to be of negligible import when compared to the overwhelming numbers of authenticated conversations. Of perhaps the greatest significance are those conversations which suggest that aesthetic issues were discussed with Beethoven. To these belong the metronome markings for the Seventh Symphony, the program to either Op. 90 or 97, the commentary to "Melancholie," and the

"Zwei Principe"; none of these can be said to stem from authenticated conversations, but who can say with absolute certainty that they did not in fact take place? These provocative passages will doubtless continue to stimulate scholarship for many years to come.

Our brief survey of these unique documents recalls an expression that arose in Beethoven's circle of friends: one could say everything about a great man; it could not harm him. Yet whatever we write about men of genius is valuable only if it leads ultimately to insights about the works which give meaning to the lives of their creators.

Beethoven and Schiller

Maynard Solomon

Friedrich Schiller's "An die Freude" was written in 1785 and published in February of the following year in the second volume of his magazine, the *Thalia*. Written during the decade that saw the culmination in the German-speaking lands of the Enlightenment ideal of a benevolent social order devoted to spiritual freedom and secular reform, it achieved an instantaneous popularity through its quasi-religious evocation of a condition in which all conflicts were dissolved in brotherhood, love, and reconciliation. Schiller was then an adherent of "Glückseligkeitphilosophie" (philosophy of happiness), a doctrine derived from Locke, Shaftesbury, and other philosophers of the English Enlightenment, which saw joy and love as the motive forces and goal of creation, overseen by a loving father who seeks to bring his creatures to perfection and enjoins them to promote the welfare of their fellow man. The ode's appeal to young idealists was reinforced by a similarity in tone and outlook to poems that were then current in the lodges of German Freemasons,[1] a similarity not altogether accidental, for Schiller was then living in Dresden within a circle of Freemasons that included his closest friend, the jurist and amateur composer Christian Gottfried Körner.

Körner almost immediately wrote what appears to have been the first musical setting of the "Ode to Joy."[2] The poem rapidly became a popular subject for German composers: more than forty settings are known, mostly for solo voice and piano, but including several for mixed choir, for mixed choir with soloists, and for male chorus.[3] More than a few of these were written in the later 1780s and early 1790s, so it was not an occasion for surprise when, in January, 1793, Schiller's disciple and friend, Bartholomäus Ludwig Fischenich, wrote to Schiller's wife from Bonn with the news that yet another composer was contemplating a setting.

I am enclosing with this a setting of the "Feuerfarbe" on which I would like to have your opinion. It is by a young man of this place whose musical talents are universally praised and whom the Elector has sent to Haydn in Vienna. He proposes also to compose Schiller's "Freude," and indeed strophe by strophe. I expect something perfect, for as far as I know him he is wholly devoted to the great and the sublime.[4]

The details of Beethoven's friendship with Fischenich are not fully known, but it is clear that they both frequented the Josephinian reading society (the Lese-Gesellschaft) and the widow Koch's literary tavern (the Zehrgarten) and they probably were associated at the university as well.[5] Although Fischenich was but two years older than Beethoven, it would appear that the young professor of philosophy and jurisprudence regarded Beethoven as his protégé and attempted to impart to the young composer his own passion for Schiller's works and ideas.

There is no reason to believe that Beethoven's attraction to Schiller—or his devotion to "the great and the sublime"—began only in late 1792, when he told Fischenich of his resolve. Schiller's first dramas, *The Robbers* and *Fiesco*, were presented at Bonn as early as the season of 1782–83[6] by the Grossmann and Helmuth theater company, a troupe that is closely intertwined with Beethoven's early biography: its director was a frequent visitor, with his wife, at the Beethoven lodgings, and its music director, Christian Gottlob Neefe, was Beethoven's teacher. Schiller's early works were widely circulated in Bonn, and his first applications of Kantian ideas to aesthetic and literary subjects contributed to the Kant fever that swept German intellectual life during the period. So great was Schiller's popularity that, upon Beethoven's departure for Vienna in 1792, no fewer than three of his friends chose passages from *Don Carlos* (1786) for their entries in his farewell album (*Stammbuch*).[7] That Beethoven shared this enthusiasm for Schiller's exuberant blend of *Sturm und Drang* sentiment and enlightened aestheticism is evident from his own inscription of quotations from *Don Carlos* in the autograph albums of friends during his early Vienna years. For example, on May 22, 1793, he wrote in one such album:

I am not wicked—Hot blood is my fault—my crime is that I am young. I am not wicked, truly not wicked. Even though wildly surging emotions may betray my heart, yet my heart is good— [Act 2, sc. 2][8]

And to his dearest friend, Lorenz von Breuning, he wrote on October 1, 1797:

> Truth exists for the wise,
> Beauty for a feeling heart.
> They belong to each other. [Act 4, sc. 21][9]

There was no personal contact between Beethoven and Schiller, nor is there any mention of Beethoven in Schiller's writings.[10] In addition to Fischenich, however, Schiller and Beethoven had another close mutual friend, the Viennese piano manufacturer and musician, Johann Andreas Streicher, who was one of Beethoven's unwavering friends for three decades, beginning in the mid-1790s. He and Schiller had studied together at the military academy in Stuttgart during the early 1780s, and in 1782 Streicher assisted Schiller in deserting from his regiment and accompanied him to Mannheim, where he provided him with sorely needed funds to maintain himself. They separated permanently in 1785, vowing, according to Streicher's memoir of the relationship, "not to write to each other till Streicher was a Kapellmeister and Schiller a minister of state."[11]

One of the Schiller entries in Beethoven's Bonn farewell album might have been inscribed as an epigraph on the Ninth Symphony.

> Tell him, in manhood, he must still revere
> The dreams of early youth, nor ope the heart
> Of Heaven's all-tender flower to canker-worms
> Of boasted reason,—nor be led astray
> When, by the wisdom of the dust, he hears
> enthusiasm, heavenly-born, blasphemed. [*Don Carlos*, act 4, sc. 21]

Ultimately, as we know, Beethoven indeed proved that he had not forgotten "the dreams of early youth." But evidently he could not pursue such dreams until he had first achieved maturity, until the past had been—or seemed to be—irrevocably lost. The reaffirmation of early enthusiasms could, perhaps, occur only after those enthusiasms had been tempered by experience, by doubt, and even by disillusionment. Thus it was necessary for Beethoven's "Ode to Joy" project to undergo a long process of germination. But, as in the similar case of *Faust*, which Goethe claimed to have carried with him for more than half a century, completion of Beethoven's "Ode to Joy" was not simply the long-postponed maturation of an early idea. Rather, it was at the same time a qualitatively new idea, one which could not have been brought to fruition at an earlier time.

And so it may be altogether appropriate that the "Ode to Joy" should have been set aside. Surprisingly, however, it seems probable that Beethoven actually did set the poem to music during his early Vienna years: a sketchbook of 1798–99 contains music for one line of the poem ("Muss ein lieber Vater wohnen"),[12] and in 1803 Ferdinand Ries wrote to Nikolaus Simrock in Bonn, offering for publication Beethoven's "Ode to Joy" as one of eight lieder which had been composed within the preceding "four years."[13] If it was indeed composed, it has disappeared without a trace. Although it is possible that Beethoven withdrew this song as musically unworthy, political factors may also have been at play in the failure to publish it. Schiller's works were banned for fifteen years by the Habsburg censors, beginning in 1793, when *The Robbers* was declared "immoral" and "dangerous." Beethoven had written to Simrock in 1794: "You dare not raise your voice here or the police will take you into custody."[14] It seems that for some years he exercised caution in the expression of his antifeudal, rebellious attitudes, and perhaps he moderated his enthusiasm for Schiller in deference to Emperor Franz's imperial censor, if not his police. Schiller's early radicalism, too, had long been tempered by discretion and by a more stoical view of historical events. He had repudiated the consequences of the French Revolution, had found safe havens (first at Jena and then at Weimar), and had both sought and obtained the insignia of princely approval, including, in 1802, a patent of nobility. Thomas Mann observed with a mixture of curiosity and regret that Schiller "always transposed his enthusiasm for liberty and liberation to other nations: to the Netherlands in *Don Carlos*, to France in *The Maid of Orleans*, to Switzerland in *William Tell*."[15]

But it would be trivial to suggest that either Schiller's or Beethoven's art was seriously affected by such matters as political timidity. Although Schiller had long since abandoned the frenzied tone of his early rebellious dramas, he had remained true to his antityrannical sentiments and to his recurrent themes of fraternity and national liberation. And it was during the very years 1803 and 1804 that Beethoven not only contemplated dedicating his Third Symphony to France's First Consul but apparently seriously considered taking up residence in the capital of revolutionary France. And, in view of the censorship, it is worth noting that in 1805 the closing quatrains of Sonnleithner's text to *Fidelio* contain a couplet from the second verse of Schiller's "Ode."

Wer ein holdes Weib errungen
mische seinen [stimm in unsern] Jubel ein.

It was for aesthetic rather than political reasons that Schiller seems to have lost his passion for the "Ode to Joy" during his later years. In September, 1800, he sent Körner a new edition of his poems, advising him that he would "look in vain for several of them."[16] Körner, who often acted as Schiller's literary and political conscience, wrote reproachfully on September 10: "Many will not forgive you for having excluded the 'Artists' and the 'Ode to Joy.' "[17] Schiller responded: "I regard the 'Ode to Joy' . . . as decidedly faulty; and although it has a certain quantity of fiery enthusiasm to back it, it is nevertheless a bad poem, and denotes a degree of cultivation which I must leave far behind me if I am to produce anything at all decent; but as it is written against the bad taste of the age, it has acquired a certain degree of popularity." He concluded, wistfully but firmly: "Your admiration of this poem may be attributed to the time at which it was written; but that is its only merit, and that only *for us*, and not for the world, or the art of poetry."[18] Despite his seeming firmness, it was not long before Schiller once again took up the "Ode to Joy." In 1803, two years before his death, he published a revised version of the poem. It is this revised version that provides the basis for Beethoven's eventual setting of the ode in the Ninth Symphony.

Apart from the ode, Beethoven set few texts by Schiller: a single verse of a ballade, "Das Mädchen aus der Fremde," in 1810; a twelve-bar setting of "Gesang der Mönche" (WoO 104) from *William Tell* in 1817; and two canons on the closing lines of *The Maid of Orleans*, one written in 1813 (WoO 163) and the other in 1815 (WoO 166). This did not signal any lessening of his regard for Schiller. On the contrary. Beethoven told Czerny: "Schiller's poems are very difficult to set to music. The composer must be able to lift himself far above *the poet*; who can do that in the case of Schiller? In this respect Goethe is much easier."[19] Nevertheless, in 1809, when offered a choice of composing incidental music to either *William Tell* or *Egmont*, he chose *Tell*, but was assigned the Goethe play by theater director Joseph von Hartl. It was at this time that the censorship of Schiller was virtually ended in Vienna, and his dramas soon came to dominate the programs at the Theater-an-der-Wien. Perhaps this is one reason why we find Beethoven writing to Breitkopf and Härtel in August, 1809, for editions of Goethe's and

Schiller's complete works. "These two poets are my favorites, as are also Ossian and Homer."[20] Beethoven did not receive the editions from his Leipzig publishers: they advised him of the cost, overlooking his broad hint that he hoped to receive them gratis. He did acquire a volume published in 1810 that included *The Maid of Orleans* and *William Tell*,[21] and in a letter to Bettina Brentano of early 1811, he sought to impress that literary lady with several allusions to Schiller. Referring to Bettina's impending marriage, he sighed, " 'Pity my fate,' I cry with Johanna."[22] Perhaps also deriving from this period is Ignaz von Seyfried's famous observation that when Beethoven was questioned about the sketchbook he invariably carried on the street, he again paraphrased Schiller's Joan: "Without my banner I dare not go."[23]

In 1812, the "Ode to Joy" project was momentarily rekindled. Beethoven interrupted the sketching of his Seventh and Eighth symphonies to jot down some ideas on "Freude schöner Götterfunken," intended either for a D-minor symphony or a choral overture; in 1814–15, this thematic material was utilized in the *Namensfeier* Overture, Op. 115.

During the last fifteen years of his life, passages from or allusions to Schiller's works appear frequently in Beethoven's correspondence,[24] his conversation books,[25] and his Tagebuch. From these it is clear that Beethoven was quite familiar with Schiller's poetry, with at least some of his essays, and with such plays as *The Maid of Orleans*, *William Tell*, *Maria Stuart*, *Fiesco*, and *The Bride of Messina*. Three Schiller quotations appear in Beethoven's Tagebuch in 1817.[26] The first of these is the transcription of the "Gesang der Mönche" from *William Tell*—in anticipation of the setting for three male voices in memory of Beethoven's friend, the violinist Wenzel Krumpholz. Also from *William Tell* is the phrase, "He who wishes to reap tears should sow love," an apparent reference to Beethoven's relationship with his nephew Karl. And, perhaps as an expression of his remorse over separating Karl from his mother, Beethoven noted these rather pre-Freudian lines from the close of *The Bride of Messina*:

> This one thing I feel and deeply comprehend:
> Life is not the greatest of blessings,
> But guilt is the greatest evil.

From Schiller's essay, "The Mission of Moses," Beethoven copied out three Egyptian ritual inscriptions and kept them under glass on his desk until the end of his life.

I am that which is.

I am everything that is, that was, and that will be. No mortal man has lifted my veil.

He is of himself alone, and it is to this aloneness that all things owe their being.[27]

The reminiscences of those who knew Beethoven in his later years indicate that Schiller remained one of Beethoven's favorite German writers. Franz Grillparzer reported that Beethoven "held Schiller in very high regard,"[28] and Karl Holz recalled that Beethoven "had underlined everything in Schiller's poems that constituted his [own] confession of faith."[29] Some contemporaries—including Aloys Weissenbach and Johann R. Schultz—relate that Beethoven habitually equated Schiller and Goethe, as was conventional at that time; however, several members of Beethoven's conversation book circle—a group not often given to disagreements with Beethoven—expressed their own preference for Schiller. "Goethe is more of an egoist," wrote Karl Bernard;[30] Holz declared that Schiller is "more exalted" in his attitude toward humanity.[31] And Schiller was the special passion of nephew Karl. He memorized many of his poems and declaimed them at school; he preferred Schiller, not only to Goethe, but to Shakespeare as well. Beethoven would not go quite that far, and one of their conversations closed with Karl grudgingly acknowledging Shakespeare's preeminence. "That is generally said," he wrote, "but Schiller is much dearer to me."[32]

As early as May, 1820, Beethoven determined to buy an edition of Schiller's works for Karl.[33] The boy repeatedly brought up the subject, chiding his uncle on the condition of his library, and on several occasions Schindler was reminded to pursue the matter with the booksellers. But Schindler, who despised Karl, was in no hurry to bear him gifts; it was not until the appearance in 1824 of the Grätz pocket edition of Schiller's *Werke* by the Viennese publisher Jacob Mayer, that the works of Schiller in twenty-one volumes, plus three brochures of engravings, found their way into Beethoven's library.[34]

It remains an open question whether the striking convergence between Schiller's and Beethoven's ideas is a matter of affinity or of Schiller's direct influence. Naturally, they shared a common intellectual heritage,[35] one that included worship of classicism and the ancients, adherence to German varieties of Enlightenment philosophy (especially to Kantian conceptions of morality, religion, and art), and a rejection of tyranny and arbitrary rule in favor of government by an idealized aristocratic elite. Neither man was a democrat. (Goethe said of Schiller that he was "far more of an aristocrat than he himself.")[36] Schiller's famous phrase, "The majority is nonsense," finds its echo in Beethoven's "They say *vox populi, vox dei*. I never believed it."[37] Both men placed their faith in princely saviors to rectify injustice and to cleanse society of irrational tyranny. Schiller's Karl Moor decried "this weak, effeminate age," and called for a sword that he might "strike this generation of vipers to the quick."[38] Similarly, Beethoven raged: "Our epoch requires powerful minds to scourge these frivolous, contemptible, miserable wretches of humanity," adding—for he was really a gentle soul—"repulsive as it is to my feelings to cause pain to any man."[39] Both men insisted that excellence and genius could not be measured by ordinary standards of morality. Beethoven, in a famous letter, wrote: "*Power* is the moral principle of those who excel others, and it is also mine."[40] And Schiller, in the Preface to *The Robbers*, insisted: "An exuberance of strength which bursts through all the barriers of law, must of necessity conflict with the rules of social life."[41] The simultaneous acceptance and defiance of necessity is a striking characteristic of these men. Schiller's thought, "Happy is he who learns to bear what he cannot change!"[42] has its parallel in Beethoven's oft-quoted "Plutarch has shown me the path of resignation,"[43] and in his Tagebuch notation from the *Iliad*: "Fate gave man the courage of endurance."[44] Despite such sentiments, neither man consistently advocated the acceptance of suffering; Beethoven's famous affirmation of free will—"I will seize Fate by the throat; it shall certainly not bend and crush me completely"[45]—has its close equivalent in Schiller's "Let evil destiny show its face: our safety is not in blindness, but in facing our dangers."[46] It is also echoed in Schiller's "On the Pathetic," in which he wrote: "The first law of the tragic art was to represent suffering nature. The second law is to represent the resistance of morality to suffering."[47]

There is a deep kinship between Beethoven's touching Tagebuch entry, "All evil is mysterious . . . when viewed in solitude; discussed with others it seems more endurable, because one becomes entirely familiar with that which we dread, and feels as if it had been overcome,"[48] and Schiller's aesthetic universalization of this thought: "Man rises above any natural terror as soon as he knows how to mold it, and transform it into an object of his art."[49] And although Beethoven left us no formal expression of his religious theory, it is apparent from his many extracts from a wide range of religious texts that he fully agreed with Schiller, who wrote: "Religion itself, the idea of a Divine

Power, lies under the veil of all religions; and it must be permitted to the poet to represent it in the form which appears the most appropriate to his subject."[50]

I cannot refrain from a speculation concerning Schiller's possible influence on Beethoven's decision to close the Ninth Symphony with a choral movement. In 1818, Beethoven planned what he called a "symphony in the ancient modes" which would utilize two rather unusual innovations. It would unite pagan and Christian style elements—"Greek myth" and "Cantique Ecclesiastique"—and it would use a chorus.[51] It seems to me possible that both of these innovations were sparked by a reading of the central ideas of the Preface to Schiller's *Bride of Messina*. That Preface, entitled "The Use of the Chorus in Tragedy," urges that the tragic poet reinstate the chorus of the Attic tragedians as a means of penetrating "to the most simple, original, and genuine motives of action." The chorus, writes Schiller, "appeals to the sense with an imposing grandeur. It forsakes the contracted sphere of incidents to dilate itself over the past and future, over distant times and nations, and general humanity, to deduce the grand results of life, and pronounce the lessons of wisdom." Of course, Schiller had reference here to a dramatic rather than a musical chorus, but the musical implications of this theory are readily apparent. Schiller notes that the chorus infuses a "bold lyrical freedom" into tragedy and that it achieves its effect "in conjunction with the whole sensible influence of melody and rhythm, in tones and movements." As for the fusion of Greek mythology and Christianity, Schiller wrote: "I have blended together the Christian religion and the Pagan mythology, and introduced recollections of Mohammedan superstition."

Beethoven never composed his "Adagio Cantique"—as he called it in 1818—but the notion of using a chorus to climax a symphony was not forgotten. Furthermore, the fusion of pagan and Christian religious motifs in the text is central to the "Ode to Joy" and gives it much of its emotional power. And although Beethoven's Ninth is not his "symphony in the ancient modes," the "Seid umschlungen Millionen" passage of its finale is firmly rooted in the ecclesiastical modes.

This is, of course, highly speculative, for there is no direct evidence that Beethoven read the introduction to *The Bride of Messina*, although it seems clear enough from his Tagebuch that he knew the play, which was customarily printed with it. And there is no evidence that Beethoven actually read or was influenced by Schiller's major aesthetic writings,[52] such as *Letters on the Aesthetic Education of Man*, in which Schiller elaborated his theories of art's humanizing function and of the *Spieltrieb*, or "Concerning Naive and Sentimental Poetry," in which the distinction between Classic and Romantic art was clearly set forth for the first time.

But if Beethoven was not directly influenced by Schiller's visionary writings on art and politics, there is a sense in which certain of his compositions can be regarded as musical embodiments of Schiller's aesthetic utopianism. Schiller, in his desire to heal what he described as the "wounds" that civilization had dealt to an innocent humanity, in his quest for a social condition that would restore man's harmony with nature and permit the unfettered development of human creativity, proposed that art's function was to hold out the "effigy of [the] ideal" as a goal toward which mankind could strive.[53] He proposed that the idyllic vision of such a future condition is modeled upon memories of a lost paradise. "All nations that have a history have a paradise, an age of innocence, a golden age. Nay, more than this," he wrote, "every man has his paradise, his golden age, which he remembers with more or less enthusiasm, according as he is more or less poetical."[54] However, he insisted that the artist's responsibility was not to advocate a contemplative return to Arcadia, but to portray a future Elysium, a condition of harmony and joy that would transcend both the idealizations of memory and the malaise of an alienated present. "A state such as this is not merely met with before the dawn of civilization; it is also the state to which civilization aspires. . . . The idea of a similar state, and the belief of the possible reality of this state is the only thing that can reconcile man with all the evils to which he is exposed in the path of civilization." It is therefore, he wrote, "of infinite importance for the man engaged in the path of civilization to see confirmed in a sensuous manner the belief that this idea can be accomplished in the world of sense, that this state of innocence can be realized in it."[55]

Naturally, this yearning for a paradisaic condition is not without its biographical sources, but we cannot explore here those experiences which predisposed both Schiller and Beethoven to their passionate desire for brotherhood and reconciliation, to their shared dream of a world of innocent joy. Beethoven's life and his art can be envisaged as a search for Elysium, for "one day of pure joy" ("Heiligenstadt Testament"), for fraternal and familial harmony, as well as for a just and enlightened social order. With the "Ode to Joy" of the Ninth Symphony, that search found its symbolic fulfillment, though not its conclusion. And it is both fitting and inevitable that Beethoven returned to Schiller for assistance in mapping the geography of Elysium.[56]

Notes

1. Hans Vaihinger, "Zwei Quellenfunde zu Schillers philosophischer Entwicklung," *Kant-Studien* 10 (1905):386–89; Gotthold Deile, *Freimäurer Lieder als Quellen zu Schillers Lied "An die Freude"* (Leipzig, 1907).
2. Körner wrote a second setting of the "Ode to Joy"; see Karl Goedeke, ed., *Briefwechsel zwischen Schiller und Körner*, 2d ed. (Leipzig, 1878), I:368 (letter of April 23, 1790).
3. For a list of settings of "An die Freude," see Julius Blaschke, "Schillers Gedichte in der Musik," *Neue Zeitschrift für Musik* 72 (1905):397–401. See also Franz Brandstaeter, *Schillers Lyrik im Verhältnisse zu ihrer musikalischen Behandlung* (Danzig, 1863). For settings of Schiller's dramas, see Albert Schäfer, *Historisches und systematisches Verzeichnis sämtlicher Tonwerke zu den Dramen Schillers, Goethes, Shakespeares, Kleists, und Körners* (Leipzig, 1886).
4. Thayer-Forbes, pp. 120–21 (letter of January 26, 1793). Beethoven's "Feuerfarb," Op. 52, no. 2 is set to Sophie Mereau's text concerning the harmony of beauty and truth.
5. For Fischenich, see Max Braubach, *Die erste Bonner Universität und ihre Professoren* (Bonn, 1947), pp. 155–59, 199; and Braubach, *Eine Jugendfreundin Beethovens: Babette Koch-Belderbusch und ihr Kreis* (Bonn, 1948), pp. 48–49.
6. Thayer-Forbes, p. 31; *Kabale und Liebe* also may have been performed: see Ludwig Nohl, *Beethovens Leben* (Vienna, 1864; Leipzig, 1867–77), I:136.
7. Hans Gerstinger, *Ludwig van Beethovens Stammbuch* (Bielefeld and Leipzig, 1927), pp. 17–18, 21. The entries are those of Klemmer, the widow Koch, and her son. The last also includes a quotation from Schiller's "Züricher See."
8. Anderson 4; the entry was in the album of A. Vocke.
9. Anderson 21; trans. from Thayer-Forbes, p. 192. Ludwig Nohl described what were probably tracings of two additional album leaves in Beethoven's handwriting, containing verses from "An die Freude": *Beethovens Brevier* (Leipzig, 1870), p. 105.
10. There is only a sparse literature on Beethoven's relationship to Schiller. The most thorough—though long outdated—study is A. C. Kalischer, *Beethoven und seine Zeitgenossen* (Berlin and Leipzig, [ca. 1908–10]), IV:101–30. For the influence of Schiller's thought on Beethoven, see the standard works by Ludwig Schiedermair, Arnold Schmitz, Jean Boyer, Adolf Sandberger, and especially Otto Baensch, *Aufbau und Sinn des Chorfinales in Beethovens neunter Symphonie* (Berlin and Leipzig, 1930), pp. 22–30. For Schiller and music in general, see Hans H. Knudsen, *Schiller und die Musik* (Greifswald, 1908), now largely superseded by R. M. Longyear, *Schiller and Music* (Chapel Hill, N.C., [1966]). For further literature, see Longyear, pp. 167–77; *Die Musik in Geschichte und Gegenwart*, XI, cols. 1719–20; and Jürgen Mainka, "Schiller und die Musik: Eine Literaturübersicht," in *Wissenschaftliche Zeitschrift der Friedrich-Schiller-Universität Jena*, vol. 5, *Gesellschafts- und Sprachwissenschaftliche Reihe*, no. 1, pp. 217–19.
11. Andreas Streicher, *Schillers Flucht von Stuttgart und Aufenthalt in Mannheim* (Stuttgart, 1836), p. 215.

12. N II:479.
13. *Simrock Jahrbuch* 2 (1929):26 (letter of September 13, 1803).
14. Anderson 12 (August 2, 1794). The lieder were refused by Simrock; they were published as Op. 52 in Vienna (by Kunst- und Industrie-Comptoir) in 1805. On another level, it seems possible that the large number of prior settings of "An die Freude" may have discouraged Beethoven from offering yet another straightforward setting for voice and piano; in view of the competition—which eventually included such well-known composers as Zelter, Rellstab, Zumsteeg, Romberg, Schobart, Winter, Kanne, and Gyrowetz—Beethoven clearly would have to offer something rather special.
15. Thomas Mann, "On Schiller," *Last Essays* (New York, 1959), p. 64.
16. *Briefwechsel zwischen Schiller und Körner*, II:356; Eng. trans. Leonard Simpson, *Correspondence of Schiller with Körner* (London, 1849), III:218.
17. *Briefwechsel*, II:356; Eng. trans., p. 219.
18. *Briefwechsel*, II:358–59; Eng. trans., p. 221 (letter of October 21, 1800). Vaihinger attributes Schiller's disenchantment with the ode to its pre-Kantian character. (*Kant-Studien* 10 [1905]:387.)
19. Thayer-Forbes, p. 472.
20. Anderson 224 (August 8, 1809); see also Anderson 226 (September 19, 1809, to Breitkopf and Härtel).
21. Albert Leitzmann, ed., *Ludwig van Beethoven: Berichte der Zeitgenossen, Briefe und persönliche Aufzeichnungen* (Leipzig, 1921), II:380; see Eveline Bartlitz, ed., *Die Beethoven-Sammlung in der Musikabteilung der Deutschen Staatsbibliothek: Verzeichnis* (Berlin, [1970]), pp. 211–12.
22. Anderson 296 (February 10, 1811); the quotation is from *The Maid of Orleans*, act 5, sc. 2. Beethoven also refers to Schiller's poem "Die Flüsse" in this letter.
23. Ignaz von Seyfried, *L. v. Beethovens Studien* (Vienna, 1832), Appendix, p. 20; the quotation is from *The Maid of Orleans*, act 5, sc. 14.
24. In addition to letters already cited, see Anderson 483 (to Treitschke, early July, 1814); 502 (to Kanka [autumn, 1814]); 948 (to Archduke Rudolph [June, 1819]); 1079 (to Peters, June 5, 1822); 1260 (to the directors of the GdM, January 23, 1824); 1269 (to Probst, March 10, 1824); 1270 (to Schott's Sons, March 10, 1824).
25. Entries concerning Schiller appear on the following pages of the published conversation books: I: 130, 297, 341; II: 19, 89–90, 105, 123, 299, 323, 324, 334; III: 99–100, 169, 236, 273, 384, 396; IV: 47, 114, 233; V: 37, 78, 95, 147, 175, 249, 258; VI: 20, 340. Karl-Heinz Köhler et al., eds., *Ludwig van Beethovens Konversationshefte*, I–II, IV–VI (Berlin, 1968–76); Georg Schünemann, ed., *Ludwig van Beethovens Konversationshefte*, III (Berlin, 1943). I omit the references to Schiller in III, Heft 26, for these are included in the renumbered Heft 20 in II. See also Jacques-Gabriel Prod'homme, *Les Cahiers de conversation de Beethoven* (Paris, 1946), pp. 342, 399, 428. Also Thayer-Dieters-Riemann, V:49, n. 2.
26. Leitzmann, II:260 (nos. 123, 124, and 130).
27. Matthias Artaria wrote in a conversation book of 1825: "Have you read 'Ueber die Sendung Moses' by Schiller?" (A. C. Kalischer, *Beethoven und seine Zeitgenossen*, IV:120).
28. Leitzmann, I:319.
29. Friedrich Kerst, *Die Erinnerungen an Beethoven* (Stuttgart, 1913), II:184. Nevertheless, Beethoven did not respond to urgings that he set such works as *Fiesco* or "Burgschaft" to music. (See Köhler-Beck, *Konversationshefte*, II:323; Kerst, II:76–77.)

For additional reminiscences by contemporaries pertaining to Beethoven and Schiller, see Kerst, I:206–7 (Anselm Hüttenbrenner); Kerst, I:278 (Braun von Braunthal); Kerst, II:62 (Johann R. Schultz); Kerst, II:76–77 (Ferdinand Leopold von Biedenfeld); Ludwig Spohr, *Autobiography* (London, 1865), I:198–99 (Spohr); Ludwig Nohl, *Beethoven nach den Schilderungen seiner Zeitgenossen* (Stuttgart, 1877), p. 110 (Aloys Weissenbach). Not located is a reported reference by Johann Sporschil.

30. Köhler-Beck, *Konversationshefte*, II:105.
31. Prod'homme, *Cahiers de conversation*, p. 428.
32. Köhler-Herre, *Konversationshefte*, IV:47.
33. Köhler-Beck, *Konversationshefte*, II:123.
34. Leitzmann, II:382. One wonders if any other books in Beethoven's *Nachlass* actually belonged to, or were intended for, his nephew Karl.
35. René Wellek notes that in this period "the question of priorities, of sources and influences, is hopelessly entangled. . . . [There existed] a community of thought and speculation which accounts for the wealth of crosscurrents and crossfertilization" among the leading German thinkers of the period: *A History of Modern Criticism*, I (New Haven, 1955), p. 228.
36. Mann, *Last Essays*, p. 19.
37. Thayer-Forbes, p. 1046. It is worth noting that both men derived much gratification from popular approval. Schiller commented that "the assertion so commonly made that the public degrades art, is not well founded. . . . [The people] derive the greatest pleasure from what is judicious and true" ("The Use of the Chorus in Tragedy"); and Beethoven, basking in the popularity that attended his *Wellington's Victory*, wrote: "It is certain that one writes prettier music when one writes for the public": Leitzmann, II:245 (no. 26).
38. *The Robbers*, act I, sc. 2. This and the following translations are from *Works of Friedrich Schiller*, ed. N. H. Dole (Boston, 1902).
39. Anderson 1423 (August, 1825).
40. Anderson 30 (to Zmeskall [1798]).
41. Schiller, Preface to *The Robbers*.
42. Schiller, "On the Sublime."
43. Anderson 51 (to Wegeler, June 29, 1801).
44. Leitzmann, II:246 (no. 37); the quotation is from the *Iliad* 24:49.
45. Anderson 54 (to Wegeler, November 16, 1801).
46. Schiller, "On the Sublime."
47. Schiller, "On the Pathetic." It seems to me likely that Beethoven read this essay, which was first published in 1793. It is tempting to speculate that the title "Sonate pathétique" derives from Schiller, but the term was applied to music by Rousseau in his *Dictionnaire de musique* (1767) and even earlier by Athanasius Kircher in *Musurgia Universalis* (1650); see Edward E. Lowinsky, "Musical Genius—Evolution and Origins of a Concept," *MQ* 50 (1964):328, 336. Eric Blom notes that Dussek gave the designation "patetico" to a movement of his C-minor sonata composed in the early 1790s: *Beethoven's Pianoforte Sonatas Discussed* (London, 1938), pp. 56–57.
48. Leitzmann, II:262 (no. 148).
49. Schiller, *Letters on the Aesthetic Education of Man*, Letter 25.
50. Schiller, "On the Use of the Chorus in Tragedy."
51. See Thayer-Forbes, p. 888.
52. One authority believes otherwise, but the only proofs he adduces are several conversation book references of 1825–26 to general histories of aesthetics that include descriptions of Schiller's aesthetics: Baensch, *Aufbau and Sinn*, p. 27. For modern

evaluations of Schiller's aesthetics, see Wellek, *History of Modern Criticism*, I:232–55, with further bibliography; Georg Lukács, *Goethe and His Age* (New York, 1969), pp. 101–35; Herbert Marcuse, *Eros and Civilization* (New York, n.d.), pp. 164–76.
53. See especially Schiller, *Letters on the Aesthetic Education of Man*, Letter 9.
54. Schiller, *Naive and Sentimental Poetry*, "The Idyll."
55. Ibid.
56. For further discussion of Beethoven, Schiller, and the Ninth Symphony, see the present author's *Beethoven* (New York, 1977), pp. 309–14. (See also pp. 38–39 for further parallels between Beethoven's and Schiller's social thought.)

The Sketches for the "Ode to Joy"

Robert Winter

In December of 1822, Ludwig van Beethoven would have celebrated—had it been customary in Vienna to draw attention to such things—his fifty-second birthday. He did not cut an especially happy figure. Since the death of his brother Karl Kaspar just over seven years earlier, Beethoven had embroiled himself in a progressively degrading series of legal struggles for the custody of his nephew. The already strained family relations of the early Vienna years had turned into outright war with his sister-in-law Johanna and periodic eruptions directed at his prosperity-oriented brother Johann. Like most wars of attrition, this one was as difficult to halt as it was detrimental to the participants.

No less saddening was the fact that, probably as much as a decade before, Beethoven had given up hope of finding a woman who would marry him and with whom he could reach a seemingly unattainable happiness. The "greatest happiness of his life," whom he refers to in 1816 as having met five years before, also turned out to be an "impossibility, a chimera." (If she was Antonie Brentano, as Maynard Solomon has convincingly argued in *Beethoven* [1977], one formidable obstacle was that she already had a husband and three children.) Except for the consolation of old friends, whose number was shrinking, Beethoven had less to look forward to than many far less gifted artists.

It seems undeniable that Beethoven's often depressing surroundings had a deleterious effect on his powers of musical creation. Can it be simply coincidental that the letter to the Immortal Beloved marked the end of his symphonic output for more than a decade? This same decade, while the breeding ground for works like the Bb Piano Sonata, Op. 106, witnessed a drastic shrinking in both the quantity and, to some extent, the quality of output. Beethoven never again achieved the productivity of his earlier years; indeed, the last years are easily grouped around three musical mastheads: the *Missa solemnis* (1819–22, years which also spawned the last three piano sonatas and many of the Diabelli Variations); the Ninth Symphony (1823); and the late string quartets (1824–26). Beethoven thought of the *Missa solemnis* as perhaps the greatest achievement of his lifetime.[1] Yet there is another level at which this work could not have expressed Beethoven's ultimate faith in the future of mankind. The doctrines of the Catholic church were deeply impressed upon him from his childhood in Bonn, and the far-reaching uses to which he put archaic devices throughout the mass demonstrate sufficiently his affirmation of a thousand years of church tradition.[2] But the mass could scarcely have encompassed the personal, nonclerical nature of Beethoven's own credo. Maynard Solomon has argued persuasively in "Beethoven and Schiller" in this volume that Beethoven's return to Schiller's "Ode to Joy" was inevitable and necessary. It is significant that after the Ninth Symphony, only a few humorous canons provided texts to attract his attention; after the Ninth he had, quite literally, nothing more to say in words. Beethoven's *Missa solemnis* was—as the year 1823 makes clear—his Ninth Symphony.[3]

What form did Beethoven's return to Schiller's ode take? In 1792, we find B. L. Fischenich writing that the young Rhinelander planned a "strophe by strophe" setting of it.[4] That this aspiration elicited mention at all suggests both Beethoven's enthusiasm for the proposed subject and the novelty of such a comprehensive treatment. In the form that Beethoven first knew the "Ode to Joy," published by Schiller in the 1785 volume of his *Thalia*, it included nine eight-line strophes, each with the rhyme scheme *a b a b c d c d*, followed by a four-line chorus (specifically labeled "Chor" by Schiller) with its own independent rhyme scheme of *a b b a*. Hence Beethoven had expressed to Fischenich his intention to set more than a hundred lines in praise not only of joy, but also of long-suffering millions and the overthrow of tyrants. There is no reason to believe that he ever fulfilled his youthful ambition. We possess today most of Beethoven's pre-1803 sketchbooks (Grasnick 1, Grasnick 2, Landsberg 7, Sauer, Kessler, and Wielhorski) and many loose sketchleaves he used before 1798, when he first began to use bound sketchbooks. The few sketches for the ode found in these sources show only fragmentary entries for occasional lines that especially attracted him, as, for example, the segment from 1798–99 illustrated in ex. 1 (Grasnick 1, fol. 13r, st. 4). Surrounded as it is by sketches for the Gellert songs, including "Denk O Mensch an deinem Tod" (on fol. 13v,

Example 1

[N II, p. 479, Ex. 1]

muss ein lieb - er Vat - er wohn - en

[not shown by Nottebohm]

[muss ein lieb - er Vat - er wohn - en]

st. 1–2), it is hard to imagine what Schiller is doing in such sombre surroundings.[5]

It is perhaps no coincidence that Beethoven did not take up the ode again until he was completing the Seventh and Eighth symphonies, the last large-scale examples of absolute symphonic music he was to produce. More interesting than the simple C-major sketches (which Gustav Nottebohm rightly showed to form the basis of the *Namensfeier* Overture, Op. 115),[6] are the prose entries which accompany the draft: "Freude schöner Götterfunken Tochter / Overture ausarbeiten" ("working out Overture on 'Joy sweet gods-spark, daughter' "); "abgerissene Sätze wie Fürsten sind Bettler u.s.w. nicht das ganze" ("disconnected sentences like 'princes are beggars' etc. not the whole"); "abgerissene Sätze aus Schillers Freude zu einem Ganzen gebracht" ("disconnected sentences from Schiller's 'Joy' brought to a whole"). Otto Baensch insisted that Beethoven in no way meant to confine himself to an overture—for Baensch the notion of a "vocal overture" was comical. But more important—and never to my knowledge noted—is that in 1811–12 Beethoven was still using the *first* edition of Schiller's poem. It is this version which included as the seventh line of the first strophe the words "Bettler werden Furstenbrüder" ("Beggars will become princes' brothers"), instead of the 1803 revision: "Alle Menschen werden Brüder" ("All men will become brothers"). We would then also have to assume that the composer was at least considering the lines of the ode's last strophe, which was dropped by Schiller in 1803.

> Rettung von Tyrannenketten,
> Grossmut auch dem Bösewicht,
> Hoffnung auf den Sterbebetten,
> Gnade auf dem Hochgericht!

(Rescue from tyrants' bonds,
　Generosity even to the scoundrel,
Hope on the deathbed,
　Mercy on the gallows!)

It is easy to see why such proclamations were an embarrassment for the now ennobled Schiller in 1803, but for Beethoven they still had not lost their revolutionary allure. Finally, we would render Beethoven a disservice were we not to note his transformation of Schiller's forceful yet graceful line in the first strophe into the roundly defiant characterization of "Fürsten sind Bettler," a sentiment he was to paraphrase many times in the ensuing years during the legal struggle for the guardianship of his nephew.

Beginning with the shattering experience of the Immortal Beloved in 1812, followed by years of compositional doubt and inactivity, Beethoven's view of the "Ode to Joy" seems to have changed dramatically. By 1812, he had already realized that a convincing musical setting could not proceed "strophe by strophe." Just how the winnowing process developed over the next decade is hard to pinpoint, and at all events it is inextricably linked with the genesis of the Ninth Symphony itself. Because the last published account based on primary sources is that of Nottebohm in 1876,[7] the chronology and evolution of Beethoven's epic hymn to the brotherhood of man requires some elaboration. It is not that Nottebohm's essay lacks his usual directness and lucidity; the outline he offers for the genesis of the work requires only moderate revision after more than a century (though he was completely unaware of one important source). But the coverage, not surprisingly in a work so vast, is highly selective; even had Nottebohm been inclined to attempt some explication of the sketches he transcribed, he would have been doomed to failure.

Following the documented interest of Beethoven in Schiller's ode in 1792, 1798, and 1811–12, the brief entry for a "Fuge" in the Scheide sketchbook of 1815 (cited by N II, p. 157, but not by Kinsky-Halm) inaugurates the thematic history of the symphony, although the work itself was not yet even dimly conceived. In the first half of 1818, during the main work on the B♭ Piano Sonata, Op. 106, Beethoven was distracted more than momentarily by ideas for a "Sinfonie in D"; rather detailed sketches for the opening of the present first movement as well as tentative ones for two further movements (the Scheide theme, somewhat altered, was to be the "3tes Stück") appear on eighteen consecutive pages in the pocket Boldrini sketchbook, now lost. No sketchbooks of the large type used by Beethoven on his work desk at home survive from this period. The flock of loose leaves for all movements of the Bb Piano Sonata suggests Beethoven may not have been using the large books at this time. Nevertheless, 1818 is the first year in which serious efforts associated with the work we now know can be ascertained (perhaps because of the brevity of Nottebohm's account, Kinsky-Halm understates the importance of the sketches in Boldrini). A single fragmentary notation for a finale ("letztes"; N II, p. 160) in D major denotes only that an orthodox instrumental conclusion was envisaged.

The composition of the *Missa solemnis* apparently engulfed the symphony project, for it is not until after the last sketches for the Dona nobis pacem in the late summer and early autumn of 1822 that Beethoven turned once again to the Ninth Symphony—as we may now legitimately call it.[8] He did not proceed systematically at first. The sketches which occupy the last dozen pages or so in Artaria 201 do include the *a* phrase of the eventual "Freude" tune (p. 111, system 10), but the first movement looks little different from its shape in Boldrini. The mission of these leaves, in fact, is conceptual and not comprehensive; they present an overview rather than a working out. Among the entries for "Sinf.," "2tes Stück," "3tes Stück," and so forth is a plan for a five-movement work similar to, though less complex than, those I have elsewhere described among the sketches for the C♯-minor String Quartet, Op. 131.[9] Three of the movements—the first, second, and fifth (the latter represented by the untexted "Freude" tune)—present themes found in corresponding positions within the final work; this layout should not be taken too seriously, however, since only a few pages earlier Beethoven had written: "auch statt einer neuen Sinfonie eine neue Overtüre/auf Bach sehr fugirt mit 3 Posaunen" ("also, instead of a new symphony, a new overture on Bach, very fugato with three trombones").[10]

Such efforts habitually served as a prelude to intensive focus on a single work. But one of the great undertakings which had interrupted work on the Ninth in the earlier sketchbook remained incomplete. The *Missa solemnis*, the last trilogy of piano sonatas, and the Op. 119 Bagatelles were now in the hands of copyists or publishers. It was those variations on a "Schusterfleck" (as Beethoven dubbed Diabelli's trivial waltz tune) that Beethoven had abandoned in early 1819 and that now demanded their due, in no fewer than fourteen further variations to complement the original nineteen. Beethoven seemed driven to wipe the compositional slate clean before giving his undivided attention to a work that must have been growing irresistibly inside his head. The witness is the Engelmann sketchbook of April–May, 1823, a volume completely unknown to Nottebohm, but of pivotal importance for a study devoted to the genesis of the Ninth Symphony. The more than twenty-five pages of sketches for the symphony (with the first movement predominant) cannot, because of internal chronological relationships, have been penned before the beginning of April, 1823.[11] From one vantage point, then, we must regard the lion's share of this massive creation as the product of some ten months in the sketches, or eleven months "bis zur letzten Feile" ("up to the final polish") in the score. This provides a healthy antidote to the more popular vision of Beethoven toiling year after year on major opuses.

The *Missa solemnis*, for example, fits the Romantic image neatly; Beethoven's labors on it not only lasted the better part of five years, but they also were interrupted on several occasions by other experiments, largely for piano. The mass elicited his religious ideals, his desire to pay tribute to his extraordinary patron, and his wish to secure for himself a position of honor among the distinguished composers of sacred music. Whether flagging interest or compositional hurdles occasioned the stop-and-start evolution of the work, the sketches offer persuasive evidence that it could not keep his undivided attention. The Ninth Symphony, on the other hand, was Beethoven's exclusive interest for almost a year. Indeed, the only composition to intervene at all is a four-bar entry for a (complete? two-voiced?) canon, "Grossen Dank . . . für solche Gnade," which Beethoven promised near the end of July, 1823, to Archduke Rudolph. This little offering is, in fact, our sole anchor point for the relative chronology of this eventful year. On July 31, Rudolph answered Beethoven's earlier disclosure of the canon by voicing the hope that he had finished it.[12]

With my reconstruction of the sketchbooks for the Ninth Symphony, we can now see further that "Grossen Dank" falls neatly between the end of sketching for the scherzo and the beginning of sustained sketching on the slow movement.[13] Hence the third and fourth movements were drafted during the last two months in Baden (August–September) and the four months following the return to Vienna (October–January). Much if not most of the work on the finale must have taken place after the long migrations, first to Hetzendorf and then to Baden; Beethoven's fresh return to Vienna marked in one sense a double homecoming.[14]

At one level the Ninth Symphony evolved like the vast majority of Beethoven's multimovement works. Beginning in April, 1823, concentrated work on the first movement was accompanied by short, exploratory drafts for remaining movements. It is important to remember—and this distinction has generally been lost in the popular literature from Nottebohm on—that Beethoven almost never worked intensively on two movements simultaneously, much less two separate works.[15] The physical layout of several dozen sketchbooks bears eloquent testimony to this, and it detracts nothing from the mystery of the creative process to know that by habit the composer began with the first movement and proceeded step-by-step to the last. Once the opening Allegro of the Ninth was almost complete after some thirty-five pages in the sketches, for example, we encounter over the next five leaves a series of fragmentary, largely unrelated entries for successive movements. Out of these emerges the scaffolding for the second movement, which then occupies the spotlight for the following fourteen pages. It would be a mistake to view the numerous preliminary ideas, most of which do not exceed a few embryonic phrases, between bundle 2, gathering I, p. 8(36) and gathering II, p. 9(45) as "work upon two or three movements simultaneously." Once serious sketching for the finale commences on bundle 2, gathering VI, p. 1(85), it continues virtually uninterrupted for forty-eight standard-format pages until the symphony was completed. Within this natural compositional rhythm, however, the varieties of Beethoven's response to the "Ode to Joy" are seemingly inexhaustible.

Nottebohm printed so few sketches to the Ninth that the vast majority of transcriptions will necessarily be first publications. I wish to focus on a dimension ever present in Beethoven's late style, but by no means restricted to this symphonic finale: direct expression. The curious and unique vocal language which is projected so strongly in the preliminary sketches has its analogue in Schiller's text, one that had spoken directly to Beethoven for more than thirty years when he began the serious drafting of the "Ode" in the autumn of 1823. By restricting ourselves to the two principal "tunes" of the movement—a soloistic one for Schiller's stanzas and a choral one for his choruses—we will touch only incidentally upon its architecture, the proper subject for an extended monograph. It is nevertheless possible to peer into the heart of Beethoven's compositional concerns in his last symphonic work.

The special qualities of the finale are due not only to its setting of Schiller, but to its unfolding from a tune rather than from a large skeletal framework. Indeed, the casting of the initial "Freude" melody

Key to exs. 2a–2r

	Sketchbook	Bundle	Gathering	Page	Stave(s)	Phrase(s)
a	Artaria 201	—	—	111	10	a
b¹	Artaria 201	—	—	119	12	a
b²	unidentified location quoted in N II, p. 182					a
c	Engelmann	—	—	25	—	a
d	Landsberg 8	2	II	9(45)	1/2	aa'ba''
e	Landsberg 8	2	II	9(45)	6	aa'ba''
f	Landsberg 8	2	VI	1(85)	5/6, 1/2	aa'b
g	Landsberg 8	2	VI	2(86)	13–14	bb'
h	Landsberg 8	2	VI	4(88)	1–4	aa' + text
i	Landsberg 8	2	VI	4(88)	6–8, 5	bb'
j	Landsberg 8	2	VI	4(88)	12–14	bb'
k	Landsberg 8	2	VI	4(88)	16	bc
l	Landsberg 8	2	VI	5(89)	1–2	a'ba''
m	Landsberg 8	2	VI	5(89)	5, 11/12	aa'b(a')
n	Landsberg 8	2	VI	5(89)	15/16, 13/14	b(a')
o	Landsberg 8	2	VI	6(90)	1/2, 3/4, 5/6, 7/8	b, then last 2 bars 4 times
p	Landsberg 8	2	VI	7(91)	6/7	last 2 bars of b
q	Landsberg 8	2	VI	7(91)	7, 8	b, last 2 bars of b
r	Landsberg 8	2	VI	7(91)	9–10	aa'ba'

took precedence over virtually all other concerns. The melody was the first element to emerge, and until it reached its definitive shape, Beethoven could not deal at length with any of the larger structural concerns of a movement that was to attain the length of many Classical symphonies. The schematic presentation in the key to ex. 2 has the drawback of compressing a longer, more irregular evolution, but it offers the advantage of showing clearly nineteen stages in the hammering out of this synthetic folk tune. Echoing the regular scheme of each eight-line strophe of Schiller's poem, Beethoven divided the theme into four four-bar phrases (shown as *a*, *a'*, *b*, and so on).[16]

The two brief entries in Artaria 201 represent, in effect, the two poles of vocal writing throughout the finale: on the one hand, the stepwise, even-rhythmed flow of the first; on the other, the angular, dancelike bursts of the second. Both share in the harmonic simplicity which stamps the finale with a special glow. Some six months later, the identical phrase (though an octave down) was copied into Engelmann. Hence by June, 1823, nothing beyond the initial *a* had been drafted, a state of affairs inherited by bundle 2 of Landsberg 8. However, in the last preliminary sketches for the "Freude" tune—sandwiched between intensive work on the first and second movements—we find a rounded, surprisingly forward-looking theme (ex. 2d) which insists only upon varying each statement of *a*. From here to the tune we know would have required a modicum of refinements, surely fewer than the dozen drafts made some four months later. Already only four lines under his *Bass* version, Beethoven enters another, clearly marked *Sopra*, which cancels altogether the Schenkerian descent from mediant to tonic characteristic of the initial *a* phrases. Was this soprano to have served as a descant to the bass? The parallels are not close enough.

With the beginning of almost fifty pages of finale sketches in bundle 2, gathering VI, the final working out of the theme became Beethoven's first order of business. After he returned to the mediant emphasis in the opening *a* phrases, the biggest challenge was to find answering phrases which were both contrasting and complementary. Aside from abortive beginnings like that of ex. 2f—almost certainly instrumental—others offer plenty of contrast. Ex. 2g, for instance, abandons the rounded structure altogether for two complementary *b* phrases, the first of which is the most arresting. Beethoven entered a clear five-bar unit in which the words "was die Mode" would presumably have been repeated. This version also hammers away mercilessly at the mediant. Ex.

Example 2

deine Zauber binden wieder was die Mode streng getheilt
alle Menschen werden Brüder wo dein sanfter Flügel weilt

189

2h symbolizes the difficulties. After setting down the *a* and *a'* phrases with obvious confidence (reinstating the cadential dotted rhythms of ex. 2d), the composer laid out the remainder of the text of the first strophe with generous spacings. And then he could enter nothing.

Returning to the problem a few lines below, Beethoven constructed two parallel concluding phrases derived in part from ex. 2g, but embarking from dominant rather than tonic harmonies. It is this stage, in fact, which allows the only significant role to the leading tone throughout the sketches (exs. 2i and 2j). On the bottom staff of the same page, the leading tones are joined by a fourth phrase different from any of the previous three. This little sketch huddled at the base of more imposing drafts marks the most extreme stage in the evolution of the tune and offers a good vantage point from which to assess its development thus far.

Whether one views Beethoven's setting as a "three-part song form,"[17] as a "Reprisenbar mit doppeltem Abgesange,"[18] or as a "plain strophic song,"[19] it should be clear from these drafts that for once the composer was less concerned with overall shape than with an elusive style he was straining to capture or create. At least three different designs, all without the choral response, were considered: *aa'ba"*, *aa'bb'*, and *aa'bc*. Rather than moving unerringly towards an increasingly obvious solution, each reading departs further from the now familiar one of *aa'ba'*. It was not, then, with fixed notions of its eventual shape that Beethoven began to form the "Freude" theme, and the goal he sought can only be understood with reference to Beethoven's particular view of the popular style.

At the height of their compositional powers, both Mozart and Haydn (though especially the latter) had achieved a fusion—perhaps for the first time in the history of western art music—between popular and serious styles, one that has remained unique well into the twentieth century. High art music, of course, has never been immune from popular influence, but between 1785 and 1800, the integration was so complete and seemingly effortless that it seems more miraculous the farther it recedes in time. We are scarcely in any better position today to characterize the elusive nature of this popular dimension. Unlike Bartók, who preserved in detail his findings about Hungarian, Romanian, and Czechoslovakian folk songs, neither Haydn, Mozart, nor Beethoven showed the slightest interest in sharing their folk roots. Yet few musicians would fail to recognize the popular undercurrents in the finale of Haydn's Symphony No. 104, whether they hear an English street cry ("hot cross buns"), a Croatian folk song, or simply the opening tune.

What are the salient characteristics of a style about which Beethoven would have found it impossible to remain ignorant following his southward migration to Vienna in 1792?

An essential ingredient seems to have been diatonic simplicity. Many of these tunes are restricted to unadorned tonic-dominant alternations, often in a regular or patterned harmonic rhythm. Tonic or dominant pedals recall the sound of the hurdy-gurdy. Even the simplest chromatic alterations, like neighboring tones or secondary dominants, are avoided. The phrasing is four-square. Internal cadences are strong and directional, frequently I–V, I–I. Thematic material operates within these parameters, but large (though diatonic) leaps coexist with stepwise and repeated-note motion. Within phrases the forward impetus is regularly provided by sequences.[20]

There is no question that the success of the popular style within art music depended upon its being a synthetic concoction; it can be doubted whether the dozens of readily identifiable instances in Haydn and Mozart have real points of contact with examples from a folk tradition now irretrievably lost. But we can be certain that Beethoven knew this tradition intimately as it manifested itself in the High Classical style, and we can be equally sure that for most of his life he ignored it. In just those places where Charles Rosen detects the strongest traces of popularism in Haydn and Mozart—closing material in expositions, the openings of finales, and the trios of minuets—Beethoven refuses to go for the bait. The closing groups in both the first and last movements of the First Symphony are too vigorous and rhythmically sophisticated; the phrase structure of the opening theme in the finale to the C-major Piano Concerto is too rich and complex; the Trio of the *Eroica* is orchestrated with too much daring. And so it goes. Even when Beethoven made efforts (probably less than enthusiastic) at meeting his idol Goethe halfway, the results are curiously ambivalent. The performer of "An die ferne Geliebte" or "Ruf vom Berge" is somehow left with the feeling that he has just sung an art song clothed in "Volksweise" garb. It is not that Beethoven is insincere, just faintly uncomfortable, as he seems to have been with too much hobnobbing among the aristocracy.

In spite of Beethoven's near obsession with direct expression in the late string quartets, the "Freude" theme is perhaps his only incontestable triumph over the popular style. I speak intentionally of "triumph over" rather than "assimilation of," for his setting of Schiller bespeaks an altogether unique relationship to the remarkable achieve-

ment of Haydn and Mozart. With the exception of the sketches shown
in exs. 2b[1] and 2b[2], the only common feature of the first eleven draft
segments is an almost perfect allegiance to stepwise motion and even
rhythmic flow. That it was fully conscious is suggested by the supreme
awkwardness of entries that might have been salvaged by a few well-
placed leaps (exs. 2e and 2k, for instance). Nowhere, not even in the
most fervently religious portions of *Die Zauberflöte*, do we find a similar
restriction to seconds and occasional thirds. Beethoven's restriction derives from the hymn rather than the dance, and it is significant that exs.
2b[1] and 2b[2]—the only sketches to suggest a dancelike setting of the
ode—make their appearance early and vanish immediately. Indeed, the
tune we know has more points of contact with the chorale "Ein' feste
Burg" than with the blatantly popular opening of the finale to Haydn's
Symphony No. 104 (ex. 3), even though the phrase structure of Haydn's
work is identical to the *aa'* of the sketches, and in spite of a common
range and an aversion to the leading tone. As a result, the solidarity
among the sketches is scarcely challenged by even the most bizarre
characteristics of phrase structure, such as the asymmetry of ex. 2g.

An almost habitual feature of Beethoven's compositional process may seem unnecessarily contrary to us today, for it contrasts sharply
with our evolutionary view of creation. Exs. 2a, 2c, and 2d bring the

Example 3

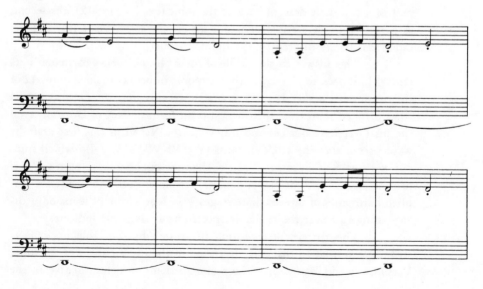

theme to a stage that is closely related to the final version, but one that is taken up again only in ex. 21. The seven intervening drafts are not only irrelevant to the straight-line development of the tune, but they move successively farther away from the version we are bound to see as inevitable. What function do they serve? Beethoven seems to have been best able to make responsible aesthetic choices after a compositional or expressive problem had been defined in terms of extremes. Ex. 2k suggests a solution so radical in both thematic and formal terms that any further experimentation would have undermined what fragile thread of continuity remained; Beethoven also knew when enough was enough.

The return to a rounded theme in ex. 21 occurs fresh on the heels of ex. 2k at the bottom of the previous page. Curiously enough it is canceled, although this probably occurred after a more satisfactory version had been worked out in exs. 2m and 2n. Beethoven needed to gather momentum for the final assault on the *b* phrase; hence the scarcely necessary repetition of both *a* and *a'* phrases (but note the surprising dominant cadence at the tag end of *a'* in ex. 21). But perhaps the most fascinating dimension of the final working out of *b* is the added stimulus of harmonic underlay in no less than six sketches and sub-sketches on the ex. 21 page and the following page. No longer satisfied with simple tonics and dominants, and unable to complete a simple sixteen-bar period without recourse to figured bass, Beethoven injects on two occasions the major mediant at the end of the *b* phrase, the first as part of a coloristic descent back to the tonic (ex. 2m, m. 12), the second as part of a moderately strong cadence on the submediant (ex. 2n; the cadence is partly diluted by the tonic six-four).

The answer to the riddle of the *b* phrase, then—particularly its crucial link back to *a'*—lay in the harmonic impetus provided in m. 12 of the tune after the sketches had reached a seeming impasse. Once again the triad invoked represents the furthest orbit from the key of D major: even the final version does not move beyond the VofVI of this first draft. It would seem that the circle of fifths (V^7ofVI-VI-VofV-V-I)n which spins out so effortlessly in mm. 11–12 of the tune ought to have been self-evident to any competent Kapellmeister, let alone Beethoven. But the implied harmonies of intermediate stages—with or without the major mediant—range all over the available spectrum, as the table indicates.

The pattern of evolution illustrated by the table is, in fact, strikingly similar to that already traced in the overall shape of the tune. Versions A and B toy with the major mediant so determinative in the

Version		m. 11	m. 12	m. 13
A	Fig. 2m	I— V	IV^6— ii^6— III— $V^4_2 of\,vi$	I
B	Fig. 2n, st. 13/14	ii^6— I^6_4	III—vi^6_4— vi— I^6_4	I
C	Fig. 2n, st. 15/16	IV^6— I^6_4— ii^6— vi^6_4	IV^6— I— V	
D	Fig. 2n, st. 14/15		ii— ii^6— I^6_4	
E	Fig. 2o, st. 1/2 (left)	I— V— V— vi	vi— ii^6— I^6	
F	Fig. 2o, st. 1/2 (right)	IV^6—IV^6— I^6_4— ii^6	I^6— V— V— I^6_4	I
G	Fig. 2o, st. 5/6	V^7— I— ii^6— $V^6_5 of\,V$	V— I— V	
H	Fig. 2o, st. 7/8	V^7— I— ii^6— $IV^{6\sharp}$	V— I— V	

final outcome. Versions C, D, and E then discard the major triad on the third degree, to rely instead on its dominant-tonic resolution, the submediant. Version E can claim the simplest harmonization, renouncing both the mediant and submediant. Versions F and G simply ornament this plain framework, first with the dominant of V and finally with an audacious augmented sixth chord. At all events, the major mediant has long since been excluded from participation. Hence its sudden reappearance on the following page (ex. 2p) follows logically from version B, in spite of several intermediate stages. A few small melodic changes permit the switching of dominant and tonic six-four functions, leading to an orthodox cadence on the submediant, a promising but ultimately unsatisfactory solution. When, a few lines later, the theme is fixed except for one or two remaining details, we are left hanging as to its harmonic fate—but by now a *b* phrase that does not circle back via V*of*vi is almost unthinkable. Beethoven had secured the best of two worlds: the unadorned simplicity of the *a* segments complemented by the comparative richness of the secondary dominant chain at the end of *b*. To this point we have seen no harmonization of *a*, and it is not unlikely that the energy of the interior phrase prompted some of its otherwise unwarranted complexity.[21]

The absolute clock time during which this elaborate sequence of events took place—if my reconstruction of the sequence is flawed, it is so only in details—could scarcely have been very long. The composition of the sketches in exs. 2f through 2r, for instance, found on seven nearly consecutive pages, probably consumed no more than a few days. Everything from the shading of inks to the symbiotic relationship among successive sketches speaks for the intensity of the process. Armed now with a concrete vision of his folk hymn, Beethoven was prepared to face larger issues of form.

He had prepared himself in characteristic fashion with three small drafts during the sketching of the "Freude" tune. None of them is greatly significant for the theme itself, but all have profound bearing upon the rapid growth in size and scope of the movement. The first shows that the wellspring of the finale was contained not just within the "Freude" idea, but in the traditional technique of variation as well. The very first page to be devoted entirely to the last movement abounds with such ideas (ex. 4: Landsberg 8, bundle 2, gathering II, p. 1(85)). Only one of the ideas struggles past the opening *a* phrase, and its =*de* continuation into *b* is especially awkward. The variations themselves are as

Example 4

much orchestrational as figural, and it is striking to catch the reluctant composer of opera and song hatching essentially instrumental plots upon an inherently vocal idea.

Beethoven probably never intended to commence the movement without some kind of orchestral introduction. Already in bundle 1, gathering II, p. 4(12), directly before the beginning of continuous sketching on the first movement, we find the notation shown in ex. 5 (bundle 1, gathering II, p. 4(12), st. 1/2). The inscription suggests none of the well-publicized wavering on Beethoven's part over the inclusion of the "Freude" in the finale, a commitment dating back to the previous fall.[22] The classically proportioned, heavily sequential eight-bar phrase portends little of the terror of the "Schreckensfanfare," but does make clear that the triumph of major over minor is to be resolved within the movement—a small hint of its scope even at this infant stage. At the conclusion of the sketches for the first movement, we find the entry which could not have failed to catch Nottebohm's sharp eye: "Vielleicht doch {auch?} der Chor Freude schöner Götter {funken}" ("perhaps however {also?} the chorus Joy sweet gods' "; bundle 2, gathering II, p. 1(37); N II, p. 180). Even if my reading of the adverb as "also" is incorrect, there can still be no question that Beethoven was wavering in his commitment to Schiller's ode. Perhaps in the flush of having just

Example 5

completed an instrumental movement of revolutionary bent, the composer registered fresh doubts about either the necessity or appropriateness of a choral finale; at all events, he had invested almost nothing in the project at this stage beyond a few tantalizing entries.

Nottebohm injects into his discussion the three examples that serve as the prototype for the finale to Op. 132, all offered as further proof of Beethoven's vacillations. But the evidence is rather softer than he suggests. The first two entries are not found in Landsberg 8 at all, but must have come from a now lost pair of pocket volumes once owned by Schindler, or possibly to a recently discovered pocket volume.[23] In any case, when Nottebohm describes a volume as containing "vor- und nachher fast nur Entwürfe zur Composition des Schiller'schen Textes" ("before and after [this point] almost exclusively sketches on the Schiller text"), a great deal of latitude remains. We may never know more precisely where these sketches came, but there is no reason to assume that they were entered when the chorale finale was especially advanced. Nottebohm's third example no longer has anything to do with the history of the Ninth; it is found two pages after the last finale sketches and keeps company with the first of the Op. 126 Bagatelles, to which Beethoven turned his attention—no doubt with some relief—after the symphony had been scored up.

Example 6

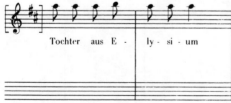

The brief introduction among the sketches for the "Freude" tune, shown as ex. 6 (bundle 2, gathering II, p. 3(87), st. 1/2), prompts wonder, if not outright amusement. Even Beethoven found it necessary to inscribe "seque" at the entrance of the voice, silent acknowledgment that a piccolo Hauptstimme was not altogether satisfactory. But the third entry, shown as ex. 7 (bundle 2, gathering VI, p. 3(87), st. 5/6), assumes an importance in the evolution of the movement far beyond its modest position directly below the curious introduction draft. Here, weeks before this structural juncture was reached in the sketches, Beethoven drafted the crucial link between the developmental passage of mm. 432–528 and the recapitulation of mm. 543ff. For a Classical composer, this bridge—regardless of how hybrid the form—was the most dramatic event in the movement; we have here an equally dramatic

Example 7

example of Beethoven's unfashionable commitment to the Classical aesthetic. It is not so much the draft itself (which recalls the deflection to B major in the closing group, mm. 108–15 of the first movement, and anticipates a similar common-tone deflection at the Poco adagio, mm. 832–42, in the finale), but its emergence even before the tune has been hammered out that captures our attention.

We tend to forget that Beethoven did not, after all, set Schiller's entire text; a rigorous selection process must have been in motion for a considerable period before the serious drafting began. Only a few traces of the process are left among the sketches themselves. Out of the eight stanzas (in the 1803 revision) Beethoven drew in order upon the first three. Musically this trio seems to have been associated from the start with successive variation. Their themes of idealized joy, friendship, and nature are touchstones of Beethoven's personal credo. The remaining stanzas either repeat the spirit of earlier ones (stanza 4: "Freude heisst die starke Feder / in der ewigen Natur"; "Joy bears an upright plume in eternal nature") or wallow in hopeless metaphors (stanza 7: "Freude sprudelt in Pokalen, in der Traube goldnem Blut / trinken Sanftmut Kannibalen"; "Joy bubbles in goblets, savages imbibe gentleness from the golden blood of its grapes"). There is reason to suspect that in his own way Beethoven had become as keenly aware of the limitations of the poem as Schiller himself.

The use to which the choruses were put involves a more complex history. That Schiller offered a division of function between stanza and chorus has gone unnoticed in the musical literature, but the direct

Example 8

sejd um - schlung - en   mil - li - o - nen   Brü - der ü - ber[m]

Stern -en - zelt   muss ein lieb - er   Vat - er wohn - en

Example 9

influence upon Beethoven's musical composition is an even more glaring omission. The startling interjection of the angular theme at the Andante maestoso (mm. 595ff.) to the text "Seid umschlungen Millionen" takes its cue directly from Schiller. Besides the poet's obvious bow in the direction of ancient Greek drama—a gesture that doubtless pleased Beethoven—the chorus of millions is the only text in the finale which is sung only and always by choral forces, declaimed in a broad yet sharply rhythmical style that may have represented an attempt on Beethoven's part to revive a lost performance tradition.

The first chorus of the "Ode to Joy" seems to have held a special fascination for Beethoven. It is just this portion of the poem which Beethoven seized upon early with the sketch in Grasnick 1 (ex. 1). It is also, following the first eight-line stanza, the first text to be set within Landsberg 8, though initially it is forced to adapt rather clumsily to the "Freude" tune, as ex. 8 (bundle 2, gathering II, p. 5(45), st. 3/4) illustrates. The omission in this sketch of line 2, with its "all-embracing kiss," is carried even further in the sketch shown as ex. 9 (bundle 2, gathering VI, p. 5(89), st. 7), where, during the intense working out of the *b* phrase, Beethoven launches a much grander vision of his favored lines. The inscription "Chor" says it all, and this vision of a loving father dwelling "above the canopy of stars" is doubtless what led him to append the third chorus, creating an indivisible eight-line unit. The working out in the sketches, however, offers another fascinating perspective on compositional extremes. At the foot of bundle 2, gathering VIII, p. 2(102), just as the second and third stanzas are being introduced in variation, Beethoven noted the following: "zwischen Verse / Brüder über Sternenzelt muss ein lieber Vater wohnen" ("between verses: 'Brothers, above the canopy of stars there must dwell a loving Father' "). The

Example 10

phrase first singled out in 1798 would thus serve as a refrain binding the entire musical structure. But only a few lines later, Beethoven exploits in as radical a fashion as possible the thoroughgoing parallels between the first and third choruses, homogenizing the lines sharply profiled in the previous quotation (ex. 10: bundle 2, gathering VIII, p. 3(103)).

To be sure, the draft cries out for musical explication, but it is the text which provides the impetus for the parallel structure. The loose inversions which answer each line in the ascending sequence are an obvious reference to the correspondence between alternating lines of the first and third choruses. In one sense they are not musical sketches at all, but arise from Beethoven's effort to draw every possible meaning from the poetry. It is true that the direct intertwining evidenced in these sketches is absent from the final version, yet Beethoven continued, after deciding that the third chorus merited successive and not simultaneous treatment, to treat both together (successively) as a single unit (cf. the Andante maestoso and the Adagio ma non troppo, ma divoto, as well as the Allegro energico). Only the sketches preserve the dimensions of his initial fascination.

Given Beethoven's use of the first three stanzas and the first and third choruses, we are obliged to inquire after the fate of the second chorus. Arguing from the content of the two chosen refrains, with their culmination in a "loving father" and "creator," it is hardly surprising that the composer evinced no apparent interest in the "Unbekannte" ("Unknown") of the second chorus. And what of the fourth chorus, used in the "Turkish" Alla marcia, curiously absent until now? The enigma is that these lines do not occur at all throughout the extensive finale sketches in Landsberg 8. It is not because the sketches yield no references to exotic musics: the two illustrated in ex. 11 (bundle 2, gathering VIII, p. 103(103)) can be found sandwiched among drafts for the "3tes Verse" and "Seid umschlungen" already quoted.[24] As might be expected, the annotations in these sketches are purely instrumental and contain no hint of a move toward B♭ major. The sole explicit reference to any secondary key occurs just a few pages later, after a bridge passage restating—much as in the final version—the last line of stanza 3 ("und der Cherub steht vor Gott"): "auch F dur/Freude" ("also 'Joy' in F major"). But in spite of the resolute tone of its first mention in ex. 11, there is no reference to the Turkish arsenal, and none of course to the fourth chorus. For Beethoven, then, the single notation in ex. 11 seems

Example 11

to point toward an instrumental variation, not to an episode which in the final version fulfills some of the functions of a secondary key area. In fact, it may well have been Schiller's fourth chorus (the first and third were already pressed into service, and the second had been passed over) which stimulated Beethoven to establish a dramatic new key center (the "transition" occurs in a single chord from m. 329 to m. 330; parallels with the secondary key of the opening Allegro have been drawn many times). These four lines, with their colorful references to "flying" and "running," are the only passages in the entire ode to paint a vision of rapid motion. Otherwise, we either "sneak weeping from this band" or "fall to our knees," neither as suggestive of a modulation as the brothers of the fourth chorus. At all events, the sketches permit us to be fairly certain that Beethoven did not incorporate a last group of lines from Schiller until this most topical of styles had been removed from the tonic. As one of two representatives in Beethoven's output of a universally popular, if ersatz, genre, we can be sure that the composer wished to exploit as sharply as possible this self-conscious burlesque in support of his utopian brotherhood of man.[25]

There remains only the task of completing the anatomy of a vocal style for choruses one and three, one that both complements and supplements Beethoven's musical image for the initial three stanzas. I have already suggested how the "Freude" tune goes beyond simple popular roots to create its own synthetic devotional language, slavishly committed to stepwise motion, flat (if symmetrical) rhythms, and narrow compass. Yet the four-square phrase structure retains an element of uncomplicated folk origins; even this slim connection to an historical past is dissolved in the sketches for "Seid umschlungen." Immediately following ex. 10, a parallel setting of choruses one and three, shown in ex. 12 (bundle 2, gathering VIII, p. 4(104)), was entered without intervening drafts. We would be justified in concluding that both examples are about awe. The musical language is stepwise as before, and only a single quarter note disturbs what is otherwise, with chaste half and whole notes, a feast of notational purity. If ex. 12 represents an attempt to diversify the rigid schematicism of the first setting, it is no less insistent in its pictorial ascent to the "Sternenzelt." The intriguing dominant of III at the end of ex. 10 offers only the suggestion of a modulation, and the reiteration of "Freude" in the tonic at the end of ex. 12 reaffirms what we have observed from the earliest sketches: the portrayal of various states of exaltation did not mean for Beethoven the

Example 12

Ex. 12 (cont)

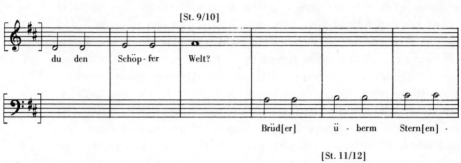

[St. 9/10]

du den Schöp-fer Welt?

Brüd[er] ü - berm Stern[en] -

[St. 11/12]

zelt such ihn ü - berm Stern - en zelt

muss ein

Brüder

ü - berm Stern - en muss er

lieb - er Vat - er wohn - en

überm Sternen zelt

[St. 13/14]

?

wohn - en muss ein lieb - er Vat - er wohn - en

über Sternen geht auch Freude schöner Götter - funk[en]
muss er wohnen hiermit

Example 13

obvious application of a dynamic modulatory scheme which received its impetus from instrumental models, hybrid or otherwise.

The relationships among sketches were anything but analogously static. If there was ever a pair of themes which might be said to result from simultaneous creation, it is the "Freude" tune and the "Seid umschlungen" chorus. After all, much less obvious interrelationships—for example, between the slow movement of the F-major String Quartet, Op. 135 and the finale of the C♯-minor Quartet, Op. 131[26]—have been documented in the sketchbooks. In the case of the Ninth, we have Beethoven's own synthesis of both at the Allegro energico (mm. 655ff.) as proof of his intentions. The composer does not disappoint us, but the relationship is nonetheless a curious one, as shown in ex. 13 (bundle 2,

Example 14

gathering VII, p. 70(2)), which appears among the much publicized introduction drafts.[27]

The contrapuntal marriage is explicitly instrumental and vocal, with "Freude" intoned only silently over square rhythms. The simple descending scale in the bass (where "Seid umschlungen" always commences) may figure as excessively simplified even when compared to other finale drafts, but it accomplishes its main mission of movement from tonic to dominant (and back again with the answer) with ease and efficiency. The remaining evolution, illustrated in ex. 14a (bundle 2, gathering VIII, p. 3(103)) and 14b (bundle 2, gathering X, p. 1 [15 in Landsberg 12]), delights the critic's eye and ear. Even though Beethoven left no tracks to the final dominant, the fundamental process of variation so dear to students of linear insights could scarcely be improved upon, even for posterity.

The next stage in the history of the evolution of this wholly unique finale would chart its gradual but inexorable shift toward a dynamic form nourished continually by the wellsprings of sonata style. But it is precisely this dimension of the work that is best known and has been documented most sympathetically in the twentieth-century literature. The models, both archaic and synthetic, have remained silent until now, slumbering among the transcriptional thorns of the Engelmann sketchbook and Landsberg 8. When we acknowledge that thirty-two of the thirty-six lines of text are selected, the first three stanzas set in variation, the intent to bring in Turkish music articulated, and the essentials of "Seid umschlungen" worked out, then we must also acknowledge that virtually every element crucial to the success of the movement is present—even, so it appears, the double exposition commenced in bundle 2, gathering VII, p. 8(76), and cited in N II, p. 184, ex. 9—before any sign of a modulatory scheme makes its presence felt. For a man who spent most of his compositional life not only developing and perfecting sonata style within its normative realm of multimovement instrumental music, but even extending it into formal areas where it was usually unwelcome (the slow movement of the Fifth Symphony, the theme-and-variation finale of Op. 111, and the Diabelli Variations, to name only a few), such restraint can only be understood against the backdrop painted in this essay of profound allegiance to archaic and associative styles perhaps not wholly understood by Beethoven, but simply raised by him to immortality.

Appendix: The Three Principal Standard-Format Sketchbooks for the Ninth Symphony

Engelmann Sketchbook (SV 107, SBH 664)

Today the book consists of nineteen leaves that can be supplemented by two further leaves once part of the manuscript: BSk 21/69 (SV 176), between pages 8 and 9; and Grasnick 20b (SV 54), fol. 20, between pages 12 and 13. The single sheet (consisting of two bifolia, one inside the other) is the gathering unit. The last leaf marks the beginning of a new gathering, and may have continued at one time to three further leaves.

Contents: Variations for Piano on a Theme by Anton Diabelli, Op. 120
      Variation 32: p. 1
      Variation 33: pp. 2–6
      Corrections for the copy sent to Ferdinand Ries in London: pp. 16–18
      Reference to theme: p. 30
      Correction to variation 12: p. 33
      Complete version of the theme, probably intended for a copyist: p. 37

Symphony No. 9 in D, Op. 125
    First movement: pp. 7–15, 21–33, 36
    Preliminary drafts for other movements, largely unused,
    including the finale: pp. 7–12, 19–20, 24–28, (36?)

Landsberg 8, bundle 1

Bundle 1 consists today of fifteen leaves of twelve-stave paper bearing two complementary watermarks. It can be supplemented by five further leaves in the Bibliothèque nationale, Paris. Since the present ordering of gatherings (the great majority of which are single sheets) within both bundles of Landsberg 8 is largely arbitrary, the following system for indicating locations within the manuscript has been adopted throughout my article: bundle, gathering, page number within the gathering (manuscript page number).

The correct sequence of gatherings within bundle 1 is:

I   MS 96 (SV 248), pp. 1–8
II   Landsberg 8, pp. 9–16
III   "   pp. 17–20; MS 57 (SV 206), part 2;
                      Landsberg 8, pp. 21–22
IV   "   pp. 23–30
V   "   pp. 1–8

Contents: Op. 120, Variation XXXII: gathering I, pp. 1–3(1–3)
           Op. 125/I: gathering I, p. 5(5); II, p. 1, 6–8(9, 14–16); III,
           pp. 1–8 (17–22 and MS 57, pt. 2); IV complete; and V,
           pp. 1–7 (1–7); included are drafts for all parts of the
           movement, concentrated heavily on the exposition and de-
           velopment
           Op. 125 concept sketches: gathering I, p. 8(8); II, pp. 10–
           13(10–13)
           Unused Dona nobis pacem idea: gathering V, p. 8(8), proba-
           bly entered before Beethoven stitched the book together

Landsberg 8, bundle 2

Bundle 2 consists today of forty leaves of sixteen-stave paper bearing two complementary watermarks. It can be supplemented by eighteen leaves from collections in the DSB, GdM, and BH. The correct sequence of gatherings is:

I	Landsberg 8,	pp.	29–36
II	"	pp.	37–52 (double sheet gathering)
III	"	pp.	93–100
IV	"	pp.	61–68
V	"	pp.	53–60
VI	"	pp.	85–92
VII	"	pp.	69–76
VIII	"	pp.	101–4 (single bifolium)
IX	"	pp.	105–8 (single bifolium)
X	Landsberg 12,	pp.	15–18 (single bifolium)
XI	Landsberg 8,	pp.	77–84

(Leaves probably missing here)

XII	A50 (GdM),	pp.	1–8
XIII	" "	pp.	9–16
XIV	" "	pp.	17–24
XV	" "	pp.	25–28, plus an inner bifolium of SBH 676 (BH), pp. 1–4

Contents: Op. 125/I: gathering I, pp. 1–8(29–36), continuity drafts for development, recapitulation, and coda

Op. 125/II: gathering II, pp. 6–16(42–52); III, pp. 1–6(93–98)

Op. 125/III: gathering III, p. 7; IV, pp. 1–8(61–68); V, pp. 1–8(53–60); VII, pp. 3–5(71–73)

Canon, "Grossen Dank" (2 voices? incomplete?), Hess 303: gathering III, p. 8(100)

Op. 125/IV: gathering II, p. 5(45); VI, pp. 1–8(85–92); VII, pp. 1–2, 5–8(69–70, 73–76); VIII, pp. 1–4(101–4); IX, pp. 1–4(105–8); X, pp. 1–4 (Landsberg 12, pp. 15–18); Landsberg 8, gathering XI, pp. 1–8(77–84); XII, pp. 1–8 (A50, pp. 1–8); XIII, pp. 1–3(A50, pp. 9–11)

Mixed ideas for Op. 125: gathering II, pp. 1–9(37–45), between work on movements I and II

Six Bagatelles for Piano, Op. 126: gathering XIII, pp. 5–8(A50, pp. 13–16); XIV, pp. 1–2(A50, pp. 17–18); XV, pp. 1–4(A50, pp. 25–26; SBH 676, pp. 1–2)

Bundeslied, Op. 122: gathering XIV, pp. 3–4(A50, pp. 19–20)

Canon, "Te solo adoro," WoO 186: gathering XIV, p. 5(21)

C-major fanfare, Hess 57: gathering XIV, p. 6(22)

Op. 127/I, introduction and first group: gathering XV, p. 5(SBH 676, p. 3)

Notes

1. In letters to Probst in Leipzig and Schott in Mainz drafted on the same day (March 10, 1824), Beethoven declared that the *Missa solemnis* was "undoubtedly the greatest work I have ever composed" and "I consider this to be my greatest work." It must not be forgotten, however, that Beethoven frequently exaggerated in letters to publishers, and that he must have felt at least somewhat compelled to justify the high fee demanded for the mass (more than half again as much as for the Ninth Symphony), particularly after his difficulties with marketing the C-major Mass fifteen years earlier. Perhaps more temperate was a letter of a year later (April 9, 1825; Anderson 1358) to Ferdinand Ries in Bonn, where the Kyrie and Gloria are described as "two of my most excellent compositions."

2. Various aspects of this tradition are mirrored—often accurately—in Warren Kirkendale, "New Roads to Old Ideas in Beethoven's 'Missa Solemnis'," *MQ* 56 (1970):665–701.

3. It is true that Beethoven toyed with the idea of writing an oratorio, or an opera, or even another mass during the last three years of his life, but none of these appears to have proceeded beyond the discussion stage.

4. Thayer-Forbes, p. 121.

5. N II:479, ex. 1 gives the first reading of this line but omits the variant second reading.

6. N I:41–42.

7. In an essay entitled "Skizzen zur neunten Symphonie," published in N II:157–92.

8. To the group of preliminary sketches for the Ninth Symphony belongs the well-publicized leaf BSk 8/56 (SV 161, Bonn BH): "Adagio Cantique—Frommer Gesang in einer Sinfonie in den alten Tonarten." By analogy with the Boldrini sketchbook (SV 71, missing since World War II), A45 (SV 275, Vienna GdM), and the Op. 106 scherzo sketches on its verso, the most plausible time frame for this leaf is May, 1818, or even a month earlier; Nottebohm offers no support for his dating "in the second half of the year 1818." Hence BSk 8/56 most likely predates the symphony sketches on pp. 92–109 in Boldrini. If this view is correct, then Boldrini shows Beethoven already to have focused on a single symphony in mid-1818. And whatever the meaning behind the purported remarks to Friedrich Rochlitz in the summer of 1822 about composing "two great symphonies" and "an oratorio," two of these works almost certainly received no voice in the sketches, remaining, as Beethoven remarked, "in my head." Nottebohm's contention that the "Sinfonie allemand" alluded to on p. 119 of Artaria 201 offered proof that Beethoven still intended late in 1822 to bring "twins" into the world (N II:168) does not wash; multiple layouts for a single work were not uncommon at this stage in the drafting.

9. Robert Winter, "Plans for the Structure of the String Quartet in C sharp Minor, Op. 131," in Alan Tyson, ed., *Beethoven Studies*, vol. 2 (London, 1977), pp. 106–37.

10. The entry is found on p. 119, st. 4–5 in Artaria 201 and transcribed in N II:167, where the correct final word is "Posaunen" and not "Subjekten."

11. Since pp. 2–6 of the Engelmann sketchbook contain a very full sketch for the final variation of Op. 120, and since a copy of the entire work sent to Ferdinand Ries in London is dated "am 30ten April/1823," the main portion of the book was probably filled in April or May. Ninth Symphony sketches are found pp. 7–36. The meaning of the inscription "am 12ten Maj" in the margin of p. 30 is not clear, but supports the general time frame proposed here.

12. Beethoven's letter (Anderson 1214) is undated, but the archduke's reply is quoted in full in A. C. Kalischer's German edition of the letters (1907–8), vol. 4, pp. 300–301.

13. A reconstruction, with general contents, of sketchbooks for the Ninth Symphony is given as an appendix to this article.

14. This supposition is supported by the oft-quoted remark of nephew Karl to Beethoven: "Mich freut es, dass Du das schöne Andante hineingebracht hast" ("I'm glad that you have brought in the beautiful Andante"). Nottebohm was surely right in linking the Andante with that in the slow movement of the Ninth Symphony, but his date of "fall 1823," drawn from Schindler's inscription on the relevant conversation book (Heft 43, but catalogued as 44 in the DStB), can now be specified with much greater precision. Indeed, an entry only two pages after Karl's can be dated September 24. The first appearance of the idea in the sketches is bundle 1, gathering II, p. 2(10) though not linked specifically to the symphony. By the middle of bundle 2, gathering IV, the relationship had solidified; Karl's enthusiastic words of support doubtless stem from slightly later. Since Beethoven returned to Vienna around the end of October, Karl's entry is fully compatible with the bulk of the finale having been composed in Vienna. Nottebohm's hunch was that the Adagio was "finished in the sketches in about October" (N II:173).

15. The account of the Ninth Symphony's genesis in Thayer-Forbes—drawn from Nottebohm—is typical: "When the foundation of the work is firmly laid we have the familiar phenomenon of work upon two or three movements simultaneously" (p. 890). Or Nottebohm himself: "We confront once more the phenomenon of Beethoven working on two or three movements simultaneously" (N II:170).

16. It is not surprising that Nottebohm's access to sources now lost produces a series of examples for the "Freude" theme which are no longer traceable. This is particularly true of the pocket complex aut. 8 (SV 25), two books of thirty and thirty-seven leaves, both lost since World War II. N II:183, exs. 2–4 and p. 184, exs. 1–8—a dozen consecutive examples—appear nowhere in the Engelmann-Landsberg 8 complex, and must have been entered into either aut. 8 or, less likely, SV 362. (The latter book has recently been purchased by the Beethovenhaus in Bonn, but is not yet available for inspection.) None of these untraceable examples has been included in my main discussion, for two seemingly contradictory reasons. First, there is no way to verify the transcriptions for accuracy. Second, assuming they are generally accurate, they simply lend further support to the findings presented in the body of my article.

17. Heinrich Schenker, *Beethovens Neunte Sinfonie* (Vienna, 1912), p. 259, where the theme is said to be in a three-part song form: a_1-b-a_2, consisting of $8+4+4$ bars. Like Beethoven in the big batch of tune sketches, Schenker does not take the repeat of b-a^2 into account; he also does not explain why a_1 should be twice as long as a_2.

18. Otto Baensch, *Aufbau und Sinn des Chorfinales in Beethovens neunter Symphonie* (Berlin, 1930), p. 7. Baensch includes the choral repeat of the last eight bars in his scheme; each "Stollen" consists of four bars, each "Abgesang" of eight (including a repeat of the second "Stollen"). Baensch's terminology is borrowed freely from Alfred Lorenz's *Das Geheimnis der Form bei Richard Wagner* (Berlin, 1924–33), but the theme type described by both Baensch and Lorenz is restricted to neither Beethoven nor Wagner, nor to a rigid view of bar-form. See, for example, the second group in the first movement of Mahler's Fourth Symphony, where an a-a'-b-a'' period is divided into units of 4, 5, 5½, and 5½ bars. Many other more and less symmetrical examples are found throughout the late eighteenth and nineteenth centuries.

19. Ernest Sanders, "Form and Content in the Finale of Beethoven's Ninth Symphony," *MQ* 50 (1964):75. Although Sanders does not supply a historical content for his invocation of "song," his account of the finished form of the finale counts as the most balanced to date.
20. The best discussion of the relationship between the popular style and art music is found in Charles Rosen, *The Classical Style* (New York, 1972), pp. 329–50.
21. It is no surprise to discover that even in the autograph Beethoven first harmonized the "Freude" tune with a simple tonic and dominant, only then (in the second layer) to enrich the downbeat of m. 117 with the softer subdominant.
22. Nottebohm is again the source for the belief in Beethoven's indecision. See figs. 2a and 2b for the sketches of ca. October, 1822, and N II:180–82, for further evidence of an instrumental finale, discussed below.
23. Aut. 8, in Schindler's possession before he sold it to the Prussian State Library in 1846 (SV 25), or SV 362, a similar pocket volume formerly owned by Marie Romain Rolland and purchased recently by the Beethovenhaus in Bonn.
24. Nottebohm quotes, as does Alfred Kalischer, several references to Turkish music from the second bundle of aut. 8 (N II:186). Is it coincidence that Beethoven quotes the line from the second stanza, "Wer das nie gekonnt, stehle—," then breaking off, almost as if to suggest the inadequacy of the image?
25. The other example is the "Marcia alla turca" (no. 4) from *The Ruins of Athens*, Op. 113, but this is simply a piece of skilled and fashionable imitation.
26. See Robert Winter, "Compositional Origins of Beethoven's String Quartet in C♯ minor, Op. 131" (Ph.D. diss., University of Chicago, 1978), particularly chapter 7.
27. N II:188–91.

General Index

Index of Beethoven's Compositions, Sketches, and Letters

Vienna, Gesellschaft der
Musikfreunde

SV 263: A34, "Kessler," 134, 177
SV 297: A67, 29, 32–34

Other Locations

SV 325: Geneva (Bibliotheca Bodmeriana), 177
SV 343: Moscow (Glinka Museum), "Wielhor-
sky," 177
SV 362: Skizzenheft (now in SBH), 198
SV 364: Princeton, N.J. (Library of William
Scheide), 179
SV 380: Stockholm (Stiftelsen Musikkulturens
främjande), 177
SV 394: Vienna (Stadtbibliothek), 177
Bergamo (Donizetti Institute) bifolium (not in
SV), 29

Letters

Numbering and dates of the letters are in accordance with Anderson.

4: May 22, 1793, 163
12: August 2, 1794, 165
16: February 19, 1796, 24–25
21: October 1, 1797, 163–64
30: 1798, 169
51: June 29, 1801, 169
53: July 1, 1801, 24
54: November 16, 1801, 169
224: August 8, 1809, 166–67
296: February 10, 1811, 167
610: February 12, 1816, 61
933: January 1, 1819, 151
939: ca. March 20, 1819, 151
1136: February 8, 1823, 35
1423: August, 1825, 169

Robert Winter is professor of music at the University of California at Los Angeles, where he has taught since 1974. The recipient of Fulbright and Rockefeller awards, he holds advanced degrees from the State University of New York at Buffalo and the University of Chicago in performance and historical musicology. He has published widely in the areas of compositional process and performance practice, and is an editor of *Nineteenth-Century Music*.

Bruce Carr, who has been assistant manager of the Detroit Symphony Orchestra since 1977, earned degrees in history and musicology at Harvard College and the State University of New York at Buffalo. He was on the editorial staff of *The New Grove Dictionary of Music and Musicians* from 1973 to 1976, and has published several articles and reviews in the field of nineteenth-century music.

The manuscript was edited for publication by Sherwyn T. Carr. The book was designed by Richard Kinney. The musical examples were prepared by Leo Kellis. The typeface for the text is Merganthaler's VIP Garamond, based on an original design by Claude Garamond in the sixteenth century.

The text is printed on IP's Bookmark Natural text paper, and the book is bound in Holliston Mills' Kingston Natural Finish cloth over boards. Manufactured in the United States of America.